Pictorial Contents

Storm-Petrels, pp. 232–279

Tropicbirds, pp. 280–285

Frigatebirds
pp. 286–293

Skuas and Jaegers
pp. 308–321

Gannets and Boobies
pp. 294–307

Gulls and Terns, pp. 322–337

Phalaropes, pp. 338–339

Oceanic Birds of the World:
A Photo Guide

Steve N. G Howell and Kirk Zufelt

Princeton University Press   Princeton and Oxford

For humans it is easiest to view penguins on land, at their colonies, yet these birds spend most of their lives at sea, where we know far less about them. King Penguins, South Atlantic, 2 April 2018.

Published by Princeton University Press, 41 William Street, Princeton, New Jersey 08540
In the United Kingdom: Princeton University Press, 6 Oxford Street, Woodstock, Oxfordshire OX20 1TR
press.princeton.edu

Cover photo credits: Gray-headed Albatross, Hornby's Storm-Petrel, Emperor Penguin © Kirk Zufelt
Atlantic Puffin © Steve N. G. Howell

Library of Congress Control Number: 2019936028

ISBN (pbk.) 978-0-691-17501-0

British Library Cataloguing-in-Publication Data is available

This book has been composed in Adobe Garamond Pro

Printed on acid-free paper. ∞
Printed in Singapore
10 9 8 7 6 5 4 3 2 1

Oceanic Birds of the World: A Photo Guide

Contents

PREFACE

The world's oceans are amazing places, among the last wildernesses on Earth, and to us they are inspiring, challenging, and marvelous. Yet some of the most conspicuous creatures inhabiting the oceans—birds—are not well known, and even a seemingly simple question defies easy answer: "What is an oceanic bird?" (also known as a seabird). There is no formal definition, and different authors have employed different criteria. Our definition is based on years of experience at sea throughout the world's oceans, but we realize that some readers will view it as somewhat idiosyncratic—why treat Peruvian Booby but not Inca Tern? Why Pigeon Guillemot but not Ivory Gull? We make no apologies for the inevitably subjective nature of which species to include. Part of our reasoning is based on the identification (hereafter ID) challenges that birders face at sea, on boats, and part is based on the simple practicality of what can fit into a small book, a true field guide. Our definition is grounded in taxonomy, but we also make a subtle but important distinction between seabirds and 'seaside' birds.

Thus, some readers may be surprised to learn that we do not consider most gulls (or 'seagulls') to be seabirds—how can this be? Humans are ostensibly land-based mammals, and when we go to a beach we often see birds such as gulls, terns, and cormorants, which we then think of as 'seabirds.' But really these are coastal birds, or seaside birds, and many can be found inland on lakes. When you travel more than a few miles offshore, most or all gulls, terns, and cormorants, among other 'seabird' species, are no longer present. Then you are in the world of true sea-birds, many of them wide-ranging citizens of the world, not limited to this coastal area or that country. Thus we do not include cormorants, pelicans, most gulls, and most terns, which are usually well covered by relevant regional field guides.

To our mind, true seabirds are birds of the ocean, birds you generally go on a boat to see. Yes, some of these species can be seen from shore (and almost all come ashore somewhere to breed), but the birds we include here are species that make their living from the ocean for all or most of the year, and often not from coastal waters. How and where we encounter the different species of seabirds varies, and we have tried to include photos that reflect how people typically see a given species. For example, we often see alcids on land, even though these birds spend most of their lives at sea. On the other hand, most sightings of petrels are of birds out at sea. Some species (such as large shearwaters) are often seen resting on the ocean, whereas others (such as storm-petrels) are usually seen in flight.

In a short guide like this it is impossible to cover the many facets of field identification for what are some of the most challenging of all birds to identify. We concentrate on the essentials, using succinct text and carefully chosen images to enable anyone to come up to speed with the latest developments in practical at-sea ID criteria, along with the related subjects of taxonomy, molt, and distribution.

Moreover, by largely avoiding the quagmire of gull identification we can devote more space to true oceanic birds, many of which have not been treated in a modern ID format for many years, in some cases never. For example, Peter Harrison's pioneering photographic seabird guide published in 1987 treated 107 tubenoses, but today the total is in excess of 175. A few of these additions are newly described taxa, but most result from 'upgrading' subspecies to species. In this guide we treat 270 or so species of 'oceanic birds,' while acknowledging that the definition of a species is also subjective and sometimes controversial; of this total, we have field experience with all but about ten cryptic and recently described taxa.

W. B. Alexander pioneered the modern seabird field guide with his *Birds of the Ocean*, published in 1928. Although rudimentary by today's standards, Alexander's work stood essentially alone for about 50 years, before a few other guides appeared. The nascent pelagic dreams of birders were truly kindled with the publication in 1983 of Peter Harrison's classic *Seabirds: An Identification Guide*, followed in 1987 by his photographic guide. Since then, knowledge of seabirds has increased dramatically, sometimes in the field, sometimes in the genetics lab. Individuals such as Hadoram Shirihai and colleagues are forging the way in rediscovering and even discovering taxa, in pushing the frontiers of our ID knowledge to new levels. A few modern ID guides have appeared for some regions and some groups of seabirds, as for North American tubenoses (Howell 2012), but a handy field guide to the world's oceanic birds has been lacking. This guide aims to summarize what has been learned 'since Harrison' and present it in a field-friendly format.

Presumed Antipodes Wandering Albatross, a taxon described only in 1992 and for which identification criteria are still evolving. Southern Chile, 11 March 2016.

HOW TO USE THIS BOOK

As in any kind of birding, breaking your possibilities into manageable groups is a good way to start. The pictorial contents inside the front cover show the 12 main groups of seabirds, which should get you quickly to the right group of species. The introduction to each group then summarizes characters of the group as a whole and may further divide the species into subgroups. When you reach the group or subgroup that probably contains your bird, *check distribution and season first*, then other ID characters. It's realistic, though, to accept that many birds at sea get away as unidentified, and that quite a few species (such as cryptic storm-petrel taxa) are not known to be safely identifiable in the field.

FORMAT OF THE SPECIES ACCOUNTS

Each group (penguins, petrels, gulls and terns, etc.) starts with an overview, often with representative images of the group broken into genera or other subgroups. Particularly challenging and common ID problems may get expanded or separate treatments.

Names. Few groups of birds have had a more-checkered taxonomic history than seabirds. We have used familiar and established names for the most part, but in some cases we had to coin new names for taxa that lacked them. A list of potential splits and newly coined or less familiar English names is given in Appendix B.

Size. After the English and scientific names comes a value for length, sometimes followed by other measures, such as wingspan (WS). These measurements were taken mostly from museum specimens; 'length' is tip of bill to tip of tail, measured from birds laid on their back, with due regard to different styles of specimen preparation. In some cases, wingspans were calculated from wing chord/wingspan ratios of related taxa (see Howell 2012). These measurements may not reflect 'size' as you see it in the field (e.g., King Penguin measures 85–90cm, but it stands only 60–70cm tall), but they offer at least a rough measure of relative size, assuming birds are of similar proportion.

Something few birders seem aware of, however, is that lengths in field guides can be misleading when trying to translate them into 'size' in the field. For example, Least Storm-Petrel measures 14cm with a wingspan of 34cm, whereas Black Storm-Petrel is 22cm with a wingspan of 53cm. From this, you might consider Black about 1.5 times the 'size' of Least. However, from a diagram drawn to these dimensions, most people would say Black is at least twice the 'size' of Least, and in the field Black can appear almost 3 times 'larger' (Fig. 1).

Identification. The main ID characters are highlighted on the plates in pale yellow text boxes; this information, along with the images and geographic range, should allow most species to be identified. Secondary information (such as age, sex, other ID features) is noted elsewhere on the plates or in the species account text.

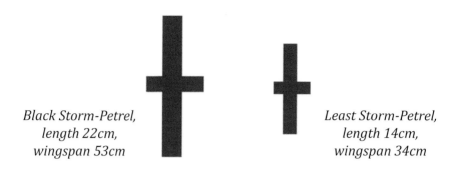

Black Storm-Petrel,
length 22cm,
wingspan 53cm

Least Storm-Petrel,
length 14cm,
wingspan 34cm

Figure 1. *Translating 'size' (= length) in a field guide to what you see in life can be challenging because area is a square of length (upper) and volume is a cube of length. Black (left) and Least Storm-Petrels off Baja California Sur, Mexico, 20 August 2010.*

Most species accounts start with a summary of **distribution and breeding periods**, because an ID can often be reached simply by knowing where and when a species occurs. For example, a small black-and-white shearwater around Hawaii is almost certainly a Newell's, but around Iceland it is almost certainly a Manx. Yes, seabirds can wander far from their known range, but geographic distribution is a good place to start.

Distribution maps (see Fig. 3, p. 11) are not provided for all species, mainly for those in regions less well traveled, or when a comparison of similar or related species' ranges might be useful. Ranges are inevitably provisional, but at least give a general idea of where a species can be found. Colored spots may indicate breeding areas—sometimes single islands, sometimes several sites combined to convey a general idea of breeding distribution. In some cases it is better to describe distribution by habitat and regional terms rather than to imply false precision with maps. Maps do not generally show areas where a species is very rare or occurs as a vagrant. The main sources for maps are noted in the references (see p. 353).

Figure 2. An adult male frigatebird, but which species—Magnificent or Ascension? For many seabirds, identification at sea is often a matter of reasonable assumption. This bird was in the Pacific Ocean, so Ascension Frigatebird is 'eliminated' by probability. Baja California Sur, Mexico, 3 December 2015.

Breeding periods given are from typical or average egg laying to typical or average fledging. Many species (such as petrels and storm-petrels) visit their colonies 1–2 months before the start of 'breeding' as defined here. As a rule, oceanic birds in tropical regions have protracted or even less than annual breeding cycles; those in temperate regions, with their well-marked and often short seasons, tend to have more-synchronized breeding. Non-breeding periods and seasons refer to adults, but immatures of many species occur year-round in the non-breeding ranges.

At-sea distributions generally relate to **feeding habitats**, which often equate to different water masses. Although the ocean may appear largely uniform to humans, it comprises numerous different habitats defined by features such as temperature, salinity, density, and productivity. As a rule, deep tropical 'blue waters' are relatively lifeless, and you can travel many hours seeing few or even no birds. Conversely, cooler temperate 'green waters' are more productive, especially in areas of upwelling, and often support larger numbers of seabirds. Because continuous ocean currents encircle the Southern Hemisphere, you may travel around the world there and stay in the same water mass with the same species, but if you travel only a short distance north or south the species can change quite quickly.

Abundance. All species are rare somewhere, but most species tend to be fairly common or relatively common in their normal range. If we do not mention specific abundance, we assume a species occurs regularly in the area mentioned or mapped, taking into account habitat and season. It may occur in low or patchy

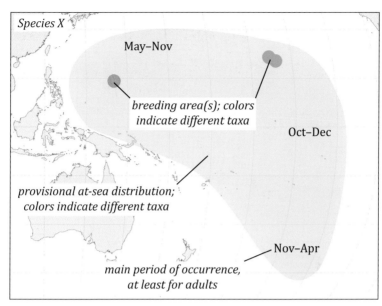

Figure 3. *Range map symbols.*

density, but seeing it would be expected. When a species is notably rare or poorly known we mention abundance and status, or when relative abundance is useful in ID; for example, Salvin's Albatross is common in Chile, whereas both Buller's Albatrosses are uncommon, and Chatham Albatross is scarce.

Because marine habitats are so mobile, a species' abundance in an area often varies daily, as well as between years and over longer cycles, so the status sections should be interpreted with this in mind—what is common in some years in an area can be rare or absent in other years.

ABBREVIATIONS AND SOME TERMS EXPLAINED

We use cen. for central and n., s., ne., etc., for north, south, northeast, etc. (capitalized for major regions, such as N Pacific or SE Australia); I. for island and Is. for islands; and WS for wingspan. For months we use 3 letters: Jun = June, Sep = September, etc. For ages and sexes we use juv. for juvenile (a bird in its juvenile plumage = first non-downy plumage) and imm. for immature (any non-adult plumage, including juvenile). Finally, we use the Latin abbreviation 'cf.' for compare with.

Adult A bird in 'adult' plumage, i.e., a plumage whose appearance does not change appreciably with age, other than seasonally. Does not necessarily reflect sexual maturity.

Adult Wing Molt Molt of breeding adults, although most species at more than a year of age have adult-like molt timing (see *Imm. Wing Molt, 1st-year Wing Molt*).

Alar Bar Pale bar on upperwing of frigatebirds, starting from bend of wing.

Bleaching Fading or becoming colorless, primarily as a result of exposure to sunlight.

Bonnet Head pattern comprising a dark cap and neck sides, as on some plumages of the Wandering Albatross complex.

Clade A group of organisms distinguishable from other groups by shared characteristics and derived from a common ancestor.

Continental Shelf The relatively shallow seabed bordering large land masses and geologically part of the continental crust.

Cookilaria Small gadfly petrel in the genus *Pterodroma*.

Cowl Partial hood covering sides of head and neck, often deepest at the rear.

Cryptic Species Species that have been or are overlooked because they closely resemble other species, such as the numerous taxa of Band-rumped Storm-Petrel.

Culmen Base The base of the bill where it meets the forehead.

Cycle A regularly repeated phenomenon, such as a molt cycle. A basic molt cycle extends from the start of one prebasic molt to the start of the next prebasic molt.

1st-year Wing Molt An 'extra' wing molt inserted into the 1st cycle of some birds, such as skuas and Wilson's Storm-Petrel (see *Imm. Wing Molt*).

Flight Feathers Collectively, the primaries, secondaries, and tail feathers; in some literature (as in Britain) the term excludes tail feathers.

Gadfly Petrel Mainly used for petrels in the genus *Pterodroma*; here also includes the genera *Pseudobulweria*, *Bulweria*, and *Aphrodroma*; derives from their often impulsive and impetuous flight, as if goaded by a gadfly.

Genus (plural Genera) Group of closely related species that share a common ancestor.

Imm. Wing Molt The 2nd prebasic wing molt (1st being attainment of juvenile plumage in the nest), usually at around a year of age (see *1st-year Wing Molt*).

Leucistic Milky-colored or white plumage due to deficiency of pigmentation.

Lores Area between the eyes and bill, above the gape; can be naked or feathered.

Molt A period of normal and regular growth of feathers (i.e., molting), by which plumages are attained; feather loss is a passive by-product of molting.

Monotypic Literally of one type. A monotypic species is one with no subspecies described, and a monotypic genus contains a single species.

M-pattern A contrasting dark pattern on the upperwings, formed by dark outer primaries and primary coverts joined to a dark diagonal band on the secondary coverts (ulnar band), sometimes connected across the rump.

Pelagic Waters beyond the continental shelf. Also an abbreviation for pelagic trip, a broad term for any birding trip in a boat going offshore in search of seabirds (whether or not it reaches pelagic as opposed to shelf waters).

Polymorphic Having 2 or more plumage morphs, such as dark morph and light morph; e.g., jaegers and some petrels.

Prebasic Molt The molt producing basic plumage, a plumage common to all birds and typically renewed completely on an annual basis.

Primaries The primary wing feathers, attached to the hand (carpal) bones and numbering 10 in oceanic birds, their bases protected by primary coverts.

Saddlebags White 'flank patches' (actually feathers of the femoral tract) behind the upperwings on flying small shearwaters.

Scapulars A group of feathers that originate from a point at the base of the humerus and fan out to protect the base of the wings at rest; they form a seamless join between the wings and body in flight.

Secondaries The secondary wing feathers attached to the forearm (ulna) bone (numbering 11–38 in seabirds), their bases protected by secondary coverts (often simply called wing coverts).

Shelf Break Where the continental shelf ends and the seabed starts to slope off into deeper waters; can be an area of productive upwelling.

Subadult An imprecise but convenient term for older immature plumages that mostly resemble the adult plumage, as opposed to younger immature plumages that look more like juvenile plumage.

Subspecies A taxonomic category below the level of species, referring to populations that can be distinguished by differences in plumage, measurements, etc., but that are not considered distinct enough to be treated as species. The colloquial term *race* means the same as subspecies.

Taxon (plural Taxa) A unit of taxonomy, used mainly when uncertainty exists as to whether something is a species or subspecies.

Tertials The inner secondaries, which act as coverts on the closed wing.

Tubenose Bird in the order Procellariiformes, in which the nostrils are housed in tubes on the bill. Includes storm-petrels, albatrosses, petrels, and diving-petrels.

Wear The abrasion of feather tips and pale edgings through day-to-day exposure with the elements and such; compounded by weakening due to bleaching.

Wing-loading The relationship of body mass to wing area. Birds with heavy bodies and small wing area have high wing-loading (e.g., Sooty Shearwater), those with light bodies and big wing area have low wing-loading (e.g., Buller's Shearwater); see Fig. 7 (p. 21).

Wing-tip At rest, the exposed tips of the outer primaries. In flight, the outer portion of the wing (largely formed by the tips of the outer primaries).

INTRODUCTION

Many people, even including men, would likely look at the instruction manual before using an unfamiliar electric kitchen or workroom tool. Yet the introductions to bird books often seem to go unread, even though they represent instruction manuals that enable you use your tool more effectively. The following sections cover a few things that can help you understand and identify oceanic birds.

TAXONOMY AND TYPES OF OCEANIC BIRDS

Taxonomy is the science of classifying things. Like all traditional classifications, seabird taxonomy has relied heavily on plumage patterns and external morphology. Recent molecular studies have repeatedly shown, however, that some taxa may diverge yet show little external evidence of their genetic separation, whereas distantly related taxa can converge in appearance and morphology. An example of the former situation occurs with the Band-rumped Storm-Petrel complex, different populations of which comprise multiple species worldwide, with four species in the Northeast Atlantic alone (Robb et al. 2008)—yet they are all but indistinguishable at sea. An example of the latter situation is the so-called Little Shearwater/Audubon's Shearwater complex, which traditionally has been considered to comprise two widespread but rather variable species: the higher-latitude Little Shearwater, with a shorter tail and white undertail coverts, and the lower-latitude Audubon's, with a longer tail and dark undertail coverts. Austin et al. (2004) showed that this complex comprises multiple species, and that one population of 'Little Shearwater' from the North Atlantic is actually an 'Audubon's Shearwater.'

The state of seabird taxonomy is still fluid, and we have tried to pick a realistic course through myriad taxonomic papers (e.g., Austin 1996, Austin et al. 2004, Chambers et al. 2009, Nunn & Stanley 1998, Penhallurick & Wink 2004, Viot et al. 1993). We include the following families of oceanic birds.

Spheniscidae: Penguins. A familiar, well-defined family of flightless seabirds restricted to cooler waters of the Southern Hemisphere. Recent genetic work, supported by morphology and biogeography, indicates that Rockhopper Penguin comprises 3 species (Banks et al. 2006, Dinechin et al. 2009). Conversely, Royal and Macaroni Penguins are sometimes lumped (Cristidis & Boles 1994). The status of the white-flippered form of Little Penguin is unresolved, but usually it is lumped into Little, while some authors suggest that Australian and New Zealand populations of Little Penguin represent cryptic species (Grosser et al. 2015).

Alcidae: Alcids. A well-defined family of diving seabirds restricted to cooler waters of the Northern Hemisphere; most diverse in the Pacific. Includes murres and allies, puffins, auklets, guillemots, and murrelets. In 2012, Xantus's Murrelet was split into Scripps's and Guadalupe Murrelets; other areas of taxonomic uncertainty include Kuril [Pigeon] Guillemot (taxon *snowi*), High Arctic populations of

Black Guillemot (taxon *mandtii*), and perhaps Whiskered Auklet.

Procellariidae: Petrels. The largest, most diverse, and 'messiest' family of tubenoses when it comes to taxonomy. Petrels range from large (giant-petrels) to small (diving-petrels) and have their tubenose atop the bill, not along the sides as on albatrosses. They occur worldwide and include some of the rarest and least known of all birds; some species are long-distance migrants, others relatively sedentary. Many species appear similar in the field, and identification criteria for several species and groups of species are still evolving.

In families such as petrels, where birds exhibit high fidelity to their nesting grounds, given enough time it is likely that many island populations will evolve into distinct species. In well-studied regions such as the Northeast Atlantic, the specific status of similar-looking taxa (some of which are indistinguishable at sea) is widely accepted—for example, Zino's, Desertas, and Cape Verde Petrels, or Balearic and Yelkouan Shearwaters (Fig. 4, below). But in remote regions of the globe such studies are lacking.

Molecular studies are helping achieve consensus about the relationships among different groups of petrels. Genera are largely agreed upon, but at the species level much remains unresolved. Within the smaller shearwaters, Austin et al. (2004) elucidated the mismatch of the traditional Little and Audubon's Shearwaters, and provided clarification for several taxa. Some of their recommendations, however, mainly within the so-called Tropical Shearwater group, were poorly supported and

---

Figure 4. Not so many years ago, these two Mediterranean-breeding small shearwaters would have been called simply 'Manx Shearwaters.' Today, both are considered distinct species: the larger and bulkier Balearic Shearwater (upper bird), and the smaller, more contrastingly patterned Yelkouan Shearwater (lower bird). Castellón, Spain, 21 December 2014. © Victor Paris.

make little sense from the perspectives of biogeography, morphology, and plumage. A study by Murphy (1927) appears equally valid for a number of small shearwater taxa. Thus, our treatments are a mix of traditional and molecular studies. Petrels can be considered in the following groups, although relationships among some genera remain unresolved.

Diving-Petrels: 6+ species in genus *Pelecanoides*, restricted to cooler Southern Hemisphere waters. Traditionally treated as a separate family, but now usually merged into petrels. Species-level taxonomy has not progressed appreciably since a study conducted 100 years ago (Murphy & Harper 1921).

Fulmars: 8+ species comprising the genera *Macronectes*, *Fulmarus*, *Pagodroma*, *Daption*, and *Thalassoica*. A diverse but well-defined clade of species inhabiting cold high-latitude waters, mainly in the Southern Hemisphere. The 2 giant-petrels were not recognized as species until 1966; Snow Petrel is variably treated as 1 or 2 species; Pintado Petrel also exhibits marked geographic variation; and Northern Fulmar may comprise 2 species.

Prions and Blue Petrel: 10+ species comprising the genera *Pachyptila* (prions) and *Halobaena* (Blue Petrel). Small petrels of the temperate Southern Hemisphere. Prions share very similar plumage and differ mainly in bill structure. Their taxonomy is vexed, and the recent discovery of an overlooked yet abundant prion in the Atlantic Ocean (Ryan et al. 2014) illustrates how neglected the genus has been. Differences within Fairy and Fulmar Prions suggest that both comprise multiple species, and the same may be true of other prions. The relatively distinct Blue Petrel appears to share a common ancestor with prions (Nunn & Stanley 1998).

Figure 5. Kerguelen Petrel has often been placed in the genus Pterodroma, *and also in the monotypic genus* Lugensa. *Current thinking puts it in another monotypic genus,* Aphrodroma. *South Atlantic, 1 April 2018.*

Gadfly Petrels: 35+ species comprising the genus *Pterodroma*, which formerly included 4 species now placed in *Pseudobulweria*, along with the enigmatic Kerguelen Petrel, now placed in *Aphrodroma* (see Miscellaneous Petrels, below). Gadflies are mainly birds of subtropical latitudes, with fewer species in cool temperate waters of the Southern Hemisphere; some species are transequatorial migrants.

Species limits in gadfly petrels have undergone major upheaval in recent decades, with more surely to come. From the 1980s through 2000s it was gradually realized that some taxa subsumed into Soft-plumaged Petrel represented 3 species not very closely related to Soft-plumaged—the North Atlantic trio of Zino's, Desertas, and Cape Verde Petrels. In the 1990s, Dark-rumped Petrel was split into Hawaiian and Galapagos Petrels, and the latter exhibits local differences in breeding season, breeding elevation, morphology, and vocalizations (e.g., Tomkins & Milne 1991), suggesting that further cryptic species are involved. Dark-morph 'Herald Petrels' in Polynesia have been proposed as a separate species, Henderson Petrel (Brooke & Rowe 1996), while differences within Black-capped Petrel are of a magnitude associated with species-level distinctions in this vexing genus (Howell & Patteson 2008).

Miscellaneous Petrels: 12+ species in 4 genera. The genus *Pseudobulweria* comprises 4+ species of medium-size petrels of the tropical Indian and Pacific Oceans; 3 are very local and poorly known, with Fiji Petrel rediscovered in the 1980s and Beck's Petrel in the 2000s. Beck's has been treated as a subspecies of Tahiti Petrel, which may still harbor cryptic species. *Procellaria*: 5 species of rather large, shearwater-like petrels that breed in the Southern Hemisphere; Spectacled Petrel was split from White-chinned Petrel only in the 1990s. *Bulweria*: 2+ tropical species of small to medium-size petrels: the widespread Bulwer's Petrel (which likely comprises cryptic species), plus Jouanin's Petrel of the Indian Ocean. *Aphrodroma*: 1 subantarctic species (Kerguelen Petrel) traditionally subsumed in *Pterodroma*, but apparently more closely related to shearwaters (Nunn & Stanley 1998, Penhallurick & Wink 2004).

Large Shearwaters: 11+ species comprising the genera *Calonectris* and *Ardenna*. A well-known group found mainly in temperate and subtropical latitudes. Most *Ardenna* (except some tropical populations of Wedge-tailed Shearwater) breed in the Southern Hemisphere, whereas all 4 *Calonectris* breed in the Northern Hemisphere. Most species are transequatorial migrants. Until recently, *Ardenna* was subsumed into *Puffinus*. Within *Calonectris*, recognition of Cape Verde and Scopoli's Shearwaters as species distinct from Cory's Shearwater has occurred in the 1990s and 2000s. Careful study of Wedge-tailed Shearwater may yet reveal cryptic species.

Small Shearwaters: 25+ species comprising the genus *Puffinus*. A well-defined worldwide clade, most diverse in the subtropical and tropical Pacific; most species relatively sedentary. Some relationships clarified by Austin et al. (2004), but species limits within the 'Tropical Shearwater' complex await elucidation. Small shearwaters are arguably the most poorly known of tubenoses: a new species was described in 2011, and undescribed taxa may still roam the tropical Western Pacific and Indian Oceans.

Diomedeidae: Albatrosses. A well-defined family, albatrosses differ from other tubenoses in being generally larger and in having nostril tubes on either side of the bill, rather than on top. Traditionally treated in 2 genera, but a review by Nunn et al. (1996) identified 4 recent genera: *Phoebastria* (short-tailed albatrosses) of the North Pacific, and 3 Southern Hemisphere genera: *Diomedea* (great albatrosses), *Thalassarche* (mollymawks), and *Phoebetria* (sooty albatrosses). Robertson & Nunn (1998) recommended that 24 albatross species be recognized, a leap from the 12–13 traditional species. Most if not all of these 'new' species are probably valid, but it is not always possible to distinguish them at sea.

Hydrobatidae: Northern Storm-Petrels. Storm-petrels as a whole are small to very small tubenoses found over most of the world's oceans. They appear to represent the earliest divergences from the ancestral tubenose lineage and traditionally have been treated as southern and northern subfamilies. Molecular evidence, however, supports the view that these are better considered as families (Nunn & Stanley 1998). Most northern storm-petrel taxa occur in the Pacific, and they differ from southern storm-petrels in their longer-armed, more crooked, and relatively narrower wings, and in their shorter legs and smaller feet, which are not habitually used to kick off from the sea surface.

Traditionally, northern storm-petrels have comprised 13 extant species in 2 genera, but molecular and vocal studies, in concert with an appreciation of morphology, biology, and biogeography (Nunn & Stanley 1998, Penhallurick & Wink 2004, Smith et al. 2007, Robb et al. 2008, Howell 2012), suggest that 20+ species are involved, in 3 genera: *Thalobata* diverged first, with a subsequent split into *Hydrobates* (including *Oceanodroma*) and *Halocyptena*. Some authors have taken the retrograde step of merging all northern storm-petrels into a single genus, *Hydrobates*, thus ignoring a suite of differences comparable to those in southern storm-petrels, which comprise multiple genera.

Oceanitidae: Southern Storm-Petrels. Unlike northern storm-petrels, the southern storm-petrels have short-armed, relatively broad wings well suited for gliding, and relatively long legs and big feet often used to kick off from the sea surface; 5 genera are widely accepted.

Several distinctive taxa of southern storm-petrels are traditionally subsumed as subspecies. The conventional view of only 9 species is unrealistic, especially in view of studies highlighting cryptic species diversity in northern storm-petrels. We provisionally treat numerous taxa of southern storm-petrels as species.

Phaethontidae: Tropicbirds. A well-defined small family of plunge-diving tropical seabirds, traditionally included in the order Pelecaniformes (or totipalmates), along with pelicans, frigatebirds, sulids, and other families that share the feature of all 4 toes connected by webbing. Molecular work shows this grouping to be artificial, and the closest relatives of tropicbirds are unclear. Usually considered as 3 species, but marked differences within White-tailed and Red-billed Tropicbirds indicate that both comprise 2 distinct species; further cryptic species may exist within the White-tailed complex.

Fregatidae: Frigatebirds. A well-defined small family of large, highly aerial, and predominantly black tropical seabirds. Five species are usually recognized, but differences within Great Frigatebirds are worthy of study; a recent molecular study found Magnificent Frigatebirds in the Galapagos to be genetically distinct (Hailer et al. 2010); and it has been proposed that the South Atlantic population of Lesser Frigatebird be considered a separate species (Olson 2017).

Sulidae: Gannets and Boobies (Sulids). A well-defined family of plunge-diving seabirds comprising 3 gannets in temperate waters and 9 boobies in tropical waters. Nazca Booby of the Eastern Pacific was split in the 1990s from Masked Booby. Comparable morphological, plumage, and molecular (Steeves et al. 2003) differences within Brown Booby support treatment as 3 species.

Stercorariidae: Jaegers and Skuas. Jaegers (genus *Stercorarius*; also known as skuas in the Old World) comprise 3 well-defined species of piratic seabirds that breed on northern tundra and spend their non-breeding periods at sea. The larger skuas (genus *Catharacta*, sometimes merged into *Stercorarius*) are usually treated as

---

Figure 6. Skuas as a group are distinctive, but species limits and ID criteria remain vexed. 'Brown Skuas' breeding around New Zealand's South Island and the Chathams look distinct from other populations and in some ways more closely resemble South Polar Skua (see pp. 311–315). New Zealand, 21 November 2012. © Matt Jones.

4 species: 1 in the North Atlantic, 3 in the Southern Hemisphere. The 3 conventional southern skua species interbreed to varying degrees, yet one of them (Brown Skua) comprises 4 groups that are well separated ecologically, do not interbreed, and seem as worthy of species treatment as the 4 traditional skuas.

Laridae: Gulls and Terns. Familiar birds found worldwide, and sometimes treated as separate families. Terns comprise 2 subfamilies that may represent families: noddies and typical terns.

Gulls occur worldwide, with greatest diversity in temperate latitudes; most have a coastal or even inland distribution. Here we treat 4 gull species as oceanic birds: Black-legged Kittiwake, Red-legged Kittiwake, and Swallow-tailed Gull are pelagic year-round, while Sabine's Gull has a life cycle similar to that of jaegers and phalaropes, breeding on Arctic tundra and wintering at sea.

Noddies are a well-defined group of pelagic tropical terns that lack seasonal changes in appearance, and also show little age-related variation; most species are not strongly migratory. Species-level taxonomy has been seriously neglected and is in need of critical study. We provisionally treat the Brown Noddy complex as 2 species, the Black Noddy complex as 4 species, the Blue-gray Noddy complex as 3 species, and the White Noddies as 3 species.

Typical terns mainly have coastal and inland distributions and are most diverse in tropical and mid-latitudes. Typical terns have black caps, seasonal plumage changes, and distinct age-related variation; most species are migratory. Although several species migrate over the ocean and might be considered as seabirds (notably Arctic Tern), we limit our treatment to the dark-backed tropical terns, within which Bridled Tern seems better treated as 2 species (Western and Eastern).

Scolopacidae: Phalaropes. Red and Red-necked Phalaropes are 2 distinctive swimming 'shorebird' species within the large and rather diverse sandpiper family. They are long-distance migrants, breeding on northern tundra and wintering widely at sea, mainly in mid-latitudes.

IDENTIFYING SEABIRDS AT SEA

Many seabirds look similar, and as with identifying all birds a synthesis of characters is important, not just single field marks. In some cases, digital images can resolve details retrospectively and assist in ID, but single images can be notoriously misleading and often are all but worthless. Simply getting good views of some seabirds can be challenging enough, especially from a moving boat, and the importance of lighting and distance to evaluating an observation at sea cannot be overemphasized. Many misidentifications result from misjudging size, which is all too easy without familiar frames of reference, or from illusions produced by a combination of distance and lighting. Experienced birders thus accept that many seabirds get away as unidentified, or perhaps can be identified only to the level of genus or to a group or pair of species. Experience gained by repeatedly watching birds is the

Figure 7. *Although both have a length of 45cm and wingspan of 100cm, Sooty Shearwater (left) and Buller's Shearwater (right) have very different wing morphologies. The broad wings of Buller's, combined with its lower weight (425 grams versus 800 grams for Sooty) mean a low wing-loading and lower aspect ratio, which result in its leisurely, rather buoyant flight relative to the hurried, heavy-bodied Sooty.*

best way to learn, but appreciating a few basics can help, especially flight manner, wing morphology, and the potential for variation.

Flight Manner. Factors such as location, habitat, and season, as well as behavior, especially flight manner, are often more important for seabird ID than are small plumage differences, which tend to be difficult to discern at sea. But be aware that flight manner can vary depending on a bird's behavior (foraging, transiting, avoiding a vessel in 'freak-out' flight) and on wind strength and relative direction. Howell (2012) provides a useful explanation of flight manner in tubenoses, which should be read by anyone with a serious interest in seabird ID.

In general, flight manner relates to wind direction, wind strength, bird behavior, and wing morphology. Leach's Storm-Petrel flies very differently in calm conditions than when foraging into the wind, or when transiting across a moderate wind; it also flies quite differently from Wilson's Storm-Petrel, because of structural differences between the 2 species, especially their wing morphology.

Wing Morphology. This can be described by 2 ratios: wing-loading (body mass relative to wing area) and aspect ratio (wing length divided by width). Light-bodied and broad-winged birds have lower wing-loading and lower aspect ratios, and they fly more buoyantly than do heavy-bodied and narrow-winged birds, which have higher wing-loading and higher aspect ratios. As a rule, tropical seabirds range widely over food-poor environments with low wind speeds, and they

Figure 8. A first take on this bird (here a composite image) would be 'dark petrel with white belly,' followed by a look for white-bellied birds in a field guide. Usually this approach works, but there remain mysteries in the world of oceanic birds. This white-bodied Bulwer's Petrel is one such enigma: Is this a rare localized morph of one population (species?), or simply an aberrant or heavily worn plumage variant? Tropical Central Pacific, 23 September 2017. © Michael Force.

Figure 9. This petrel's plumage features, in combination with large size (similar to that of White-faced and Black-faced [Black-capped] Petrels seen with it), suggest it might be a hybrid between one of those taxa and Fea's Petrel. Or might it be 'simply' an aberrantly plumaged Black-faced Petrel? In some cases, even birds seen well and photographed are best left as unidentified. North Carolina, USA, 28 May 2017.

feed mainly by seizing fast-moving prey from the surface, for which a lighter body and broader wings are well suited. Conversely, temperate tubenoses inhabit windier environments with food-rich areas, where they dive after slower-moving prey, for which a heavier body and narrower wings are better suited (see Fig. 7, p. 21).

Variation. The degree of inherent variation in characters such as size and plumage varies among groups of birds. For example, all ages and sexes of storm-petrels appear similar, whereas variation relating to age and sex in frigatebirds is greater within a species than differences between species. Any bird's appearance can also be affected by sun bleaching and wear, and by molt. In general, and given the same lighting conditions, fresh feathers on petrels and storm-petrels are usually grayer and often look reflective, or frosty, whereas worn and faded feathers tend to be browner and duller, without a strong sheen. Aberrant plumages (such as partially white birds) are seen occasionally, and some can be puzzling. In such cases, check structure and flight manner to try to help resolve an ID.

Because many oceanic birds nest on islands, their breeding ranges are not continuous, and given time any island population might develop distinctive characters. In some cases, geographic variation may be consistent enough for subspecies to be distinguished, such as by differences in wing length or bill size, less often by slight differences in plumage patterns. Whether one treats such populations as species or subspecies is a matter of opinion.

Figure 10. White-faced [Black-capped] Petrels. The white stripes on the upperwings of the left-hand bird (3 June) are formed by the white bases of the secondaries, which are revealed when the overlying greater coverts are shed. Also note the browner tones of worn and faded plumage relative to the grayer tones of a fresh-plumaged bird (right; 16 August).

Figure 11. *Molting birds can appear atypical and even suggest other species. Left: the normally neat upperwing pattern of Southern Royal Albatross can be spotted white when underlying feather bases are exposed during molt, suggesting the more coarsely spotted pattern typical of Snowy Wandering Albatross. Right: the long forked tail of Ashy Storm-Petrel (upper bird) alters during molt (lower bird), inviting confusion with Least Storm-Petrel.*

MOLT—YES, IT CAN BE USEFUL

Feathers are not permanent—they wear out and need to be replaced. Molt is simply the normal and regular growth of feathers, by which plumages are renewed. The most conspicuous molt tends to be in the wings, especially among the primaries (like most birds, all oceanic birds capable of flight have 10 primaries). Among most seabirds, primary molt starts with the inner primaries and proceeds sequentially out to the outermost primary.

Often the inner 3–4 primaries (p1–p3/p4) are dropped almost simultaneously, so that there is an obvious gap in the wing; the middle primaries (p5–p7) tend to be molted gradually, 1–2 at a time; the long outer primaries (p8–p10) may molt gradually or, in some species, may all grow at once, which can compromise flight for short periods. Species that molt several outer primaries at once tend to do so because they have only limited time available for molt, such as long-distance migrants (e.g., Great and Sooty Shearwaters) or species with short periods between breeding seasons (e.g., Black-footed Albatross). Species that rely on flight agility for feeding, such as frigatebirds, molt their primaries very slowly, usually 1 at a time.

When wing molt has progressed out to around p4 or p5, many species, such as petrels, synchronously shed most or all of their upperwing greater secondary coverts; species with white bases to the secondaries often show white upperwing stripes at this stage of molt, before the coverts grow out and cover the white bases (see Fig. 10, p. 23).

Most seabirds do not molt when they are breeding, because gaps in the wings can compromise foraging ability when a bird needs to feed itself and its young. Immatures often molt appreciably earlier in the season than adults, as they are not involved in nesting, while failed and non-breeding adults often molt slightly earlier than breeding adults. As well as helping in age determination, wing molt timing can be helpful for species identification if similar-looking species breed (and therefore molt) at different seasons. Among cryptic populations of storm-petrels, wing molt timing may be the only way to distinguish different taxa.

Albatrosses have novel wing molt strategies. Primary molt in Southern Hemisphere species is split into 2 phases that alternate between cycles: thus, the outer 2–3 primaries (*phase 1 molt*) are renewed in 1 cycle, the middle primaries (*phase 2 molt*) inwards in the next cycle, and so on. The first wing molt always involves outer primaries (at around 20–23 months after fledging in mollymawks, at around 27–30 months in great albatrosses). Identifying phase 1 or phase 2 primary molt can assist with ageing immatures, and consequently with ID of different taxa and

---

Figure 12. *Because this image of a 'Wandering Albatross' was taken in early April, the uniform age, rather faded upperwings and frayed tips to the outermost primary point to retained juvenile primaries and a bird about 26 months after fledging, soon to start its phase 1 primary molt. The extensively white head and body on a bird this young point strongly towards a Snowy Wandering Albatross, and probably a male (sex also supported by stout bill and by tawny neck staining, more prevalent on broad-headed males than on females). Without recourse to knowledge of wing molt strategies, however, much less could be inferred about this individual.*

sexes in the Wandering Albatross complex (see pp. 204–207). In the Northern Hemisphere genus *Phoebastria,* outer primaries and a variable number of middle and inner primaries are renewed annually, but with the same underlying pattern of and outward molt of outer primaries and inward molt of middle primaries.

Boobies, gannets, tropicbirds, and perhaps frigatebirds exhibit another variation on the standard pattern of wing molt, although their wing molts still progress from innermost primary to outermost. These birds exhibit what is known as stepwise wing molt, whereby the primaries are replaced in continuous waves, or steps (Howell 2010b; Fig. 13, opposite). Boobies are the best-studied example of stepwise molt. Their first wing molt starts with p1 rather early in life, at about 6–7 months after fledging; a second wave of molt starts again with p1 at about 14–15 months, when the first wave has reached p7–p8; the first wave completes with p10 at about 18 months, and a third wave starts anew with p1 at about 27 months. By the time birds reach breeding age, 3–4 waves of molt have been set up, which means that molt can be underway at 3 or 4 places within the primaries at the same time. This makes sense: for birds that rely on flight for foraging, a few small gaps in the wing are better than one big gap. Moreover, in this way a complete wing molt can take only a few months, rather than being protracted for a year or more if it needed to follow a sequential p1 to p10 progression.

WHERE AND HOW TO SEE OCEANIC BIRDS

Although oceanic birds might be found anywhere out at sea, some areas have a much greater species diversity than others. In general, tropical regions have fewer species than subtropical and temperate waters. Regions with the greatest diversity and largest numbers of seabirds (some breeding locally, others visiting from far-flung locations) include the Humboldt Current, the New Zealand region, the California Current, Southern Africa (where the cold Benguela Current meets the warm Agulhas Current), the Aleutian Islands/Bering Sea region, the Southwest Atlantic (where the warm Brazil Current meets the cold Falkland Current), the North Atlantic, and islands and waters near the Antarctic Convergence, which encircles the Southern Ocean.

Seabird hotspots are obviously linked to ocean productivity, but the types of species using them also relate to the proximity of islands suitable for nesting. For example, albatrosses can travel vast distances in search of food, whereas alcids are not able to make such long commutes. Depending on their location relative to feeding grounds, some islands can host breeding species adapted to very different marine habitats. For example, the Galapagos Islands are home to Galapagos Penguins that feed locally, Galapagos Albatrosses that commute south to the relatively cool upwellings of the Humboldt Current, Galapagos Shearwaters that commute north to warm waters along the coast of Central America, and Galapagos Petrels that range far offshore in the tropical Eastern Pacific.

1st wave completing
with fresh p10

2nd wave has
reached p5

Figure 13. *This immature Northern Gannet photographed in mid-February can be aged more precisely by looking for molt waves in the primaries: 2 waves of molt indicate a bird in its 2nd winter, supported by the wholly dark secondaries. Note contrast between fresher and blacker p5 and older and browner p6 (the oldest feather among the primaries), as well as a gradient within p1–p5 and within p6–p10 from browner (and older) p1 and p6 to blacker (and newer) p5 and p10.*

Seeing oceanic birds is as easy as getting on a boat and taking what is known as a pelagic trip, or simply a 'pelagic.' That said, a few tips may be helpful if you've never been on a pelagic or have tried only one or two. Because you'll be on a moving platform at all times, pelagic birding is some of the most challenging birding there is. As on land there will be slower birding days, and even on great days there will be slower periods. The number of bird species on a pelagic day trip may be only on the order of only 12–20 (with perhaps only 4–10 tubenoses), but they'll include some good birds. Given this manageable number of species you can easily review the possibilities beforehand—trying to read small print and looking at a book on a boat are good things to avoid.

Decent waterproof binoculars and a rainguard are important. You don't want to test the waterproofing of your binoculars at sea, but it's better to be prepared. Telescopes and tripods are not practical except on larger vessels (such as big ferries and cruise ships). Good 8-power or 7-power binoculars are better at sea than 10-power; the lower magnifications have a wider, brighter, and deeper field of view and are easier to hold steady—all big advantages on a moving platform while watching moving subjects over a moving surface. That said, a lot of watching is best done with the naked eye, at least until you feel comfortable being on a moving platform. Think about trying to watch birds using binoculars from the back of a pickup truck driving down a dirt road—using your naked eye is a lot easier. However, when the boat stops, or birds are close, that is the time for using your binoculars to get a good view of things.

Polarized sunglasses help greatly in cutting down glare, and particularly if you are fair skinned, sunscreen is a good idea, even on partly cloudy days, because reflection from the sea can be strong. Earplugs can be helpful, as many boats have loud engines. Keep a dry cloth or tissues handy in a resealable plastic bag for wiping off your lenses, which can be licked first to remove salt and avoid scratching. And after a pelagic it's good to rinse off salt spray residue with fresh water (assuming your binoculars are waterproof), to prolong the functional life of your optics.

Seasickness? If you've never been on a boat don't assume you'll get seasick, particularly if you take the following precautions. It may be better to try a short trip free from drugs, as some seasickness medications can make you queasy, dry mouthed, and sleepy, none of which is likely to enhance your experience. Instead, get a good night's sleep; stay outside with a breeze in your face; watch the horizon; watch the direction of prevailing waves and *let your body move with the ocean*, not fight against it (contrary to popular belief, the ocean surface does not move randomly); don't read or look down (review species you might see the day before; there really aren't that many); and use your binoculars only to look at birds you can see with the naked eye.

On small boats, it's helpful to keep food and water on your person to avoid going into the cabin; eat light meals and keep something in your stomach during the trip. Standing all day at sea can be tiring, and on longer trips you can lie down

---

Figure 14. Birders on a California pelagic trip, enjoying close-up views of Black-footed Albatrosses on the water behind the boat.

Figure 15. *Humans and seabirds often compete for the same resources, as here, where hundreds of Northern Gannets swarm around a fishing boat in the North Atlantic. Every corner of the world's oceans has been reached by humans, as one fish stock after another is pushed to or beyond the edge of sustainability.*

or sit down and take naps. And that's it—all that remains now is to get out there and see some oceanic birds!

CONSERVATION

Seabird numbers today are a mere fraction of what they once were—before humans brought non-native mammals (including themselves) to former seabird havens across the planet. Elimination courtesy of non-native predators can be easy to see and record, but the gradual declines through other processes, such as plastics in the ocean, over-fishing, and attraction to lights at night are more insidious. Humans have a great capacity for denial, only realizing something when it is too late. We can only hope that someone writing 50 or 100 years from now will not be lamenting the loss of Townsend's Shearwater, or of the wandering albatrosses, whose populations are in steady decline.

Traditionally, seabird conservation and study have focused on breeding grounds, because birds are easiest to study there. The study of birds at sea, where they spend most of their lives, involves numerous logistical factors that have limited this area of research. But problems at sea are also great, and understanding all aspects of a species' life history is necessary if we are to have any hope of conserving it. A fundamental first step in studying any organism is the ability to identify and name it. We hope this guide will aid in the identification, appreciation, monitoring, and conservation of oceanic birds.

The ocean is an infinite jigsaw, and, while each pelagic trip might contribute another small piece, we will never approach completing the puzzle. Mascarene Petrel is one of the rarest and least-known seabirds in the world, with its breeding grounds found only in 2007 and the first at-sea photos obtained in 2012. Its oceanic distribution remains ostensibly unknown, and even the genus to which it belongs, Pseudobulweria, *was not widely accepted as distinct from* Pterodroma *until the 2000s. Off Réunion Island, Indian Ocean, 5 December 2018.*

SPECIES ACCOUNTS AND PLATES

PENGUINS (19+ species in 6 genera)

Distinctive, well-known family of flightless diving seabirds, restricted to the Southern Hemisphere. Ages differ, sexes similar (male averages larger and bigger-billed in most species); juv. plumage replaced by adult plumage at about 1 year. Undergo synchronous molts on land, replacing all feathers in 2.5–5 weeks. Almost all species breed colonially; found singly or in groups at sea, where dive well and can be difficult to observe, let alone ID. Voices are mostly unmusical brays, honks, and chatters, mainly given around colonies and in interactions.

Can be considered in 5 groups: **ruling penguins** (genus *Aptenodytes*), **brush-tailed penguins** (genus *Pygoscelis*), **crested penguins** (genus *Eudyptes*), **banded penguins** (genus *Spheniscus*), and **miscellaneous penguins** (genera *Eudyptula*, *Megadyptes*). Most species distinctive, but some crested penguins and banded penguins very similar. For ID, pay attention to head and bill patterns, including color around base of bill.

Ruling, pp. 34–35

Brush-tailed, pp. 36–37

Crested, pp. 38–43

Banded, pp. 44–46

Miscellaneous, pp. 46–47

Penguins can commute long distances to their feeding grounds. When in a hurry, like these Erect Crested Penguins, they often move by repeated low-angle leaps from the water, a behavior known as porpoising.

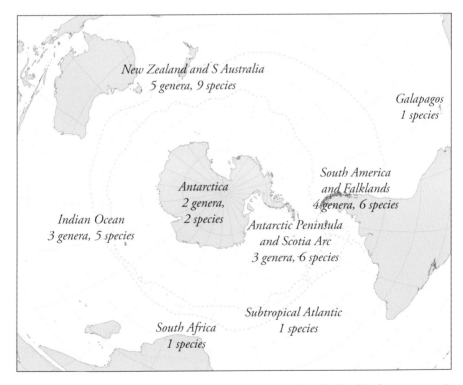

New Zealand and S Australia
5 genera, 9 species

Galapagos
1 species

South America
and Falklands
4 genera, 6 species

Antarctica
2 genera,
2 species

Indian Ocean
3 genera, 5 species

Antarctic Peninsula
and Scotia Arc
3 genera, 6 species

Subtropical Atlantic
1 species

South Africa
1 species

Present-day distribution of penguin species and genera. New Zealand is the top penguin hotspot, followed by South America and the Falklands, then the Antarctic Peninsula and Scotia Arc region (including South Georgia). Only 2 species (Emperor and Adelie) are truly birds of Antarctica.

34

RULING PENGUINS (Genus *Aptenodytes*)

Largest penguins. 2 species: Emperor breeding in Antarctica, King breeding on subantarctic islands. ID straightforward in range. Nest in colonies, with single egg incubated on feet and tucked into belly feathers.

adult, with Adelies and Chinstrap

adult with Adelie Penguins; large size not always striking

juv. has white throat

largest penguin, unmistakable in antarctic range; note relatively small, decurved bill

adult

possible 2nd-year (pale bill base)

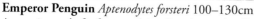

Emperor Penguin *Aptenodytes forsteri* 100–130cm
Antarctic, rarely far from pack ice. Breeds very locally in Antarctica, May–Dec; best known around Ross Sea and Antarctic Peninsula; exceptional vagrant n. of Antarctic Convergence. Away from breeding areas, usually seen as 1s and 2s standing on ice floes, often with other 'peon' penguins. Adults give wheezy brays and moans.

incubating adults

adults

distinctive, with long pointed bill; cf. larger (but smaller-billed) Emperor of Antarctic

fresh juv.

faded juv.

chick and molting juv.

adult

King Penguin *Aptenodytes patagonicus* 85–95cm

Subantarctic, mainly around Antarctic Convergence. Breeds in large dense colonies from South Georgia e. to Macquarie; smaller colonies on Falklands and (since 2000s) in s. Chile. Ranges at sea in subantarctic waters; vagrant farther n. Breeding mainly starts Nov–Dec, but cycle requires a year or more; hence colonies always have staggered activity. Adults produce trumpeting brays in display, begging juvs. give high, persistent whistles.

36

BRUSH-TAILED PENGUINS (Genus *Pygoscelis*)

Three species of colonial, medium-size, antarctic and subantarctic penguins, characterized by rather long and pointed ('brush-like') tails. ID straightforward, and all 3 breed together at some sites on Antarctic Peninsula and Scotia Arc islands. Adelie breeds earliest, then Gentoo, and lastly Chinstrap, which often nests on higher ground than the others. Nest scrapes built up with small stones; 2 eggs laid. Calls are gruff brays and chatters, sometimes given in pulsating rhythym.

juv. Adelie with Chinstraps and Gentoos

white throat, unlike black adult head

distinctive, with black head, white eyes

Adelie Penguin *Pygoscelis adeliae* 67–72cm
Stereotypical, gregarious, 'cartoon' penguin. Breeds Nov–Feb in colonies around Antarctica, also on Scotia Arc islands; molts Feb–Mar. In n. areas, breeds alongside Chinstrap and Gentoo. Ranges at sea around Antarctica, mainly in and near pack ice; rare vagrant n. of Antarctic Convergence. Regularly stands on ice floes, even fairly high on icebergs, often with Chinstraps. Juv. has white throat; dull eyes become pale in 1st year.

distinctive, with white 'headphones' and lipstick-orange bill

adult feeding juv.

Gentoo Penguin *Pygoscelis papua* 70–80cm
Attractive penguin of subantarctic islands from South Georgia e. to Macquarie; also Scotia Arc islands, Antarctic Peninsula, Falklands. Occurs alongside King and Magellanic Penguins in n. of range; usually nests in small colonies. Breeds Jul/Oct–Dec/Mar in n. of range, Nov–Apr in s. Ranges mainly in subantarctic waters; vagrant to s. South America, New Zealand, Tasmania. Two races: n. *papua* averages larger and longer-billed than *ellsworthi* of Antarctic region. Ages similar, but juv. has paler throat, averages less white on head.

distinctive, with white face, narrow black chinstrap

ground stained red by krill residue from penguin poop

molting

with Adelie

Chinstrap Penguin *Pygoscelis antarctica* 67–72cm
Striking penguin of Antarctic Peninsula and Scotia Arc islands, with >99% of population in S Atlantic region; very small numbers elsewhere, as at Balleny Is., E Antarctica. Breeds Nov–Mar, often in dense colonies; molts Feb–Mar. Ranges at sea in pack ice around Antarctica; rare vagrant n. of Antarctic Convergence. Regularly stands on ice floes, even fairly high on icebergs, at times in big groups. Ages similar, but some juvs. have dusky flecking on face and throat.

38

CRESTED PENGUINS (Genus *Eudyptes*)

Of 8 species, 4 are endemic to the New Zealand region. In most places, nest in colonies well above the sea, reaching nest sites by treks, often over steep and rocky slopes, where hop and move confidently (all could equally be called rockhoppers). Nest scrapes lined with stones and vegetation; 2 eggs laid.

Main ID features are pattern of yellow head plumes, presence or absence of pale margin around base of bill, and size of bill. ID of adults at sea often not possible (diagnostic head plumes sleeked down when wet), and 1st-years of all species very similar, even when dry—note bill size and pattern. All species give braying and chattering calls; trumpeting brays can carry far over still water.

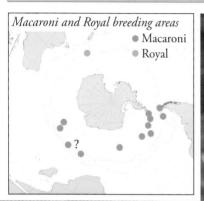

Macaroni and Royal breeding areas
● Macaroni
● Royal

many birds in normal range of Macaroni have a slightly paler, grayish throat

distinctive in normal range; lush golden head plumes meet across forehead

with Gentoo Penguin

note pink gape and big bill, cf. rockhoppers

Macaroni Penguin *Eudyptes chrysolophus* 65–75cm
Locally common on antarctic and subantarctic islands from Scotia Sea e. to Indian Ocean; also small numbers locally on Falklands (among Rockhopper colonies) and in Cape Horn region. Breeds Nov–Mar, molts Feb–Apr. Occurs at sea in antarctic and subantarctic waters; vagrant n. to S Africa, e. to New Zealand. 1st-year has paler throat, reduced head plumes. Adult plumes greatly reduced when wet and swimming.

note smaller size of presumed Macaroni (left) with typical Royal Penguins

dusky-faced birds uncommon, dark-headed birds rare in east coast colonies

50–80% of birds in east coast colonies white-faced, only 10–20% in west coast colonies; females more often dark-faced than males

Royal Penguin *Eudyptes schlegeli* 72–77cm
Locally common on Macquarie I., Australia; breeds Oct–Feb, molts Jan–Apr. Macaroni Penguin averages smaller and smaller-billed, rare vagrant to Macquarie. Only other crested penguin breeding on Macquarie is Eastern Rockhopper. Typical 1st-year has variable dusky markings on face and throat, reduced head plumes; others may be dark-faced. Taxonomic status of small numbers of white-faced, Royal-like birds on Marion I. and Crozets remains to be elucidated.

ROCKHOPPER PENGUINS

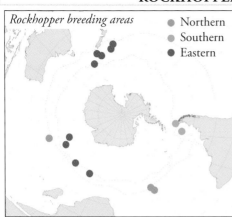

Rockhopper breeding areas
- Northern
- Southern
- Eastern

Formerly considered 1 or 2 species, but recent studies support recognition of 3 species (see map).

Subtropical Northern Rockhopper distinctive, but other 2 species subtle, differing mainly in bill pattern. Rockhoppers overlap in range with several other crested penguins, all of which are larger and can be distinguished by details of crest plumes and head pattern. Beware that shape of plumes in all species of crested penguins varies with mood (e.g., flared strongly when excited) and whether dry or wet.

distinctive; only penguin in its very local subtropical range; head plumes much less obvious when wet

1st-year

Northern Rockhopper Penguin *Eudyptes [chrysocome] moseleyi* 60–65cm
Fairly common but very local on Tristan group and Gough in Atlantic, and on Amsterdam/St. Paul in Indian Ocean; ranges at sea in subtropical waters; vagrant to S Africa and SW Ausralia. Breeds Sep–Dec, molts Dec–Mar. Adult has exuberant, 'punk' head plumes (greatly reduced to narrow eyebrow when wet); 1st-year has pale throat, duller bill, reduced head plumes.

distinctive in range; only regular overlap is with larger Macaroni Penguin (p. 38)

nesting with Black-browed Albatross

Southern Rockhopper Penguin *Eudyptes [chrysocome] chrysocome* 55–60cm
South Atlantic. Fairly common but local breeder in Falklands and Cape Horn region, ranges at sea in subantarctic S Atlantic; vagrant to S Australia, and s. to South Georgia. Breeds Nov–Mar, molts Jan–Apr. Lacks pale gape margin of Eastern Rockhopper. 1st-year has pale throat, head plumes reduced to fine yellow brow line. Cf. larger Macaroni Penguin (p. 38).

pale gape margin

smaller and smaller-billed than other crested penguins in its range, with thinner head plumes becoming a narrow line forward of eyes

Eastern Rockhopper Penguin *Eudyptes [chrysocome] filholi* 55–60cm
Fairly common but local on subantarctic islands from Indian Ocean e. to New Zealand; vagrant n. to S Africa and S Australia. Breeds Nov–Mar, molts Jan–Apr. 1st-year has pale throat, head plumes reduced to fine yellow brow line. Breeding range overlaps Macaroni (p. 38) in Indian Ocean, and Erect-crested (p. 42) in New Zealand.

NEW ZEALAND CRESTED PENGUINS

despite its smaller size and different head pattern, an Eastern Rockhopper can be overlooked easily among Erect-crested Penguins—can you find it?

with begging chicks

1st-year

crest sleeks down to neat stripe when wet; swimming birds and imms. not readily distinguished from Snares Crested; Fjordland Crested lacks pale gape margin

crest starts nearer gape than in Fjordland and Snares

crest wet

from slightly smaller Snares Crested by erect bushy brows (when dry), less stocky build

Erect-crested Penguin *Eudyptes sclateri* 65–70cm
Common endemic on Antipodes and Bounties, New Zealand. Breeds Oct–Feb, molts Jan–Apr. Some wander n. to main islands of New Zealand; vagrant n. to S Australia and Macquarie I., exceptionally to Falklands. 1st-year has paler throat, duller bill, reduced head plumes.

very like Snares Crested but lacks pale gape margin; adult usually has whitish streaks on sides of throat

1st-year

Fjordland Crested Penguin *Eudyptes pachyrhynchus* 57–62cm
Endemic to New Zealand. Breeds Aug–Nov and molts Jan–Mar, mainly along sw. coast of South Island and on Stewart I.; non-breeding range presumably in New Zealand waters, including North Island; vagrant s. to subantarctic islands (mainly Snares) and n. to SE Australia. 1st-year has paler throat, duller bill, reduced head plumes.

1st-year

crest position and length vary with mood, individual, and whether wet or dry

Snares Crested Penguin *Eudyptes robustus* 57–62cm
Common endemic on Snares Is., New Zealand; ranges very rarely n. to South Island, vagrant to SE Australia. Breeds Sep–Jan, molts Jan–Apr. Cf. very similar Fjordland Crested and slightly larger Erect-crested Penguins. 1st-year has paler throat, duller bill, reduced head plumes.

44

BANDED PENGUINS (Genus *Spheniscus*)

Four species: 3 in South America, 1 in South Africa. Only ID concern is Humboldt vs. Magellanic, especially 1st-years. Nest colonially in burrows dug in soil, and in rock crevices; 1–2 eggs laid. Some colonies number 1000s of pairs, but when birds are incubating very little activity may be apparent. Loud braying calls have earned the trio of larger species the name jackass penguins.

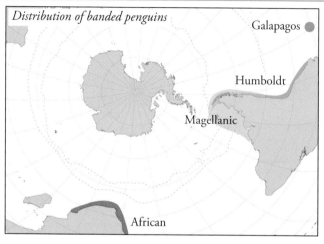

Distribution of banded penguins

Galapagos

Humboldt

Magellanic

African

distinctive, only penguin in Africa; adult has single black breast band

1st-years

adults

African (Jackass) Penguin *Spheniscus demersus* 65–70cm
Breeds South Africa and Namibia, vagrant n. to W Africa and Mozambique; breeds in any month, and cycle can be less than annual. On adult note single black breast band, variable dark spots on underparts (very rarely dense enough to create a second breast band); 1st-year has variable face and neck pattern. Mainly in shelf and inshore waters, often seen from shore.

adult has single black breast band, pink bill base, narrow white eyebrow

adult

reduced feathering, cf. Magellanic

pink at base of bill can be hard to see on imm.

Humboldt Penguin *Spheniscus humboldtii* 65–70cm
South America. Shelf and inshore waters from Lobos de Tierra I., n. Peru, s. to Chiloé I., cen. Chile; vagrant n. to s. Ecuador, exceptionally to Cen America. Breeds on inshore islands (in any month in Peru; Oct–Mar in cen. Chile), and often seen from shore. Uncommon and local; still impacted by guano harvesting in Peru. Occurs alongside Magellanic at colonies in cen. Chile. Often paler above than Magellanic (useful when the 2 species are together).

feathered base, cf. Humboldt

distinctive in most of range; all ages have dark base to bill

1st-year has variable face and neck pattern

adult has 2 black breast bands, broad white eyebrow

Magellanic Penguin *Spheniscus magellanicus* 65–70cm
South America. Locally common in s. Chile, s. Argentina, Falklands; uncommon among colonies of Humboldt Penguin in cen. Chile. Breeds Oct–Mar, molts Feb–Mar. Migrant (mainly Apr–Oct) to n. Chile and se. Brazil, very rarely n. to s. Peru and ne. Brazil; vagrant to New Zealand, SE Australia. Mainly in shelf and inshore waters, often seen from shore and ferries.

distinctive: only penguin in Galapagos; note relatively long bill

adults

1st-year

Galapagos Penguin *Spheniscus mendiculus* 48–53cm
Endemic to Galapagos Is. Breeds locally (in any month) on Isabela and Fernandina, near the coast in burrows and crevices. Wanders to other islands. Small, and can be difficult to see in open ocean. Groups often loaf in inshore waters and along coasts.

MISCELLANEOUS PENGUINS (Genera *Eudyptula, Megadyptes*)
Two distinctive species of the New Zealand region: the scarce and 'antisocial' Yellow-eyed Penguin, and the diminutive Little Penguin.

small (for a penguin) and rather plain, difficult to see in the water; no similar species

note pale eyes, small grayish bill

Little (Blue) Penguin *Eudyptula minor* 40–50cm
Southern Australia (breeds mainly May–Dec) and New Zealand (breeds mainly Aug–Jan); vagrant to s. South America. Upperpart color varies with population and plumage wear; ages similar. Nests in burrows, rock crevices; mainly nocturnal at colonies; 2 eggs laid.

Australian population averages shallower bill, has been proposed as separate species, *E. novae-hollandiae*. Population on e. side of New Zealand's South Island has more extensive white edging to flippers, sometimes treated as separate species, **White-flippered Penguin** *E. albosignata*.

unique, with yellow headband, streaked crown, staring pale eyes

1st-year

adults

Yellow-eyed Penguin *Megadyptes antipodes* 70–75cm
Endemic to New Zealand. Breeds Sep–Mar, locally on main South Island, and on Auckland and Campbell Is.; molts mainly Feb–Mar. Breeds in scattered pairs under cover; 1–2 eggs laid. Not colonial like most penguins, although flocks gather locally on beaches in non-breeding season, when does not range far from breeding areas. Juv. lacks yellow headband, throat whitish, eyes average duller.

ALCIDS (25 species in 12 genera)

Northern Hemisphere family of heavy-bodied diving seabirds, the ecological counterparts to penguins. Together with the Dodo, the flightless Great Auk of the North Atlantic is an icon of extinction. Alcids are most diverse in the North Pacific; only 6 species occur regularly in the North Atlantic. Favor cold and cooler high-latitude waters, with a few species also in subtropical waters of nw. Mexico. Most species are short- to medium-distance migrants. ID at sea can be very challenging, because alcids typically dive to avoid boats or take off and fly straight away, low and fast over the water.

Most alcids exhibit seasonal and age-related plumage differences, but the sexes appear similar; attain adult appearance in 1–2 years. Wing molt mainly in non-breeding periods (overlaps with breeding in a few species) and synchronous in several species, which thus become flightless for a few weeks. Even when full-winged, most species need to run along the water surface to gain momentum for takeoff. Feed by diving, using their wings underwater. Flight through the air direct and usually fairly low over the water, with steady fast wingbeats and no gliding. Most alcids nest colonially, usually on islands, and sometimes in huge numbers. Some species nest above ground on cliffs and steep slopes, even high in trees, but most nest hidden in burrows and crevices. Most species breeding at mid-latitudes visit colonies at night to avoid predators such as gulls and raptors. Voices are largely unmusical chatters, clucks, brays, and whistles, sometimes helpful for ID.

For ID purposes, alcids can be divided into 4 groups: **murres and allies** (4 species in 3 genera), **puffins and auklets** (9 species in 5 genera), **guillemots** (4 species in 1 genus), and **murrelets** (8 species in 2 genera).

a typical view of many small alcids, in this case a Cassin's Auklet

Murres and Allies
pp. 50–52

Puffins and Auklets
pp. 53–57

Guillemots
pp. 58–60

Murrelets
pp. 61–65

MURRES AND ALLIES (4 species in 3 genera)

Largely Atlantic and High Arctic group of gregarious, black-and-white alcids. Solid dark hoods in breeding plumage, white throats in non-breeding/imm. plumages. Braying, growling, and other guttural calls given mainly at colonies. Nest in dense colonies (large species often mixed together) on cliffs, rocky ledges, in crevices and boulder screes; visit colonies during the day. Murre and Razorbill chicks leave the nest ledges before they can fly and are accompanied at sea for a few weeks by the male parent, keeping in contact with low brays (adult) and high whistles (juvenile). Wing molt occurs in late summer–fall and is synchronous, so that birds are flightless for 2–4 weeks.

with Razorbills

breeding adult

variable dark on coverts

non-breeding

large alcid with pointed bill, dark brown upperparts, variable dark flank streaking

California adult with chick

some chicks dark-headed

some N Atlantic birds have white spectacles

Common Murre (Common Guillemot) *Uria aalge* 41–46cm Atlantic, 43–48cm Pacific North Pacific, North Atlantic. Breeds May/Jun–Jul/Aug in Pacific region from Chukchi and Bering Seas s. to n. Japan and California, in Atlantic region from sw. Greenland and Novaya Zemlya s. to Gulf of Maine and Portugal; locally common to fairly common. Winters at sea in N Pacific and N Atlantic, rarely s. to nw. Mexico and North Carolina. Northern breeding populations average darker upperparts and stouter bills than southern populations.

whiter underwing than Common

non-breeding

Atlantic

1st-winter has smaller bill, reduced pale gape line

stockier than Common Murre, with shorter bill, pale gape stripe, blacker upperparts, unstreaked flanks

breeding adult

Pacific

non-breeding (right) with molting Common Murre (Oct)

Thick-billed Murre (Brünnich's Guillemot) *Uria lomvia* 38–44cm Atlantic, 41–47cm Pacific Arctic Ocean, North Pacific, North Atlantic. Breeds Jun/Jul–Aug in Pacific region from Arctic Russia and Bering Sea s. to Kurils and sw. Alaska, also n. British Columbia; in Atlantic region from Arctic Canada and Novaya Zemlya s. to Newfoundland, Iceland, n. Norway; locally common to fairly common. Winters mainly around and s. of pack ice, in N Pacific s. to n. Japan and British Columbia (very rarely to California); in N Atlantic s. to New England (rarely to Mid-Atlantic states) and s. Norway. Pacific birds average blacker upperparts than Atlantic.

North Atlantic Winter Alcid Comparison

Thick-billed Murre

dark head, whitish throat, stout bill

Razorbill

dark helmet, thick bill, long tail

Common Murre

white cheek with dark stripe, slender bill

Black Guillemot

white head, small bill, white wing panel

breeding adults

adult non-breeding

large alcid with thick black bill, rather long and pointed tail

juv./1st-winter bill smaller, without white lines

adult non-breeding

Razorbill *Alca torda* 37–42cm; also see p. 51

North Atlantic. Locally fairly common breeder (May/Jun–Jul/Aug) from w. Greenland s. to Gulf of Maine, and from Iceland and White Sea s. to nw. France. Winters in N Atlantic, s. to Mid-Atlantic states, SW Europe, and W Mediterranean, often in nearshore waters.

dark underwings

non-breeding

small, stocky, 'bathtub-toy' alcid with stubby bill, rapid whirring flight

adult breeding

Dovekie (Little Auk) *Alle alle* 21–24cm

Arctic Ocean. Locally common to fairly common breeder Jun–Aug in Arctic Ocean from e. Baffin I. and Greenland e. to Arctic Russia; small numbers in Bering Sea on Little Diomede I., St. Lawrence I. Winters mainly around and s. of pack ice, irregularly s. over shelf and shelf slope waters to e. US and NW Europe. Nests in dense colonies; at sea, often found in flocks, usually not associating with other alcids.

PUFFINS AND AUKLETS (9 species in 4 genera)

Largely Pacific group of alcids with stout and often colorful bills, especially in breeding season; puffins require 3–4 years to attain full adult bill size and pattern. Ages and seasonal plumages differ; most species have ornamental head plumes, most distinct in breeding plumage. Purring, moaning, and clucking calls heard mainly at colonies. Nest in crevices and burrows, usually in colonies, often of multiple species in Bering Sea and North Pacific; s. populations often visit colonies at night to avoid predators.

Wing molt in larger species is synchronous, and birds are flightless for 2–4 weeks in late summer (or, in Atlantic and Horned Puffins, in late winter); wing molt of smaller auklets (Crested, Whiskered, Least, Cassin's) gradual in summer–fall, when these can still fly and continue foraging commutes.

breeding adults

note dark underwings, complete black collar

1st-summer

distinctive, medium-size, 'clown-faced' alcid with big red-and-blue bill, smoky-gray face

non-breeding adult (October)

juvenile (October)

Atlantic Puffin *Fratercula arctica* 27–30cm

North Atlantic. Locally fairly common to common breeder late Apr/Jun–Jul/Aug from Greenland and Novaya Zemlya s. to Gulf of Maine and nw. France, most numerous in Iceland, Norway, and British Isles. Winters in N Atlantic, mainly well offshore, s. to Mid-Atlantic states, NW Africa, and w. Mediterranean. Breeds colonially on grassy-topped cliffs, also crevices at high latitudes. Away from colonies, seen mainly as singles or small loose groups, usually not associating with other alcids. Adult wing molt in late winter–spring.

distinctive, fairly large alcid with huge yellow-and-red bill, dark 'eyelash' horns

breeding adults

1st-summer

subadult

Horned Puffin *Fratercula corniculata* 34–37cm

North Pacific. Locally fairly common to common breeder Jun–Sep from Beaufort and Bering Seas s. to cen. Kurils and se. Alaska (rarely British Columbia); winters mainly well offshore in N Pacific, s. to n. Japan and n. California. At sea away from colonies, usually found as singles. Non-breeding/imm. has smaller bill and darker face than breeding adult, as in Atlantic Puffin. Adult wing molt in late winter–spring, vs. fall in Tufted Puffin.

distinctive, large, black-bodied alcid with big orange-red bill

breeding adults

1st-summer

2nd-summer

with Rhinoceros Auklet

full adult bill in puffins develops in 3–4 years

non-breeding adult

juvenile

Tufted Puffin *Fratercula (Lunda) cirrhata* 37–41cm

North Pacific. Locally fairly common to common breeder May/Jun–Aug/Sep from Beaufort and Bering Seas s. to n. Japan and cen. California; winters mainly well offshore in N Pacific, s. to around 35°N. At sea away from colonies usually found as singles, separate from other alcids.

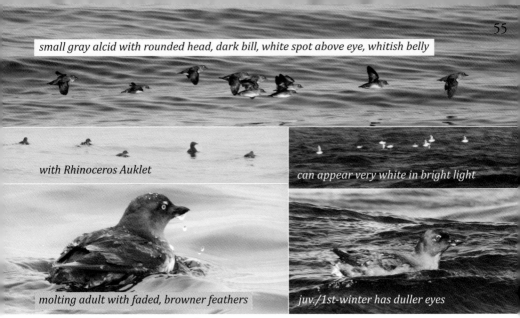

small gray alcid with rounded head, dark bill, white spot above eye, whitish belly

with Rhinoceros Auklet

can appear very white in bright light

molting adult with faded, browner feathers

juv./1st-winter has duller eyes

Cassin's Auklet *Ptychoramphus aleuticus* 21–23cm
North Pacific. Locally common to fairly common (breeds Jan–Apr in s. areas, Jun–Aug in n.) from Aleutians s. to nw. Mexico. Winters in N Pacific, with southward shift from n. breeding areas. Usually in flocks, at times 1000s, less often singles. Can be locally abundant in areas with krill; off California, often found in the same areas as Blue Whales, which also eat krill.

large gray alcid with orange bill, flat, rather anvil-shaped head

with Cassin's Auklet

subadult

belly extensively white on imm./non-breeding, cf. Parakeet Auklet (p. 56)

breeding adult has big white face stripes, 'rhino horn' on bill

non-breeding adult

1st-year bill finer and darker

Rhinoceros Auklet *Cerorhinca monocerata* 33–36cm
North Pacific. Locally fairly common to common breeder Apr/Jun–Jul/Aug from s. Kurils to Japan, from sw. Alaska to California; winters mainly in shelf waters, in Japan and from se. Alaska s. to nw. Mexico. Often in small groups, sometimes in 10s. Attains full bill horn in 2–3 years.

medium-size alcid with stout orange-red bill, extensively white underparts

breeding adult non-breeding

Parakeet Auklet *Aethia psittacula* 25–27cm

North Pacific. Locally common breeder May/Jun–Aug from Bering Sea s. to Kurils and Gulf of Alaska; winters offshore in N Pacific s. to Japan and California. Often in small groups, less often flocks of a few 100 birds. Non-breeding/imm. has pale gray to whitish throat, duller bill. Juv. has grayish bill, duller eyes, shorter and duller face plume. Cf. imm. Rhinoceros Auklet (p. 55).

distinctive, very small alcid with extensively white underparts (variably mottled slaty in breeding plumage)

breeding adult highly variable; most have white throat patch

non-breeding

extreme dark variant

Least Auklet *Aethia pusilla* 16–18cm

North Pacific. Locally common breeder late May/Jun–Aug from Bering Sea s. to cen. Kurils and Aleutians; winters in ice-free waters from Bering Sea s. to n. Japan. Often feeds and commutes in large flocks, or swarms. Non-breeding/imm. has white throat and underparts, whitish shoulder patches. Juv. like non-breeding but eyes duller.

stocky, medium-size, slaty-gray alcid with bushy frontal crest, big lipstick-red bill

lacks white belly of slightly larger and rangier Parakeet Auklet

breeding adult

1st-winter

Crested Auklet *Aethia cristatella* 24–26cm
North Pacific. Locally common breeder late May/Jun–Aug from Bering Sea s. to cen. Kurils and Aleutians; winters in ice-free waters from Bering Sea s. to n. Japan and Gulf of Alaska. Often feeds and commutes in large flocks, or swarms. Non-breeding/imm. has shorter crest. Juv. has grayish bill, duller eyes, vestigial bushy crest, no face plumes.

distinctive small alcid with long wispy crest, bold white face plumes, stubby red bill

whitish belly visible in flight

crest can be held flat

breeding adults

Whiskered Auklet *Aethia pygmaea* 19–21cm
North Pacific. Locally common breeder May–Jul/Aug from Sea of Okhotsk and Aleutians s. to Kurils; winters near and within breeding range, also s. to Japan. Often feeds in large flocks, especially in tidal rips between islands. Non-breeding/imm. has reduced head plumes. Juv. has grayish bill, duller eyes, no face plumes; cf. slightly larger, bigger-billed Cassin's Auklet (p. 55).

58

GUILLEMOTS (4 species in 1 genus)

Medium–large, slender-billed alcids (note: murres are known as guillemots in the Old World). Mostly black in breeding plumage, blackish above and white below in non-breeding/imm. plumages; 1st-summer plumage variably intermediate between breeding and non-breeding adult. High-pitched whistling calls. Nest in crevices and burrows, including human-made structures; visit colonies during day. Often seen from shore year-round, favoring rocky coasts; mainly in small groups or as singles, rarely in flocks of more than 100 birds. Wing molt in late summer– late fall is synchronous, so birds are flightless for 2–3 weeks.

distinctive in most of range; told from Pigeon Guillemot (overlap in Bering Sea) by gleaming white underwing coverts

High Arctic

non-breeding adults

breeding adults

N Atlantic

juv. variable; wing panel reduced to white tips

Black Guillemot *Cepphus grylle* 32–36cm; also see pp. 51, 60

Arctic Ocean, North Atlantic. Locally fairly common breeder May/Jun–Jul/Aug from Arctic Canada and Greenland e. to Arctic Russia and n. Alaska; in N Atlantic, breeds s. to Gulf of Maine and nw. British Isles. Winters inshore, largely within ice-free waters of breeding range, a few s. to New England, rarely to Pribilofs. High Arctic race *mandtii* is whiter overall in winter than s. populations; rare variant of *mandtii* has upperwing panel mostly to wholly blackish year-round. Some adults (especially in Iceland) and 1st-summers have dark bar in white wing panel.

distinctive: note white wing panel, dark underwings; cf. Black Guillemot

non-breeding adults

breeding adults

dark bar in white wing panel can be hidden at rest

juv. messier than Common Murre; wing panel reduced to white tips

Pigeon Guillemot *Cepphus columba* 32–36cm; also see p. 60
North Pacific. Locally fairly common breeder May/Jun–Jul/Aug from Bering Sea s. to Kamchat-ka and California. Winters in ice-free waters of breeding range and s. to n. Japan; in E Pacific, s. populations move n. in Aug–Sep to winter in protected waters of Pacific Northwest and Alaska. Like other guillemots, flight typically low and fast, more hurried than larger murres.

very local in NW Pacific; white wing panel reduced or lacking

molting, Feb

breeding adults

non-breeding with Pigeon Guillemot (behind)

Kuril (Snow's) Guillemot *Cepphus [columba] snowi* 32–36cm; also see p. 60
Split from Pigeon Guillemot. Local breeder May–Aug in Kurils (Paramushir s. to Iturup); potential overlap (and interbreeding?) with Pigeon Guillemot needs study. Winters in ice-free waters of breeding range, s. to n. Japan. White wing panel reduced or absent, and non-breeding blacker above than Pigeon; cf. larger Spectacled Guillemot (p. 60).

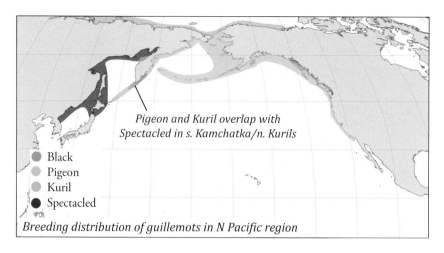

Pigeon and Kuril overlap with Spectacled in s. Kamchatka/n. Kurils

● Black
○ Pigeon
○ Kuril
● Spectacled

Breeding distribution of guillemots in N Pacific region

distinctive, bulky guillemot of NE Asia: note white goggles, lack of white wing panel

non-breeding

breeding adults

Spectacled Guillemot *Cepphus carbo* 38–42cm
Northwest Pacific. Locally fairly common to uncommon breeder May–Aug from Sea of Okhotsk and s. Kamchatka s. to n. Japan (where declining) and n. Korea; winters mainly within ice-free areas of breeding range and s. to s. Japan. Non-breeding/imm. has white underparts but retains diagnostic white 'goggles' on black head; cf. non-breeding Kuril Guillemot.

MURRELETS (8 species in 2 genera)

Small, slender-billed, relatively long-winged alcids of North Pacific, mainly found as pairs or small groups; take off from water more easily than other alcids, sometimes springing up without pattering. Ages and seasonal plumages differ in northern-breeding species, similar in southern species. Calls are varied whistles, trills, and grunts. Breed in loose colonies and scattered pairs; nest in crevices, also (Marbled and Long-billed) on branches in conifer forest canopy; visit colonies at night. Wing molt occurs in summer–fall; primaries are shed in blocks or synchronously, and birds can be flightless for 2–3 weeks.

Genus *Brachyramphus* Like most alcids, young remain in nest and fledge at night. 1st-summer birds highly variable; some have full breeding plumage, others non-breeding plumage, others intermediate. Long-billed Murrelet formerly treated as Asian race of Marbled Murrelet.

small nearshore alcid; breeding adult mottled dark brown overall, often with ghosting of distinctive non-breeding head/neck pattern

breeding adults

molting adult and some 1st-summers have variably messy head pattern

lores rarely dark

non-breeding has broken white hindcollar, white shoulder patches; lores usually white

Marbled Murrelet *Brachyramphus marmoratus* 25–29cm
Northeast Pacific; usually in twos. Uncommon to fairly common breeder Apr/Jul–Jun/Sep from Aleutians s. to cen. California. Winters in nearshore waters from s. Alaska to California. Often seen from land; rarely found more than a few miles offshore. Flight call when commuting to and from nests a strong, ringing *keeur*; at sea, also gives sharp whistled yelps. Common Murre chick can be mistaken for non-breeding Marbled; usually white-faced and with parent murre.

62

non-breeding

white tail, unlike Marbled

breeding adults

small, short-billed alcid with rather blank face; breeding adult spangled pale gray and brown, with extensively white belly

Kittlitz's Murrelet *Brachyramphus brevirostris* 23–27 cm
North Pacific. Uncommon to locally fairly common breeder mid-May/Jun to Jul/Aug from Chukchi Sea s. to Sea of Okhotsk and se. Alaska. In breeding season, mainly found as singles and pairs in fjords and inshore waters near glaciers and icebergs, often in the same areas as more numerous Marbled Murrelet. Presumed to winter in shelf waters of N Pacific.

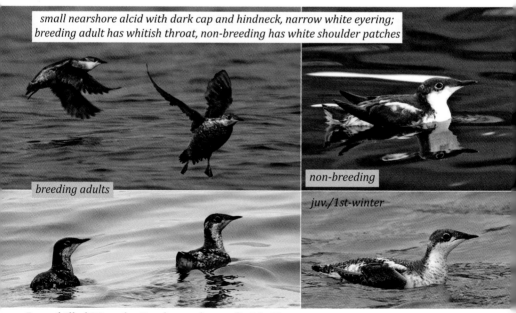

small nearshore alcid with dark cap and hindneck, narrow white eyering; breeding adult has whitish throat, non-breeding has white shoulder patches

breeding adults

non-breeding

juv./1st-winter

Long-billed Murrelet *Brachyramphus perdix* 26–30 cm
Northwest Pacific; usually in twos. Uncommon to fairly common breeder May–Aug locally from Kamchatka and Sea of Okhotsk s. to n. Japan; winters in nearshore waters from Sakhalin s. to s. Japan, around 25°N. Widespread vagrant across North America (mainly Jul–Dec), s. to California and e. to Atlantic Canada and Florida, with many records inland.

Genus *Synthiboramphus* Fluffy chicks leave nest crevices within a few days and swim off with parents, in some cases moving long distances. No age/seasonal plumage differences in the 3 southern species. Guadalupe and Scripps's Murrelets formerly lumped as 1 species and known as Xantus's Murrelet.

small, brightly patterned alcid with black head, white neck sides, steely-gray back, small pale bill

imm./non-breeding

non-breeding

breeding adults

Ancient Murrelet *Synthliboramphus antiquus* 25–27cm
North Pacific. Locally fairly common to common (breeds Apr/Jun–Jun/Aug) from Command-ers and Sea of Okhotsk s. locally to Yellow Sea, and from Aleutians s. to n. British Columbia; winters mainly in shelf waters of N Pacific, s. to Japan and California, where can be seen from shore. Often in small flocks, up to 50+ birds. White hindcrown stripes variable (even in winter), typically streaked and indistinct, but sometimes thick and bushy, recalling Japanese Murrelet.

Japan, where overlaps locally with smaller-billed Ancient Murrelet

breeding adult has black neck sides; solid white head stripes thicker than Ancient

non-breeding distinctive, with white throat and lores, streaky head stripes

crest often held flat

Japanese (Crested) Murrelet *Synthliboramphus wumizusume* 25–27cm
Uncommon to locally fairly common (breeds Mar–May) in Japan, n. to Honshu, also off South Korea. Nests on rocky islets; feeds mainly in shelf waters, not far offshore. Usually in pairs or small groups. Adult breeding plumage mainly Feb–Jul; imm. similar to non-breeding plumage.

Jul–Oct

Guadalupe Murrelet

Jun–Oct

?

Scripps's Murrelet

Jul–Oct

?

Craveri's Murrelet

?

birds that appear intermediate between Guadalupe and Scripps's are likely poorly marked Guadalupe; ID best confirmed by voice; also note finer bill of Guadalupe

most birds distinctive, with beady dark eye offset in white face

bright white underwings, like Scripps's Murrelet

extent of white face varies with angle of view and individually

Guadalupe Murrelet *Synthliboramphus hypoleucus* 24–25.5cm
Northeast Pacific; usually in twos. Locally fairly common breeder Mar–Jun on Guadalupe and San Benitos, Mexico. Uncommon post-breeding migrant Jul–Oct n. to California, rarely to Washington, mainly well offshore. Call from post-breeding birds at sea (especially when pairs are separated) is a ringing, fairly slow-paced trill, more musical than drier, more cricket-like trill of Craveri's Murrelet; also quiet hard ticks that may run into trills.

stockier and stouter-billed than Craveri's Murrelet; usually shows white notch forward of eye

upperparts grayer than Craveri's

bright white underwing coverts

large chick/young juv. has finer bill, weaker white eye-arcs than adult

Scripps's Murrelet *Synthliboramphus scrippsi* 24–25.5cm
Northeast Pacific; usually in twos. Locally fairly common breeder Mar–Jun from San Benitos n. to California Channel Is. Uncommon Jun–Oct n. to British Columbia, mainly well offshore. Call from post-breeding birds at sea is a high piping whistle, usually in short series; may suggest a baby chicken, distinct from trills of Guadalupe and Craveri's Murrelets.

thinner-billed and longer-tailed than Scripps's Murrelet; black cap comes down lower on face, below base of bill

underwings dusky overall

tail often cocked in a point

upperparts darker than Scripps's

Craveri's Murrelet *Synthliboramphus craveri* 24–25.5cm
Northwest Mexico; usually in twos. Locally fairly common breeder Feb–May in Gulf of California; also breeds on San Benitos. Post-breeding movement Jun–Jul to s. and into Pacific waters; uncommon and irregular Jul–Oct n. to cen. California, mainly in warm-water years. Call from post-breeding birds at sea is a dry, rattled, slightly reedy trill.

66

DIVING-PETRELS (6+ species in 1 genus)

Small, poorly known group of Southern Hemisphere diving tubenoses; ecological counterparts to auklets of Northern Hemisphere. Traditionally considered a distinct family, but now usually treated as a divergent group within the petrel family (see p. 70). Species-level taxonomy vexed: 4 species usually recognized, but Common Diving-Petrel complex surely comprises multiple cryptic species and is in need of critical modern study (the last overview of diving-petrel taxonomy and relationships was published in 1921!). ID at sea can be challenging if not functionally impossible, compounded by often poor views, but most taxa are not known to overlap in range.

Diving-petrels are found singly or in aggregations, locally in 100s or even 1000s at feeding areas and near colonies. Typical view is of birds flying past or away (as flushed by boats), low over the water with rapid, 'whirring' wingbeats and no gliding; often dive straight into water on 'landing' and may stay submerged a minute or longer. Diving-petrels can glide and bank briefly in strong winds, but rarely do they stop flapping for more than a few seconds—or they would fall out of the air. Run across surface to gain speed for takeoff. Ages/sexes similar. Nest in burrows and crevices on islands, visit colonies at night to avoid skuas, gulls, and other daytime predators. Often grounded on ships when attracted to lights. Rarely vocal away from breeding grounds.

Unidentified diving-petrels (suspected to be mainly or entirely South Georgia) at South Georgia, where both Subantarctic [Common] and South Georgia Diving-Petrels are 'common' (3.8 million and 2 million pairs, respectively). Field ID criteria for these 2 species are still developing, with bill size and structure being the most reliable characters.

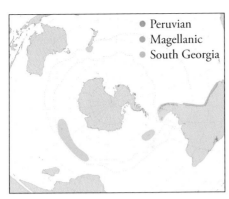
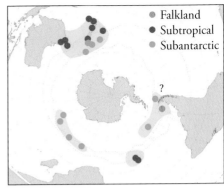

Common Diving-Petrel Complex

only diving-petrel in Humboldt Current; no similar species in range

Peruvian Diving-Petrel *Pelecanoides garnotii* 23–25cm; see map, top of page
Humboldt Current. Shelf and inshore waters from Lobos de Tierra I., n. Peru, s. to Gulf of
Arauco, cen. Chile (nests year-round, at least in Peru); can be seen from shore, at times in
groups of 10s. Largest diving-petrel; plumage lacks strong contrast, bill relatively large. Range
not known to overlap with other diving-petrels, but should be looked for around Chiloé I.,
Chile, where overlap with Common and Magellanic Diving-Petrels might be possible.

distinctive diving-petrel: white neck sides contrast with blackish hood, underwings brighter white than other taxa in range

Magellanic Diving-Petrel *Pelecanoides magellani* 22–23.5cm; see map, p. 67
South America. Fairly common from Tierra del Fuego n. to Gulf of Ancud, Chile (breeds Nov–Mar); also ranges over Patagonian Shelf, rarely e. to Falklands (where may breed). Favors inshore waters, fjords, and straits, especially around tidal rips; can be seen from shore (mainly when windy) and ferries, as in Strait of Magellan and Chilean fjords. Wing molt mainly Mar–Jun.

small bill

no toe projection (toes often project on Subantarctic)

averages smaller and 'cuter' than Subantarctic Diving-Petrel with more compact, 'bathtub toy' demeanor, smaller bill; plumage variable, but classic South Georgia has whiter throat, face, underwings, and flanks; averages bolder white braces and trailing edge to secondaries

in direct comparison, differences in bulk and bill size between South Georgia (left) and Subantarctic Diving-Petrel (right) can sometimes be appreciated

South Georgia Diving-Petrel *Pelecanoides georgicus* 20.5–21.5cm; see map, p. 67
Locally common (breeds Nov–Mar) around subantarctic islands from South Georgia e. to Heard, scarce around Macquarie; at-sea range poorly known. Wing molt believed to be synchronous. Rare in subtropical waters s. of South Island, New Zealand (breeds Codfish I.; at least formerly in Auckland Is.).

Species status proposed for relict population breeding on Codfish I., as *P. whenuahouensis*, **Codfish Diving-Petrel** (Fischer et al. 2018; see p. 346), which averages slightly deeper bill and bolder white braces than other populations; not known to be identifiable in the field.

lacks strong contrast: sides of head and chest dusky, face pattern typically weak, underwings dingy, white braces and white tips to secondaries reduced or absent; feet often project noticeably beyond tail tip, unlike South Georgia Diving-Petrel

Falkland

Subantarctic averages stockier than Subtropical, with slightly shorter, wider, and stouter bill

toes project

Subtropical

Subantarctic

Common Diving-Petrel (*Pelecanoides urinatrix*) **Complex** 20–23cm; see map, p. 67 Widespread; often common. Provisionally treated as 3 cryptic species, rarely identifiable at sea beyond presumption based on range: **Falkland Diving-Petrel** *P. [u.] berard* on Falklands (breeds Oct–Feb); **Subtropical Diving-Petrel** *P. [u.] urinatrix* on Gough and Tristan, and from SE Australia to New Zealand (breeds Jul/Sep–Jan/Feb, molts Jan/Feb–Apr, after breeding); and **Subantarctic Diving-Petrel** *P. [u.] exsul* on subantarctic islands from South Georgia (and per-haps Diego Ramírez Is., Chile, where taxon uncertain) e. to s. New Zealand (breeds Oct–Feb; molts Jan–Mar, overlapping with breeding). Falkland birds average largest and longest-tailed, with relatively slender bill. Plumage variable in all taxa, compounded by wear.

Within Subtropical Diving-Petrel, populations on Tristan/Gough have been described as race *dacunhae*, those from Chathams and Snares as *chathamensis*, which also occurs on Auckland Is. along with Subantarctic Diving-Petrel (Murphy & Harper 1921). Critical modern study needed; some of these populations may represent further cryptic species.

PETRELS (107+ species in 16 genera)

Largest, most diverse family of tubenoses, ranging from very large (giant-petrels) to very small (diving-petrels; pp. 66–69). Tubenose housings lie atop the bill, not along the sides as on albatrosses. Occur worldwide and include some of the rarest and least known of all birds. Some species are long-distance migrants, others relatively sedentary. Many species look similar in the field, and identification criteria are still evolving for several species and groups of species.

Ages similar (except giant-petrels); sexes similar, although males average larger-billed. Wing molt mainly in non-breeding periods (overlap with breeding in a few species, especially giant-petrels). Most species nest colonially, often on remote islands, and visit colonies at night (fulmars and allies visit during daytime). Mostly silent away from breeding grounds, but sometimes utter brays, clucks, and squawks in feeding interactions.

For ID purposes, petrels can be divided into 5 groups: **diving-petrels** (6+ species in 1 genus, traditionally considered a separate family; pp. 66–69); **fulmars and allies** (8+ species in 5 genera); **prions and Blue Petrel** (10+ species in 2 genera); **gadfly petrels and allies** (42+ species in 4 genera); and **shearwaters and allies** (41+ species in 4 genera).

Fulmars and Allies
p. 72–79

Prions and Blue Petrel
pp. 80–91

Gadfly Petrels and Allies, pp. 92–151

Shearwaters and Allies, pp. 152–193

FULMARS AND ALLIES (8+ species in 5 genera)

Diverse but well-defined clade comprising fulmars (genus *Fulmarus*), Pintado Petrel (*Daption*), ice petrels (*Pagodroma*, *Thalassoica*), and giant-petrels (*Macronectes*). Inhabit colder high-latitude waters, mainly in the Southern Hemisphere. Giant-petrels not recognized as 2 species until 1966; Northern Fulmar may comprise 2 species (Atlantic and Pacific; treated here in separate accounts); Pintado Petrel shows marked geographic variation; and Snow Petrel is variably treated as 1 or 2 species.

Feed mainly by scavenging, with giant-petrels often known as vultures of the Southern Ocean. Several species accompany ships for long periods. Unlike most other petrels, typically nest above ground and visit colonies during daytime. Sail and glide easily, riding updrafts off ships, cliffs, and icebergs. Only real ID concerns are between the giant-petrels, with bill tip color the most reliable feature, and between the snow petrels, which are rarely distinguishable in the field unless seen together.

Pintado Petrel and
Ice Petrels, pp. 73–75

Fulmars
pp. 76–77

Giant-Petrels
pp. 78–79

with giant-petrels and albatrosses

attractive and ostensibly unmistakable small petrel; often accompanies ships

white 'spattering' on upperparts (pintado means painted) highly variable, least extensive on n. populations in New Zealand

Pintado (Cape) Petrel *Daption capense* 34–38cm, WS 81–90cm

Southern oceans. Breeds Nov–Mar, locally around Antarctica, and on most subantarctic islands from Scotia Arc e. to New Zealand (n. to Snares and Chathams). Ranges in summer mainly in subantarctic waters, moving n. (mainly Mar–Nov) to subtropical waters off S America (regular in Humboldt Current n. to Peru, very rarely s. Ecuador), S Africa, and S Australia; vagrant n. into tropical waters. Found as singles or in groups, locally of 100s when scavenging around fishing boats. A 'professional' ship attendant, circling and following ships for hours. Nests colonially on rocky cliffs, ledges, and in crevices.

Snow Petrels and Antarctic Petrels (far left, 2 birds) often rest on icebergs

distinctive black-and-white petrel—looks like a Pintado Petrel that's been organized

tone of upperparts changes with lighting and plumage wear

faded 1st-year, molting

Antarctic Petrel *Thalassoica antarctica* 45–47cm, WS 97–107cm

Antarctic, rarely far from ice. Breeds mid-Nov to mid-Mar, locally in Antarctica and on adjacent islands. Ranges at sea mainly in areas with icebergs and light pack ice, also (mainly Jun–Nov) n. in adjacent open waters; vagrant (mainly Aug–Oct) n. of Antarctic Convergence. Found as singles or in groups, locally of 100s, resting on and wheeling around icebergs; flight often strong and fast, sailing easily in high winds. Also attracted to ships, usually briefly, when may associate with smaller Pintado Petrels. Nests colonially on snow-free ledges and in crevices.

distinctive snow-white petrel, rarely seen far from ice

can be virtually invisible when resting on ice and flying among ice floes

Greater averages larger and chunkier, with larger head and stouter bill, best appreciated when the 2 taxa are seen together; ID often inferred by geographic range

Lesser

Greater

Snow Petrel (*Pagodroma nivea*) **Complex** 37–41cm, WS 80–90cm
Antarctic, rarely far from ice. Taxonomy vexed, appears to include 2 cryptic species, which reportedly interbreed: widespread **Lesser Snow Petrel** *P. [n.] nivea*, breeds around Antarctica (except Balleny Is.), and near glaciers on South Georgia; **Greater Snow Petrel** *P. [n.] confusa*, breeds Balleny Is., locally elsewhere in E Antarctica, and perhaps w. to South Orkneys. Breeds Nov–Mar, and ranges in areas with pack ice and icebergs, s. of Antarctic Convergence. Found as singles or groups, locally of 100s, resting on and feeding around ice floes and bergs. Also attracted to ships, but usually only briefly. Flight usually quick and agile, wheeling easily; the 2 taxa mix readily where ranges overlap. Nests colonially on snow-free ledges and in crevices.

76

with immature gulls

distinctive stocky petrel with highly variable plumage;
note bulbous head, stout pale bill tipped orange

tail usually darker than rump

all but darkest morphs have
whitish wing flashes

worn and molting dark morph

fresh light morph

Pacific [Northern] Fulmar *Fulmarus [glacialis] rodgersii* 40–44cm, WS 95–110cm
North Pacific. Breeds late May–Sep, locally from Bering Sea and Aleutians s. to Kurils and se.
Alaska. Ranges n. to limit of sea ice and across N Pacific; in summer mainly n. of 45°N, in winter ranges s. to nw. Mexico and n. Japan (at s. edge of range, numbers vary greatly year to year;
in some years a few oversummer s. to Mexico). Northern breeders mainly light morph, southern
breeders mainly dark morph; majority of birds reaching California are dark morph. Flies with
slightly loose flapping of stiffly held wings, and sails easily in strong winds. Nests colonially on
cliffs, rocky and grassy slopes. Cf. dark-bodied large shearwaters (pp. 158–160).

distinctive stocky petrel with variable plumage; note bulbous head, stout pale bill tipped orange

tail usually not darker than rump

nostril tubes can be blackish, unlike Pacific Fulmar

about 5% of Svalbard birds have narrow dark distal tail band

Atlantic [Northern] Fulmar *Fulmarus [glacialis] glacialis* 42–46cm, WS 102–115cm
North Atlantic. Breeds May–Sep, locally from Arctic Canada and Franz Josef Land s. to
Newfoundland and nw. France. Ranges n. to limit of sea ice, and across N Atlantic, in summer
mainly n. of 45°N, in winter s. to e. US (at s. edge of range, numbers vary greatly year to year;
some years, a few oversummer s. to ne. US). Arctic breeders mainly dark morph, southern
breeders mainly light morph (reverse of Pacific); great majority of birds off e. US and W Europe
are light morphs. Nests colonially on cliffs, rocky and grassy slopes, even stone buildings.

distinctive, medium-size, silvery-gray petrel; note pink bill with black tip, blue tubes

unlike northern fulmars, lacks a dark morph; plumage consistently silvery

Antarctic (Southern) Fulmar *Fulmarus glacialoides* 45.5–48cm, WS 96–104cm
Cold southern oceans. Breeds Dec–Mar, locally around Antarctica and on islands s. of Antarctic Convergence. Ranges at sea s. to pack ice, and (mainly Apr–Nov) n. to subantarctic waters
(mainly s. of 40°S), rarely to S Australia and S Africa, but regular to Humboldt Current off
Chile (scarce some years, common in others), rarely to Peru. Bold scavenger, often follows boats
and associates with Pintados and giant-petrels. Nests colonially on cliffs and steep rocky slopes.

78

imm. (left) with imm. Southern Giant

giant-petrels are much larger than White-chinned and other petrels, with massive pale bills, hunch-backed flight shape

lacks white morph, but some adults very pale overall

adults

dark-tipped, cf. Southern

giant-petrels often in wing molt

adult plumage highly variable; always has pinkish bill tip (often dark reddish pink), vs. pale greenish on Southern Giant

downy chick pale grayish

with Subantarctic Skua

Northern Giant Petrel *Macronectes halli* 79–89cm, WS 200–220cm
Southern oceans. Breeds Aug/Sep–Feb/Mar, locally on subantarctic islands from South Georgia e. to New Zealand (n. to Chathams and off s. end of South Island), typically about 6 weeks earlier than Southern Giant where the 2 species co-occur. Usually less numerous than Southern Giant, except around n. breeding islands. Ranges mainly in subantarctic waters, also n. (mainly Apr–Nov) to subtropical waters in S Hemisphere and in Humboldt Current n. to cen. Peru. Flight strong and wheeling in high winds, but labored in calm, with slow deep wingbeats much like an albatross. Bold scavenger, feeding on beaches as well as at sea. Often accompanies ships and scavenges at fishing boats. Nests on flat or gently sloping ground, usually in small colonies.

all ages have diagnostic, pale greenish bill tip

with Antarctic Fulmars

bill appears uniformly pale at a distance, versus often dark-tipped on Northern Giant

adults

imm. dark morph
(some adults similar)

scarce white morph
has scattered dark
flecks and spots

rare leucistic variant pure white with wholly pinkish bill

Southern Giant Petrel *Macronectes giganteus* 79–89cm, WS 200–220cm
Southern oceans. Breeds Sep/Oct–Mar/Apr, locally around Antarctica, on most subantarctic islands, and in small numbers n. to s. Chile, Falklands, and Gough. Ranges at sea s. to pack ice, and (mainly Apr–Nov) n. to subtropical waters in S Hemisphere, and n. in Humboldt Current to cen. Peru. Habits much like Northern Giant Petrel, with which it readily associates. Like Northern Giant, juv. plumage wholly dark (except white morph, in which all ages similar) and subsequent plumage sequences undescribed; attains variable adult plumage over a few years, starting with whitish on face and throat; typical adult has whitish head and neck, vs. whitish face on Northern, but much variation and some breeding adults almost wholly dark.

PRIONS AND BLUE PETREL (10+ species in 2 genera)

Small petrels of the Southern Hemisphere, mainly in cooler waters. Prions (genus *Pachyptila*) are perhaps the most challenging of all petrels to identify to species, and field characters for some taxa still await elucidation; we attempt to summarize what is known, and to provide a foundation for testing and refinement. The Blue Petrel (genus *Halobaena*) is superficially prion-like but has relatively distinctive plumage and a different bill shape.

Prions often accompany ships, when several species can be seen together. They feed mainly while swimming and skittering over the water, using their bills to filter out krill and other small organisms. Visit colonies at night to avoid predation by skuas and gulls. Susceptible to large 'wrecks' in which 100s, at times 1000s, of dead or moribund birds wash ashore on beaches, mainly in mid-winter (May–Aug). Much distributional information is inferred from wrecks, which may not reflect the distribution of healthy prions.

Features that can help with prion ID are bill structure and coloration, head and bill size, and head and tail patterns; proximity to known breeding islands is a factor that also adds comfort to an ID. 1st-years have slightly smaller bills than adults, and within some species, especially the widespread Antarctic Prion, bill shape and face pattern vary among islands, as well as among individuals. Beware that apparent bill shape can vary greatly depending on angle of view and can look quite different from one image to the next, compounded by a gular pouch that can be distended and quite pronounced on larger-billed species.

Prions typically fly low to the water, at times forming large foraging flocks in which one species usually predominates. This silvery swarm is probably a mix of MacGillivray's and Broad-billed Prions. Off Gough Island, South Atlantic, 8 April 2009.

Blue Petrel
p. 82

Fairy Prion
Complex, p. 84

Fulmar Prion
Complex, p. 85

Slender-billed
Prion, p. 86

Antarctic Prion
pp. 87–88

Salvin's Prion
p. 89

MacGillivray's Prion
p. 90

Broad-billed Prion
p. 91

82

Blue Petrel

distinctive small petrel with white tail tip, dark cap and half-collar, thin black bill

tail tip contrast and plumage tones vary with lighting

Blue Petrel *Halobaena caerulea* 28.5–30cm, WS 67–71cm
Circumpolar in colder subantarctic waters. Breeds Oct–Feb on subantarctic islands from South Georgia e. to Macquarie, also on Diego Ramirez Is., s. of Cape Horn. Favors subantarctic waters near Antarctic Convergence and ranges s. to pack ice; in winter (mainly May–Aug) small numbers range n. to Humboldt Current of s. Chile, to South Africa, and to waters off S Australia.

Often associates with prions, such as groups accompanying ships; flight similar to prions, but when windy tends to wheel and bank higher, although not steeply or to the extent of small gadfly petrels.

PRION DISTRIBUTION

The at-sea distribution (and even breeding status) of prions is poorly known—for example, an abundant 'new' prion was discovered in the 2010s breeding on Gough Island in the South Atlantic. Thus, the maps below should be considered more tentative than for other petrels, but they give a general idea of distribution, which can be a starting point for ID. Note, though, that information in some areas is derived from dead birds found on beaches, which may not reflect the distribution of healthy prions. Careful observations, supported by digital images, could add greatly to our understanding of prion distribution.

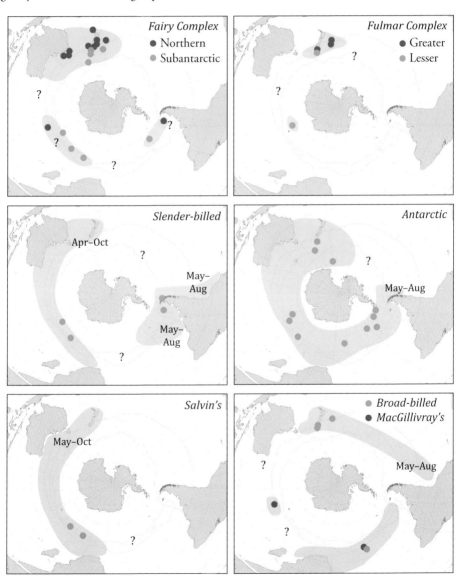

84

broad black tail tip separates fairy prions from all except fulmar prions; also note small head, variable face pattern, small bill

Northern
(New Zealand)

Subantarctic
(South Atlantic)

stockier than Northern, with softer face, beady eye, shorter bill; cf. Fulmar Prion

broad black tip

face can suggest Slender-billed but bill stouter, tail band broad

darker cheeks and longer bill than Subantarctic Fairy

Subantarctic
(New Zealand)

Fairy Prion (*Pachyptila turtur*) **Complex** 25–26.5cm, WS 58–62cm; see map, p. 83
Widespread: 2 races usually recognized, but critical revision needed; probably at least 2 species involved. At-sea range poorly known, but appears not to range widely far out to sea.
   Northern Fairy Prion *Pachyptila [turtur] turtur* breeds Oct/Nov–Jan/Feb (later southward) commonly around New Zealand and in SE Australia; perhaps also S Indian Ocean and Falklands (uncertain which fairy prions breed in those regions). Wing molt mainly Dec–Jun. Favors subtropical waters, but ranges locally into subantarctic waters.
   Subantarctic Fairy Prion *Pachyptila [turtur] subantarctica* breeds Nov–Mar on subantarctic islands from South Georgia e. to Macquarie; also reportedly on Snares and Antipodes; uncommon to locally fairly common. Disperses n. in winter, when can wreck in S Australia.

similar to Subantarctic Fairy Prion, but typically has stouter bill with bigger nail, weaker face pattern, stronger bluish wash to underparts

stout bill, large nail

whitish brow rarely strong

Greater (New Zealand)

broad black tip like Fairy Prions

face pattern typically diffuse

nail nearer tubenose than Fairy

Fairy

Fulmar

Lesser (Heard Island)

visits colony at Bounties during daytime

Fulmar Prion (*Pachyptila crassirostris*) **Complex** 25.5–27cm, WS 59–63cm; see map, p. 83 Indian Ocean and New Zealand; very local. Most authors recognize 2–3 races, perhaps representing at least 2 species, but not known to be distinguishable at sea. Males average larger-billed than females, such that male Lesser approaches or overlaps in bill size with female Greater. Other prions do not have such marked sex differences in bill size.

Greater Fulmar Prion *Pachyptila [crassirostris] crassirostris* breeds Nov–Feb on Snares, Bounties, and Chathams, New Zealand; locally fairly common to common. Considered relatively sedentary, ranging in seas around breeding islands; has occurred n. to S Australia in wrecks. Chatham birds average largest, often treated as race *pyramidalis*.

Lesser Fulmar Prion *Pachyptila [crassirostris] flemingi* breeds Nov–Feb on Heard and Auckland Is.; fairly common. Considered relatively sedentary, ranging in adjacent seas; probably occurs very rarely in S Australia during wrecks.

broad white eyebrow, white lores, and narrow dark eyestripe contribute to an 'open, smiling' face; bill narrow and rather slender (but dimensions overlap with some Antarctic Prions)

upperparts relatively pale, with poorly contrasting dark M-pattern (the weakest of all prions)

narrow dark tip

South Atlantic

fresh juv.
Mar

dark eystripe typically narrower than white brow

forehead often rather steep and squared

Falklands

Indian Ocean

Slender-billed Prion *Pachyptila belcheri* 23–24.5cm, WS 58–61.5cm; see map, p. 83
South Atlantic and Indian Oceans. Breeds Nov–Mar, commonly on Falklands and Kerguelen; smaller numbers on Crozets and in s. Chile; wing molt Feb–Jun. Mainly in subantarctic waters during summer, ranging north to subtropical waters in winter. Fairly common migrant (mainly Apr–Sep) in Humboldt Current off Chile, rarely n. to Peru; uncommon e. to New Zealand.

Antarctic Prion Variation

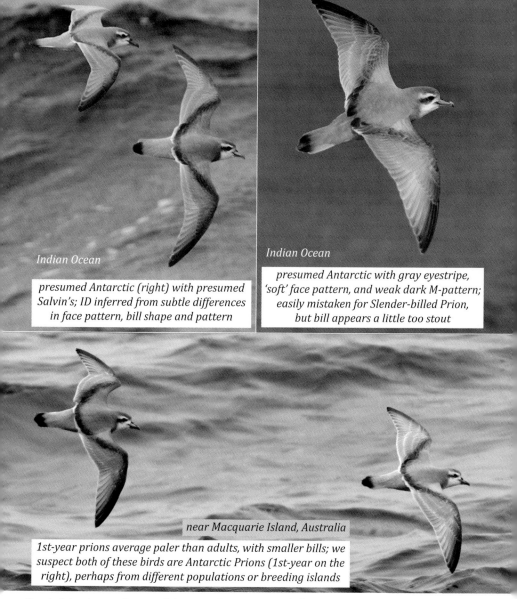

Indian Ocean

presumed Antarctic (right) with presumed Salvin's; ID inferred from subtle differences in face pattern, bill shape and pattern

Indian Ocean

presumed Antarctic with gray eyestripe, 'soft' face pattern, and weak dark M-pattern; easily mistaken for Slender-billed Prion, but bill appears a little too stout

near Macquarie Island, Australia

1st-year prions average paler than adults, with smaller bills; we suspect both of these birds are Antarctic Prions (1st-year on the right), perhaps from different populations or breeding islands

South Atlantic populations of Antarctic Prion average darkest above, with darker lores and smaller white eyebrow than other populations; birds in Australia and New Zealand average palest overall, with whitish lores, broader white eyebrow, and can closely resemble Slender-billed Prion. At the other end of the spectrum, darker Antarctic Prions may not be distinguishable from Salvin's Prion. Bill of Antarctic Prion broadest on Auckland Is., smallest on Kerguelen (where bill width overlaps with Slender-billed Prion).

88

confusingly variable, may harbor cryptic species; also see. p. 87

pale bulbous nail

face averages 'sterner' than Slender-billed, but can be similar (see p. 87); other birds resemble Salvin's, but bill averages narrower, with more prominent pale nail

slightly stockier and bigger-headed than Slender-billed

fresh juv.
Apr

fledgling, Mar,
South Georgia

like all prions, dorsal plumage tones vary with lighting and plumage wear

Antarctic Prion *Pachyptila desolata* 26.5–28cm, WS 59–63cm; also see p. 87, map, p. 83
Widespread. Breeds Dec–Apr, commonly on subantarctic islands from South Georgia e. to
Macquarie, also small numbers on Scott I.; wing molt Mar–May. Favors subantarctic waters, s.
locally to pack ice, in winter ranges n. to s. S America, South Africa, and S Australia; a few reach
Humboldt Current off Chile and very rarely s. Peru, at least in some years. Cf. Slender-billed
Prion, Salvin's Prion, juv. MacGillivray's Prion.

similar to Antarctic Prion, and often not safely identified at sea; birds with combination of classic features appear distinctive to observers familiar with prions; also see p. 87

bill averages broader and stouter than Antarctic Prion; nail typically duskier gray and less bulbous

small dusky nail

strong white eyebrow contrasts with rather broad dark eyestripe; lores whitish, often with dusky flecking, and cheeks often marked with a curly, narrow gray gape line

gray crown typically blends smoothly with back, but forehead can be darker

Salvin's Prion *Pachyptila salvini* 26.5–28cm, WS 58–62cm; see map, p. 83
Indian Ocean. Breeds Nov–Mar, commonly on Marion, Prince Edwards, Crozets; disperses w. at least to waters off S Africa and e. at least to New Zealand. Wing molt Mar–Jun. Favors sub-antarctic waters and cooler subtropical waters. Cf. Antarctic Prion, MacGillivray's Prion.

appears intermediate between Broad-billed and Salvin's Prions, bill size nearer the former

forehead averages less steeply squared and bill nail paler than Broad-billed

fresh juv.
Apr

juv. can suggest Antarctic Prion but bill darker, with less bulbous nail, and broader as viewed from above

worn adult
Apr

bill broad, with gray to blackish sides; face typically less 'stern' than Broad-billed, with whitish lores, more distinct white brow

Gough Island

primary molt in Apr
too late for Broad-billed

MacGillivray's Prion *Pachyptila macgillivrayi* 27.5–29.5cm, WS 60–64cm; see map, p. 83 Subtropical Atlantic and Indian Oceans. Breeds late Nov–Mar commonly on Gough (but only formally discovered there in 2010s) and St. Paul/Amsterdam (scarce, but increasing following eradication of non-native predators); wing molt likely Mar–May. Probably ranges mainly in subtropical waters, but largely unknown at sea; may occur off SW Africa, at least in non-breeding season. Cf. Broad-billed Prion, Salvin's Prion, Antarctic Prion.

very large, broad, 'duck-like' bill slopes up into steep squared forehead; bill sides gray to blackish, often with a paler band near cutting edge

South Atlantic

face often rather dark and 'ugly,' with dusky smudging in lores, curly gray gape line

pouch swollen

New Zealand

possible juv.

Gough Island

Broad-billed Prion *Pachyptila vittata* 29.5–31cm, WS 65–69cm; see map, p. 83
Subtropical Atlantic and New Zealand. Breeds Aug–Jan, locally on subtropical islands in South Atlantic (Gough/Tristan) and New Zealand (Chathams, Snares, around s. end of South Island); wing molt Dec–Feb. Ranges mainly in subtropical waters around New Zealand, rarely to S Australia, very rarely e. in May–Aug to waters off n. Chile and Peru; and in S Atlantic, regularly to SW Africa, rarely to Falklands. In S Atlantic, cf. MacGillivray's Prion.

GADFLY PETRELS AND ALLIES (42+ species in 4 genera)

Varied assemblage of medium-size to fairly small petrels comprising the genera *Pterodroma* (35+ species), *Pseudobulweria* (4+ species), *Bulweria* (2+ species), and *Aphrodroma* (1 species). Most diverse in subtropical latitudes of the Pacific, but found in all oceans, with some species tropical, a few subantarctic. Differ from shearwaters and allies in more dynamic and accomplished flight (even impetuous and wild-looking in strong winds, as if goaded by a gadfly), generally less gregarious nature, more offshore and oceanic habitat, and, in the larger species, a stouter and stronger bill. Species limits in several species remain unresolved.

Feed by snatching fish and squid near the surface, and by scavenging. Often attracted to ships, at least briefly, but not habitual ship attendants. Most species nest in burrows and crevices and visit colonies at night; a few tropical species nest above ground and visit colonies in daytime. Perhaps more than for most seabirds, the at-sea ranges of gadfly petrels are being elucidated through use of geolocators and other forms of tagging, at least for breeding adults; even so, the at-sea distributions of several species remain largely conjectural.

Species ID sometimes straightforward, but more often challenging, compounded by taxonomic uncertainty and frequently brief views, as well as by numerous similar-looking species and a few cases of polymorphism (with various and variable plumage morphs). **For ID purposes**, we treat gadflies and allies in 3 groups: **small white-bodied species** (subgenus *Cookilaria*); **larger white-bodied species**; and **dark-bodied species** (opposite).

Like many seabirds, Hawaiian Petrel is threatened by the usual litany of human-related pressures, such as non-native predators, habitat loss, consumption of plastics (which look like food items), and perhaps disease. Also, as with numerous seabirds, its taxonomy is vexed and it may comprise cryptic species—all of which would be endangered!

Small White-bodied (*Cookilaria*), pp. 94–106

Larger White-bodied, pp. 107–136

Dark-bodied, pp. 137–151

SMALL WHITE-BODIED GADFLY PETRELS (*Cookilaria*)

Nine species of small, snappy, fast-flying petrels with white underparts and a dark M-pattern on mostly gray upperparts; all breed only in the Pacific. It is convenient to refer to all of the small gadflies as the subgenus *Cookilaria*, although some authors limit *Cookilaria* to species with bluish feet, relatively slender bills, and narrower black underwing margins, thus excluding the stockier, pink-legged Black-winged, Chatham, and Bonin Petrels.

For ID, pay attention to head and neck patterns, head/back contrast, underwing pattern, and tail tip pattern. With experience (and good photos), subtle structural clues and bill size can also be helpful. Species-level taxonomy appears to be mostly resolved, although variation in Collared Petrel remains to be clarified.

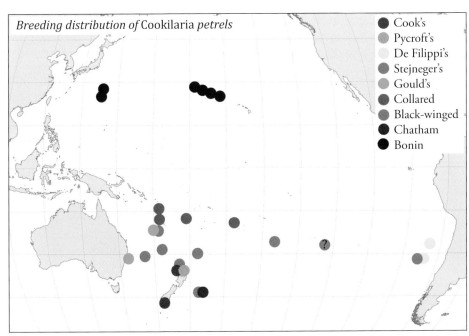

Breeding distribution of Cookilaria petrels

- Cook's
- Pycroft's
- De Filippi's
- Stejneger's
- Gould's
- Collared
- Black-winged
- Chatham
- Bonin

Thankfully, most Cookilaria *exhibit relatively little plumage variation, the notable exception being Collared Petrel, which varies from white-bodied to blackish-bodied (below). The proportion of dark morphs varies among populations, and taxonomy of this group remains vexed; dark Collared Petrels are treated on p. 148.*

COOKILARIA ID

All else being equal, species-level ID of some *Cookilaria* petrels is difficult enough. However, birds fly quickly, views may be brief, and the effects of lighting, plumage wear, angle of view, and changes in shape relating to flight manner and wind speed all add to the challenge. The images below illustrate some of the pitfalls.

Behavior of all species is broadly similar, not usually helpful for species ID. Found singly, or locally in feeding and rafting flocks, at times with other seabirds. In calm to light winds, flight usually low to the water, with bursts of quick wingbeats and buoyant glides; in moderate to strong winds flight more erratic, with high, steep wheeling arcs and short bursts of quick stiff wingbeats—at times a bird flips back on itself and arcs with near-vertical slicing action.

Cook's Petrel

wheeling gently in light wind, fresh plumage

arcing steeply in strong wind, bright lighting

gliding low, worn plumage, poor lighting

banking, worn plumage, nape bleached

Stejneger's Petrel

white cheek notch 'softens' and disappears as bird banks and turns away

Cookilaria *regularly rest on the sea but tend to flush well before you can get good views, as these Cook's Petrels did right after this image was taken*

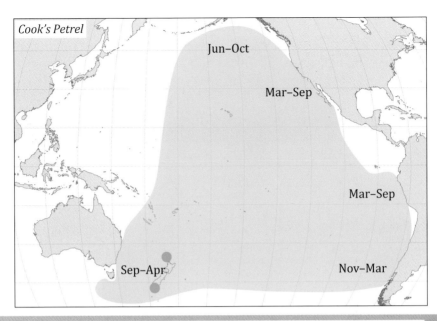

Cook's Petrel

Jun–Oct

Mar–Sep

Mar–Sep

Sep–Apr

Nov–Mar

rather long-winged, short-tailed Cookilaria *with gray cap, white brow, beady dark eye, slender bill, darker tail tip above; cf. Pycroft's and De Filippi's Petrels (pp. 98–100)*

*white brow
can be weak*

*extent and shape of gray cap/
cowl varies with angle of view*

Cook's Petrel *Pterodroma cookii* 30.5–34cm, WS 76–82cm; also see pp. 98, 100
Breeds Nov–Mar in New Zealand, ranges Sep–Apr around New Zealand and w. to SE Australia. Non-breeding range (Mar–Sep, with small numbers Oct–Feb) mainly in E Pacific off Baja California and s. California, and off Peru; small numbers range n. to NE Pacific and s. to Chile. Wing molt mainly Feb–Aug. Habits much like other *Cookilaria.*

Cook's Petrel versus Pycroft's Petrel

These 2 species co-occur around New Zealand and potentially in the tropical Pacific. Pycroft's is slightly smaller, chestier, shorter-necked, and shorter-winged than Cook's, but plumage is very similar and the 2 species are not always safely distinguished at sea. Head and neck pattern (paler in fresh plumage, darker when worn), in combination with structure, are the best ID features.

Cook's

Pycroft's

white brow accentuates Cook's beady dark eye

worn plumage

Cook's

Pycroft's

long neck and small head accentuate longer bill

short neck, 'puffy' head

fresh plumage

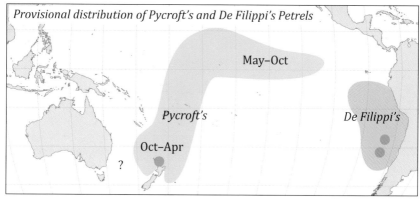

Provisional distribution of Pycroft's and De Filippi's Petrels

May–Oct

Pycroft's

Oct–Apr

De Filippi's

?

grayish cowl smudges into blacker eye patch; worn plumage darker-capped, cf. Stejneger's (p. 101)

fresh plumage

rarely has short white brow

dumpy-chested, short-necked

worn plumage

Pycroft's Petrel *Pterodroma pycrofti* 28.5–31cm, WS 69–74cm; also see opposite
Breeds late Nov to mid-Apr in n. New Zealand. Non-breeding range (May–Oct) mainly in
tropical Cen Pacific. Wing molt mainly Mar–Sep. Habits much like other *Cookilaria*.

stockier, broader-winged, and bigger-billed than Cook's (see pp. 97, 100), with gray half-collar, large black eye patch; also cf. Stejneger's (pp. 100–101)

worn plumage

completing wing molt, Mar

lacks distinct dark tip

extent of half-collar varies with angle of view, cf. p. 96

fresh plumage

De Filippi's Petrel *Pterodroma defilippiana* 30–33cm, WS 74–80cm; also see p. 100
Breeds mainly Jul–Dec off cen. Chile on Juan Fernandez and Desventuradas. Ranges at sea in
Humboldt Current region from cen. Chile n. to Peru (where reported Mar–Oct). Wing molt
mainly Oct–Mar. Habits much like other *Cookilaria*. Also known as Masatierra Petrel.

Cook's Petrel versus De Filippi's and Stejneger's Petrels

These 3 species can occur together seasonally in the Humboldt Current of Peru and Chile, while Cook's and Stejneger's can also occur together more widely in the Pacific. In relative terms, De Filippi's is large and lumbering, Stejneger's small and snappy, with Cook's falling somewhere between, but under field conditions they can all appear quite similar. The dark-capped Stejneger's is relatively distinctive, but beware the effects of lighting and plumage wear (see p. 96). Best ID features are head and neck pattern, bill size, and contrast and pattern on upperparts.

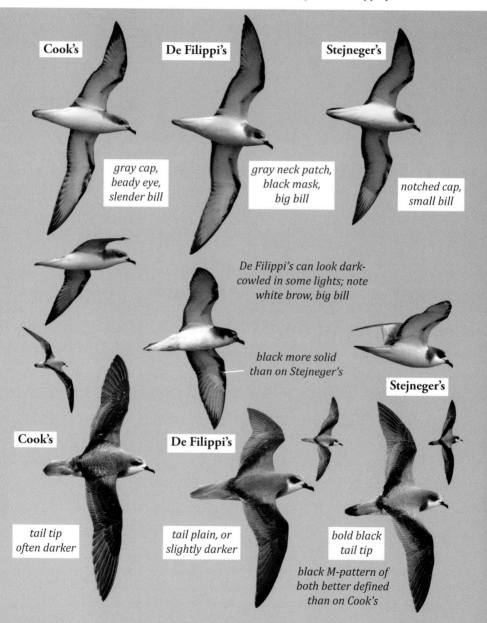

Cook's

De Filippi's

Stejneger's

gray cap, beady eye, slender bill

gray neck patch, black mask, big bill

notched cap, small bill

De Filippi's can look dark-cowled in some lights; note white brow, big bill

black more solid than on Stejneger's

Stejneger's

Cook's

De Filippi's

tail tip often darker

tail plain, or slightly darker

bold black tail tip

black M-pattern of both better defined than on Cook's

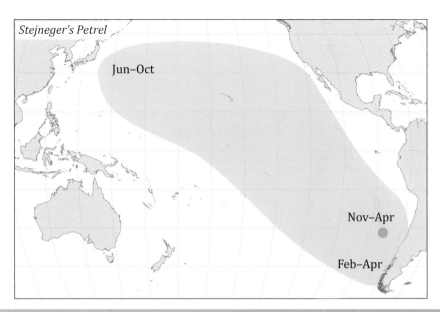

Stejneger's Petrel

Jun–Oct

Nov–Apr

Feb–Apr

small, rather contrasty Cookilaria: *note slaty cap with white notch behind cheeks, black tail tip*

worn plumage

fresh plumage

shape of slaty cap changes with angle of view, cf. p. 96

short neck accentuates rather long tail

Stejneger's Petrel *Pterodroma longirostris* 29–31.5cm, WS 70–76cm
Breeds Dec–Apr on Selkirk in Juan Fernandez Is.; ranges at sea Nov–Apr off cen. and s. Chile. Non-breeding range (May–Oct) in subtropical NW Pacific; vagrants reported Dec–Feb sw. to New Zealand. Wing molt mainly Mar–Aug. Habits much like other *Cookilaria*.

102

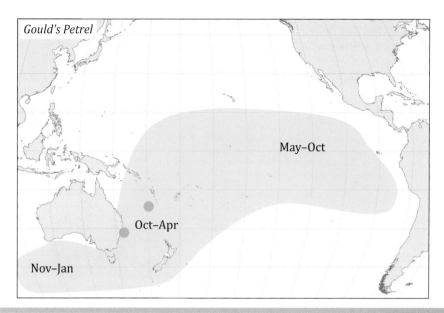

Gould's Petrel

May–Oct

Oct–Apr

Nov–Jan

cf. slightly smaller, more lightly built Collared Petrel, which has broader black underwing margins (suggesting Black-winged), dark cap vs. cowl of Gould's

often has narrow dark collar (rarely complete)

cowl shape varies greatly with angle of view, but distinct from notched cap of Collared

Gould's (White-winged) Petrel *Pterodroma leucoptera* 30.5–33cm, WS 72–79cm
Breeds late Nov–Apr on Cabbage Tree I. and New Caledonia; during breeding season ranges
w. to S Australia and subantarctic SE Indian Ocean. Non-breeding range (mainly May–Oct) in
tropical E Pacific. Wing molt mainly Feb–Oct. Habits much like other *Cookilaria*.

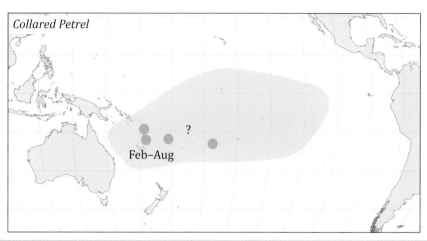

Collared Petrel

? Feb–Aug

cf. slightly larger and longer-winged Gould's Petrel, which has narrower black underwing margins, white primary bases, blackish cowl rather than cap

thicker than Gould's

underparts vary from white to dark (see p. 148)

white throat hooks slightly into dark cap, cf. dark cowl of Gould's

more extensive dark than Gould's

Collared Petrel (light morph) *Pterodroma brevipes* 29–31cm, WS 67–73cm; also see p. 148 Breeds locally in tropical SW Pacific, from Vanuatu e. to Cooks. Breeding season(s) poorly known and may vary locally; perhaps mainly Mar–Aug. Ranges at sea in tropical W and Cen Pacific. Habits much like other *Cookilaria*. Has sometimes been lumped into Gould's Petrel.

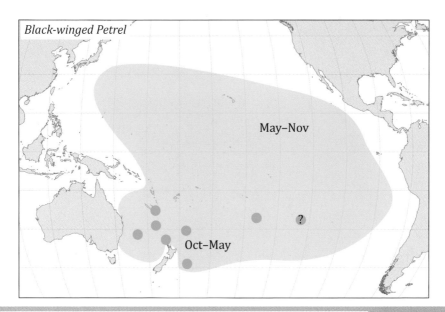

Black-winged Petrel

May–Nov

Oct–May

?

distinctive, rather stocky Cookilaria*, with gray half-collar, very wide black underwing margins, and relatively dull, often rather brownish upperwings*

black underwing margins vary with angle of view

faded 1st-year can show white hindcollar

Black-winged Petrel *Pterodroma nigripennis* 30.5–33cm, WS 73–79cm
Breeds mid-Nov to Apr, mainly Tasman Sea region, with smaller numbers on New Caledonia, Chathams, Rapa, and perhaps Easter I. Widespread non-breeding range (mainly May–Nov) in tropical and subtropical Pacific. Wing molt mainly Feb–Oct. Habits much like other *Cookilaria*.

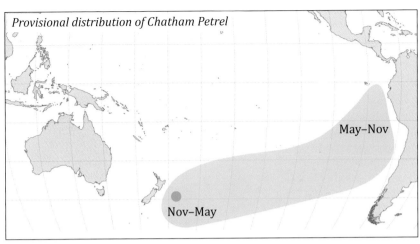

Provisional distribution of Chatham Petrel

May–Nov

Nov–May

rare, rather stocky Cookilaria, with gray half-collar, striking and diagnostic underwing pattern

bolder M-pattern than Black-winged

Chatham Petrel *Pterodroma axillaris* 30.5–32cm, WS 68–74cm
Breeds late Dec–early Jun in Chathams (mainly on Southeast I.); rare, with around 500 pairs. Poorly known at sea, but disperses in non-breeding period to E Pacific, off Peru and n. Chile. Wing molt presumed Mar–Sep. Habits much like other *Cookilaria*.

106

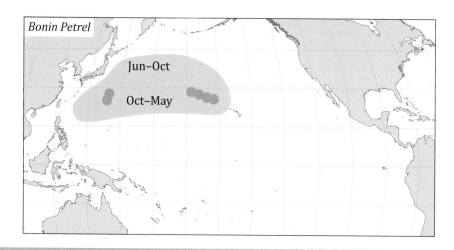
Bonin Petrel

Jun–Oct

Oct–May

distinctive Cookilaria *with long tapered tail, dark cowl, striking and diagnostic underwing pattern; cf. larger Hawaiian Petrel (p. 125; lacks gray rump contrast with black tail)*

black primary-covert wedge diagnostic

Bonin Petrel *Pterodroma hypoleuca* 29–31.5cm WS 72–78cm
Breeds Jan–Jun on Bonins, Volcano Is., and nw. Hawaiian Is., ranges in subtropical NW Pacific, mainly 15–40°N. Wing molt mainly Apr–Sep. Habits much like other *Cookilaria*.

LARGER WHITE-BODIED GADFLY PETRELS

These comprise 23+ species (21+ in genus *Pterodroma*, 2+ in genus *Pseudobulweria*) of medium-size to large gadfly petrels found in all oceans. Most are tropical and subtropical in distribution, the long-distance migrant Mottled Petrel being a notable exception—it migrates seasonally between antarctic and subarctic waters.

Species limits are unresolved in several cases, even with relatively 'familiar' species such as Black-capped Petrel, compounded by breeding areas that are difficult to access or even unknown. Four *Pterodroma* species are polymorphic; dark morphs are treated with dark-bodied gadflies (see p. 137).

For ID, besides location pay attention to general size (medium or large, often reflected in flight manner), head and neck patterns, underwing patterns, and to a lesser extent bill size and overall plumage patterns. As with other seabirds, species of cooler and windier latitudes tend to have heavier bodies and narrower wings (such as Soft-plumaged Petrel), whereas those of warmer and calmer latitudes tend to have lighter bodies and broader wings (such as the Fea's Petrel complex); these structural differences are reflected in subtly distinctive different flight manners (see p. 21–22).

For ID purposes we break larger white-bodied gadflies into 4 groups (see pp. 108–109): 6+ subtropical and North Atlantic species; 2 subtropical and tropical Indian Ocean species; 10+ subtropical and tropical Pacific species (which can be considered in terms of 5+ 'white-winged' and 5+ 'dark-winged' species based on overall underwing pattern); and 5 southern-breeding species.

As well as being viewed as dark-bodied or white-bodied, larger gadflies can be divided into large species, such as Gray-faced Petrel (lower), and medium-size species, such as Soft-plumaged Petrel (upper). In general, the medium-size species have a more maneuverable and quicker-looking flight manner, although large species usually fly faster.

LARGER WHITE-BODIED GADFLY PETRELS

Subtropical and North Atlantic

Fea's complex
pp. 114–116

Black-capped
complex
pp. 110–112

Bermuda
p. 113

Subtropical and Tropical
Indian Ocean

Barau's
p. 119

Trindade
p. 117

Subtropical and Tropical Pacific (white-winged)

Dark-rumped complex
pp. 124–125

White-necked
complex
pp. 120–121

Juan Fernandez, p. 122

Subtropical and Tropical Pacific (dark-winged)

Kermadec
p. 126

Herald
p. 127

Phoenix
p. 129

Tahiti complex
pp. 130–131

Southern-breeding

Atlantic
p. 132

Magenta
p. 133

White-headed
p. 134

Mottled
p. 136

Soft-plumaged
p. 135

Black-capped Petrel (*Pterodroma hasitata*) Complex

Taxonomy vexed. Variation within Black-capped Petrels was examined by Howell & Patteson (2008) and Manly et al. (2013), and we provisionally consider that 2 species are involved: White-faced Petrel *P. hasitata* differs from Black-faced Petrel (formally unnamed) in plumage, average larger size and bigger bill, earlier molt timing (implying earlier breeding), and apparently more northerly at-sea distribution. Whether intermediate-looking birds represent variation in one or both taxa, or perhaps a third taxon, remains unresolved (see p. 112).

two comparisons between classic examples of White-faced (on left) and Black-faced Petrels; as well as head pattern, note reduced dark chest spur, narrower black underwing margin, and more advanced wing molt of White-faced; above 27 Jul 2007, below 3 Jun 2017.

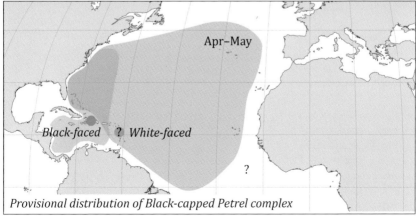

Provisional distribution of Black-capped Petrel complex

large, stocky, stout-billed gadfly with big white rump patch, small black cap; variable white hindcollar usually bold and distinct; cf. Black-faced Petrel

averages narrower than Black-faced

juv.

white exposed during molt

fresh upperparts gray, fading to show brown tones

White-faced [Black-capped] Petrel *Pterodroma [hasitata] hasitata* 39–45cm, WS 100–105cm

Breeds (mainly Dec–Jun?) probably in Lesser Antilles (Dominica, at least); perhaps elsewhere in Caribbean. Ranges n. year-round into Gulf Stream off se. US; also n. to waters off ne. US (mainly Aug–Sep), and into Cen N Atlantic (mainly Apr–May). Wing molt mainly late Mar–Aug. Associates readily with Black-faced Petrel; both often raft in the company of Band-rumped Storm-Petrels and Cory's Shearwaters. Powerful, high arcing flight in moderate to strong winds typical of larger gadflies; in calm and light winds, flight low with buoyant wheeling glides interspersed with slightly snappy wingbeats.

112

large, stout-billed gadfly with big white rump patch, black cap extending to cheeks; hindneck dusky, but can be whitish in worn plumage; cf. White-faced Petrel

Black-faced　**Bermuda**

note head/neck patterns

chest spurs average wider than White-faced Petrel

fresh upperparts gray, fading to show brown tones

affinities of birds with intermediate head patterns unclear; cf. White-faced Petrel (p. 111)

Black-faced [Black-capped] Petrel *Pterodroma [hasitata]* undescribed 38–44cm, WS 98–103cm; also see p. 110
Breeds (mainly Jan–early Jul) on Hispaniola, perhaps elsewhere in Caribbean. Ranges n. year-round (with main numbers Jun–Sep) over warm waters into Gulf Stream off e. US; extent of at-sea range requires elucidation, but may not range as far n. as White-faced Petrel. Wing molt mainly late Apr–Sep. Habits much like White-faced Petrel, with which it readily associates.

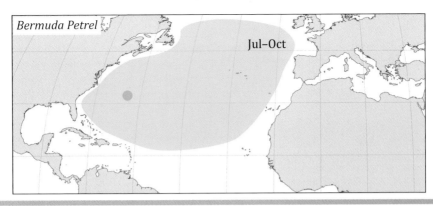

Bermuda Petrel

Jul–Oct

medium-size, fairly long-tailed gadfly with dark cowl, thick black underwing margins, narrow whitish rump band; appreciably smaller and smaller-billed than Black-faced Petrel

lacks dark chest spurs of Black-faced Petrel

extent and shape of dark cowl vary with angle of view

fresh upperparts gray, fading to show brown tones

Bermuda Petrel (Cahow) *Pterodroma cahow* 35–38cm, WS 85–92cm
Breeds Jan–early Jun on Bermuda; endangered, but with population recovery now just over 100 pairs. Ranges in subtropical N Atlantic, mainly 15–50°N. Wing molt mainly Apr–Sep. Flight buoyant and easy, typical of mid-size subtropical gadflies such as Fea's. Sometimes associates with other seabirds, but as often or more often found separately, foraging as single birds.

114

Fea's Petrel versus Zino's Petrel

The Fea's Petrel complex comprises 3 taxa: Cape Verde Petrel *P. feae*, Desertas Petrel *P. desertae*, and Zino's Petrel *P. madeira*. While usually treated as separate species, Cape Verde and Desertas Petrels are typically indistinguishable at sea (wing molt timing differs) and for ID purposes they are best treated together as Fea's Petrel. ID criteria for Fea's and Zino's Petrels were discussed by Shirihai et al. (2010): Zino's averages smaller and more lightly built than Fea's, with a smaller head and bill; some Zino's also have overall whiter underwings, a pattern not known in Fea's. Traditionally, all 3 species were considered conspecific with Soft-plumaged Petrel.

medium-size gadfly with stout bill; note gray cowl, dark underwings contrasting with white body, tapered gray tail

messy black eye patch and 'meat-cleaver' bill often create 'brutish' face unlike neater and 'gentler' Zino's Petrel

body sides vary from clean white to barred and mottled dusky

'Fea's Petrel' = **Cape Verde Petrel** *Pterodroma [feae] feae* and **Desertas Petrel** *Pterodroma [feae] desertae* 35.5–38cm, WS 87–97cm; also see opposite

These 2 species are not readily distinguished at sea except by presumption based on location, and seasonally by wing molt timing, although deepest-billed male Desertas Petrels may fall outside variation of Cape Verde Petrel. For practical purposes they are best lumped as Fea's Petrel. **Cape Verde Petrel** breeds late Dec–early Jun on Cape Verdes (wing molt mainly Mar–Sep); **Desertas Petrel** breeds late Jul–early Jan on Desertas on Madeira (wing molt mainly Oct–May). Both taxa range widely in subtropical and tropical Atlantic. Tagging data from small samples of breeding adults suggest Desertas ranges more widely (50°N–40°S), Cape Verde less extensively, (40°N–5°S). Flight buoyant and easy, typical of mid-size subtropical gadflies.

medium-size gadfly, very like Fea's but averages smaller and more compact, with deeper chest, shorter neck, smaller head, finer bill

broad whitish median panel of some Zino's is an underwing pattern not known on Fea's

Zino's Petrel *Pterodroma madeira* 34–36cm, WS 83–88cm; also see p. 114
Breeds mid-May to early Oct on Madeira; endangered, with population <100 pairs. Ranges at sea mainly in subtropical and tropical E Atlantic. Tagging data from small samples of breeding adults reveal non-breeding range from 45°N to 25°S; imms. may range more widely, recorded w. to Gulf Stream off e. US (Sep). Wing molt mainly Sep–Feb. Habits much like Fea's Petrel, but flight a little quicker and more maneuverable.

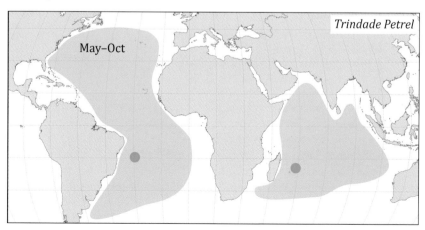

Trindade Petrel

May–Oct

medium-size, lightly built gadfly with relatively long wings, small head, variable plumage; underwing typically has whitish central panel, rarely dark overall with pale primary flashes

underparts vary from white to dark (see p. 146)

fresh upperparts have gray sheen, fading to show brown tones

bleached shafts can show as white

Trindade Petrel (light morph) *Pterodroma arminjoniana* 36–39cm, WS 94–102cm; also see pp. 118, 146

Breeds year-round in S Atlantic on Trindade (mainly Apr–Sep, Oct–Mar); also small numbers year-round in SW Indian Ocean on Round I. Ranges widely in subtropical and tropical Atlantic, n. to around 45°N (mainly dark morph), s. to 40°S (mainly light morph), and in Indian Ocean. Flight buoyant and easy in calm to light winds, when often stays fairly low; wheels high and steeply in strong winds. Hybridization with Kermadec Petrel and Herald Petrel recorded on Round I. Has been considered conspecific with Herald Petrel. Cf. Atlantic Petrel (p. 132).

118

Trindade Petrel versus Kermadec and Herald Petrels

On Round Island, Indian Ocean, it appears that small numbers of Kermadec Petrels and Herald Petrels hybridize with Trindade Petrels (Brown et al. 2011). Relative to Trindade (and Herald), Kermadec is slightly larger and stockier, with broader wings, heavier bill, and relatively shorter, less tapered tail. Kermadec and Herald typically have skua-like white patches on the underwing primaries vs. a white median panel on Trindade, and Kermadec shows white primary shafts on the upperwing (dark on the other species). Herald is slightly smaller and smaller-billed than Trindade, and light morph typically has whitish lores vs. dark on Trindade. Hybrids with Kermadec show intermediate plumage patterns, such as partially white upperwing primary shafts, but situation needs study from a field ID perspective; also see pp. 126–128, 144–147.

Trindade **Herald** **Kermadec**

skua-like white flashes

dark lores, cf. Herald

dark overall

chunky, broad-winged

white

dark

shorter, broader, dark below

Trindade

Kermadec

dark shafts (can reflect silvery in sun)

white shafts

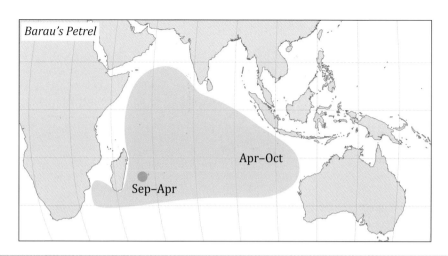

Barau's Petrel

Sep–Apr

Apr–Oct

rather large, long-tailed gadfly, distinctive in Indian Ocean range;
note dark cap, white underwings with distinct black margins

Barau's Petrel *Pterodroma baraui* 37–40cm, WS 95–102cm
Breeds Nov–early May on Réunion. Ranges in subtropical S Indian Ocean, mainly 15–35°S,
seasonally e. to W Australia (mainly Mar–Aug). Wing molt mainly Mar–Sep. Flight typical of
medium-large subtropical *Pterodroma*: buoyant and easy in calm to light winds, when can stay
fairly low; wheels high and steeply in strong winds.

White-necked Petrel (*Pterodroma cervicalis*) Complex

This complex includes widespread, large White-necked Petrel *P. cervicalis*, and slightly smaller Vanuatu Petrel *P. occulta*, described in 2001. ID criteria were proposed by Shirihai & Bretagnolle (2010): Vanuatu averages smaller overall, and averages more black on the underwing margins, but cannot realistically be identified at sea (other than by presumption around breeding island), given overlap in underwing pattern. Also cf. worn-plumaged Juan Fernandez Petrel (p. 122).

large handsome gadfly with black cap, white hindcollar, extensively white underwings; can be confused with worn-plumaged Juan Fernandez Petrel (p. 122); cf. Vanuatu Petrel

averages more black than Juan Fernandez, less than Vanuatu

white 'tongues' typical (primaries rarely dark)

fresh upperparts gray, fading to show brown tones

White-necked Petrel *Pterodroma cervicalis* 41–44cm, WS 102–110; also see p. 123
Breeds Dec–Jun on Macauley I. in Kermadecs; also small numbers on Phillip I. Non-breeding range mainly May–Oct (imms. year-round) in subtropical W and Cen Pacific, rarely in E Pacific. Wing molt mainly Apr–Sep. Flight typical of large subtropical *Pterodroma*: buoyant and easy in calm to light winds, when can stay fairly low; wheels high and steeply in strong winds.

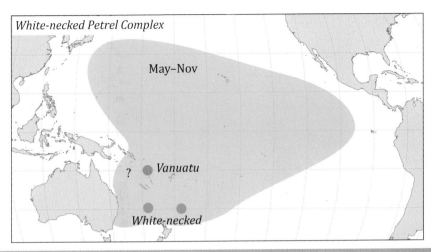

White-necked Petrel Complex

May–Nov

? Vanuatu

White-necked

poorly known, rather large gadfly, not readily separable in field from White-necked Petrel but averages smaller and smaller-billed, averages more extensive dark on underwings

big dark wing-tip

averages more black than White-necked

white extreme (primaries dark on most birds)

Vanuatu Petrel *Pterodroma [cervicalis] occulta* 38–41cm, WS 97–103cm
Poorly known; taxonomic status unresolved. Breeds (Jan–Jun?) on Vanua Lava I., n. Vanuatu. At-sea range unknown; likely ranges at least in tropical SW Pacific, rarely (?) to E Australia. Habits much like White-necked Petrel, from which not separable at sea except by presumption for birds seen around breeding island.

122

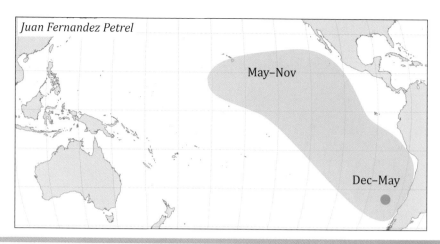

Juan Fernandez Petrel

May–Nov

Dec–May

large, rather long-tailed and long-billed gadfly with blackish mask merging into gray neck sides; nape can wear and fade to whitish, cf. White-necked Petrel

faded 1st-year

slightly worn

black comma

fresh upperparts gray, fading to show brown tones

fresh

Juan Fernandez Petrel *Pterodroma externa* 42–45cm, WS 103–114cm; also see opposite Breeds Dec–May on Selkirk in Juan Fernandez Is.; ranges at sea Dec–May off cen. and n. Chile. Non-breeding range (May–Nov; imms. year-round) in tropical Cen and E Pacific. Wing molt mainly Mar–Sep. Flight typical of large subtropical *Pterodroma*: buoyant and easy in calm to light winds, when can stay fairly low; wheels high and steeply in strong winds. Often in mixed-species feeding flocks over yellowfin tuna, with Wedge-tailed Shearwaters, Sooty Terns.

Comparison of larger 'white-winged' Pacific *Pterodroma*

In much of the tropical Pacific, 4 species of larger white-bodied and 'white-winged' *Pterodroma* petrels potentially overlap, and 2 or more species can occur together in mixed-species feeding flocks that also include Wedge-tailed Shearwaters, Sooty Terns, and other gadfly petrels.

The main ID features are head and neck patterns and underwing patterns. Note that fresh dorsal plumage is much grayer, even frosty in tone, whereas worn plumage is duller and browner. A common pitfall is 'white-necked' Juan Fernandez Petrels, in which the hindneck has bleached and worn to white (mainly 1st-year birds in Nov–Feb). Variation in Hawaiian and Galapagos Petrels remains to be elucidated; head pattern and bill size vary within both, and further cryptic species may be involved.

White-necked **Juan Fernandez** **Hawaiian** **Galapagos**

black comma

more black than Juan Fernandez

thick black wing margins; Galapagos usually also has dark 'armpit' smudge

black cap, white nape, gray neck spur

black mask, gray nape, long bill

narrow wings, medium wing-loading; dark cap

broad wings, low wing-loading; dark cowl

shorter, squarer tail than Juan Fernandez

Dark-rumped Petrel (*Pterodroma phaeopygia*) Complex

Before 2002, Hawaiian and Galapagos Petrels were lumped as a single species, Dark-rumped Petrel *P. phaeopygia*, and were considered indistinguishable in the field. With the split into 2 species (both of which may include further cryptic species), provisional ID criteria were proposed by Force et al. (2007). Variation within both taxa (relating to populations nesting on different islands and at different seasons) awaits elucidation.

fairly large, long-tailed gadfly with variable dark cowl, thick black underwing margins; little or no range overlap with very similar Hawaiian Petrel; also cf. p. 123

cowl shape changes with angle of view

fresh

black averages thicker than Hawaiian

worn

variable dark 'armpit' smudges, cf. Hawaiian Petrel

fresh upperparts gray, fading to show brown tones

Galapagos Petrel *Pterodroma phaeopygia* 39.5–42cm, WS 99–110cm; also see p. 123
Breeds on larger islands in Galapagos. Season varies with island and even elevation (Tomkins & Milne 1991): mainly May–Oct on Santiago; Jul–Dec on Santa Cruz; Mar–Aug (lowlands) and May–Oct (highlands) on Floreana; and year-round but mainly Jan–Jun and Jun–Nov on San Cristobal. Ranges in tropical E Pacific. Wing molt can occur year-round. Flight buoyant and easy in calm to light winds, when often stays fairly low; wheels more steeply in strong winds, but less so than heavier-bodied Hawaiian Petrel. Likely comprises multiple cryptic species.

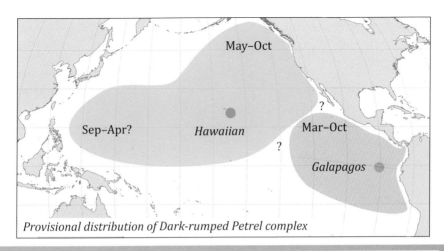

Provisional distribution of Dark-rumped Petrel complex

medium-large, long-tailed gadfly with variable dark cap, thick black underwing margins;
little or no range overlap with very similar Galapagos Petrel; also cf. p. 123

fresh

*cap shape changes
with angle of view*

worn

averages smaller bill than Galapagos;
usually has clean white flanks

*fresh upperparts gray,
fading to show brown tones*

Hawaiian Petrel *Pterodroma sandwichensis* 37.5–40cm, WS 94–104cm; also see p. 123
Breeds Apr/May–Oct/Nov on se. Hawaiian Is. Ranges in subtropical and tropical Pacific, n. to
around 50°N (breeding adults), w. to around 130°E (mainly Sep–Apr, perhaps mainly imms.).
Wing molt mainly Aug–Feb. Flight buoyant and easy in calm to light winds, when often stays
fairly low; wheels steeply and high in strong winds, more so than lighter-bodied, broader-
winged Galapagos Petrel, which tends to wheel in longer-wavelength arcs.

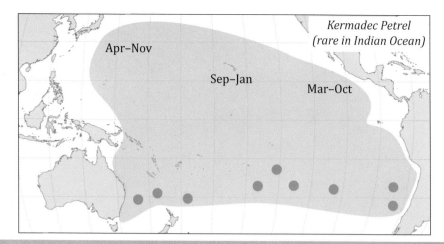

medium-large, rather stocky gadfly with broad wings, rather short and broad tail; plumage highly variable, cf. Herald and Trindade Petrels; note white primary shafts

white flashes rarely muted

skua-like white flashes below

white shafts

fresh upperparts grayish, soon fading to brown

Kermadec Petrel (light morph) *Pterodroma neglecta* 37–40cm, WS 97–106cm; also see pp. 118, 128, 144–145

Breeds (mainly Nov–May, but locally year-round) in subtropical S Pacific from Lord Howe e. to Juan Fernandez Is. Ranges widely in subtropical and tropical Pacific, n. to around 40°N. Small numbers also breed Round I., SW Indian Ocean; at-sea range unknown. Wing molt can be year-round. Flight relatively heavy for a larger gadfly; in strong winds tends to wheel in long-wavelength versus steep arcs; at times pirates petrels and other seabirds, much like a skua. Nests on surface and visits colonies during day.

127

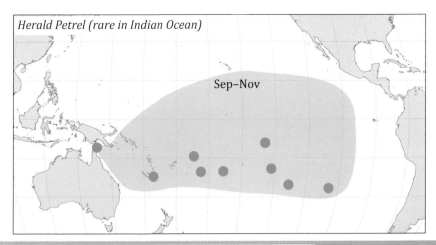

Herald Petrel (rare in Indian Ocean)

Sep–Nov

medium-size, lightly built gadfly with narrow wings, tapered tail;
plumage variable, cf. Kermadec and Trindade Petrels

white flash averages smaller
than Kermadec

dark shafts

lacks pale-headed and messy
morphs of Kermadec Petrel

Herald Petrel (light morph) *Pterodroma heraldica* 34.5–37cm, WS 90–97cm; also see pp. 118, 144, 146

Breeds (year-round, perhaps mainly Feb–Sep) in tropical S Pacific from NE Australia e. to Easter I. Ranges widely in subtropical and tropical Pacific, n. at least to 25°N in Cen Pacific (mainly Apr–Oct?). Small numbers breed Round I., SW Indian Ocean; at-sea range unknown. Wing molt can be year-round. Flight buoyant and easy in calm to light winds, when often stays fairly low; wheels high and steeply in strong winds. Nests on surface and visits colonies during day. ID criteria vs. Trindade Petrel (p. 117–118) and hybrid Trindade × Herald Petrel require study.

Kermadec Petrel Variation and Possible Hybrid Petrels

Kermadec Petrel exhibits a huge degree of plumage variation, which has yet to be studied critically (also see pp. 126, 145); some plumages are very similar to those of Herald Petrel, others unique to Kermadec. A confounding issue is potential hybridization among Kermadec, Herald, Henderson, and Murphy's Petrels, which nest together locally. Although undocumented in Pacific, hybridism has been recorded in Indian Ocean, involving Kermadec, Trindade, and Herald Petrels (Brown et al. 2011). However, potential hybrids (intermediate in plumage, bill size, overall structure) have been found in the Pitcairn group, as shown below.

Kermadec Petrel

head and body vary from creamy white to dark brown; also see pp. 126, 145

classic upperwing has jaeger-like crescent of white primary shafts; whether birds with reduced white are pure or hybrids is unknown

Possible hybrids

reduced white

classic pattern

'Henderson Petrel' × Kermadec Petrel

Murphy's Petrel × Herald Petrel (2 examples)

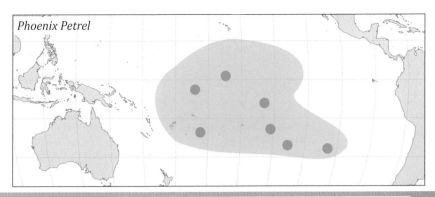

Phoenix Petrel

medium-size, lightly built gadfly, very like Herald Petrel in size, shape, flight manner; whitish chin patch and narrow leading edge to underwing visible at close range

solidly sooty chocolate-brown above

white overall

lacks white underwing flashes, but primaries can reflect paler

Phoenix Petrel *Pterodroma alba* 36–38cm, WS 90–96cm
Breeds year-round (details poorly known) in equatorial and tropical S Pacific from Phoenix e. locally to Easter I.; uncommon. Ranges in tropical Cen Pacific. Wing molt likely occurs year-round. Flight manner and habits much like Herald Petrel, quite different from Tahiti Petrel, which shares similar plumage pattern. Perhaps not safely told from some dark-hooded Herald Petrels (study needed), but Herald typically has white primary flashes, darker undertail coverts, grayer upperparts. Nests on surface and visits colonies during day.

Tahiti Petrel (*Pseudobulweria rostrata*) Complex

For many years, Beck's Petrel treated as small race of Tahiti Petrel, but its strikingly different size supports species status (see Shirihai 2008). Within Tahiti Petrel, 2 races sometimes recognized: *rostrata* from Tahiti, *trouessarti* from New Caledonia; taxonomic status of birds with broad whitish underwing stripe (not a function of plumage wear or molt, as often claimed) unresolved.

rather large, long-winged gadfly with long-armed wings, tapered tail, very stout bill

tail coverts often paler

some W Pacific birds have a broad whitish underwing stripe

Tahiti Petrel *Pseudobulweria rostrata* 38–42cm, WS 101–108cm

Breeds (lays year-round, varying with location) in tropical S Pacific. Ranges in subtropical and tropical Pacific, e. to Middle America; some also range w. into E Indian Ocean. Wing molt may be year-round. Flight languid and rather heavy in calm to light winds, with deep loose wingbeats and low glides on wings held rather straight with tips slightly curled up (long-armed wings can suggest an albatross, vs. more crooked and bowed wings of *Pterodroma*); in moderate to strong winds, wheels in long-wavelength arcs, not steeply. Feeds mainly by scavenging, thus not usually with mixed-species feeding flocks over schooling fish or dolphins.

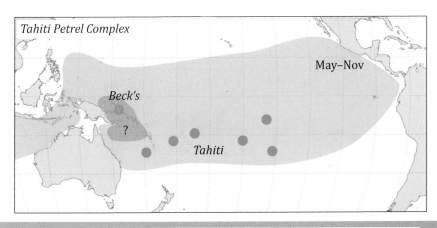

Tahiti Petrel Complex

Beck's

?

Tahiti

May–Nov

medium-size, long-winged gadfly; told from Tahiti Petrel by smaller size, flight manner

Beck's Petrel *Pseudobulweria becki* 30–34cm, WS 84–89cm
Poorly known, but locally fairly common in Solomon Sea, between Bismarcks and Solomons (may breed New Ireland, Mar–Aug). At-sea range largely unknown (overlaps with Tahiti Petrel), perhaps s. at least into Coral Sea and e. to Vanuatu. Flight quicker and more manueverable, less languid than appreciably larger Tahiti Petrel (can be seen together scavenging at slicks), with quicker, snappier wingbeats and rather buoyant glides. Simply from photos, however, with no context or flight manner, not readily distinguishable from Tahiti Petrel. Beck's can have paler underwing stripe, but not known to show a broad whitish stripe like some Tahiti Petrels.

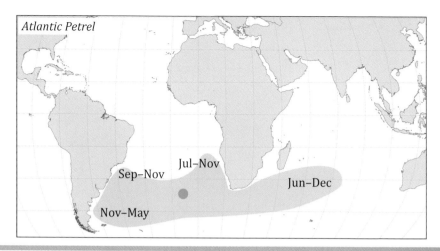

Atlantic Petrel

Jul–Nov

Sep–Nov

Jun–Dec

Nov–May

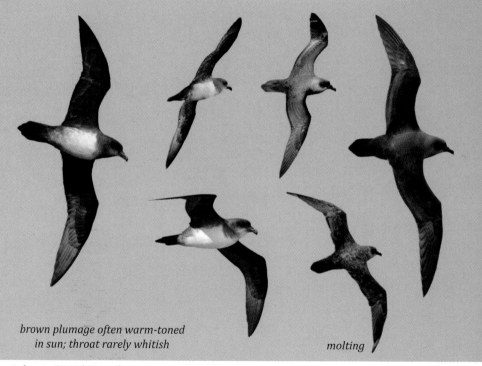

large, rather heavyset gadfly, distinctive in range, but cf. light-morph Trindade Petrel (pp. 117–118); note large size, white body contrasting with dark undertail

brown plumage often warm-toned in sun; throat rarely whitish

molting

Atlantic Petrel *Pterodroma incerta* 43–46cm, WS 105–112cm
Breeds mainly Jun–Dec on Gough (extirpated from Tristan group?). Ranges in subtropical S Atlantic, mainly 25–50°S; small numbers (imm. non-breeders?) range e. into SW Indian Ocean. Wing molt mainly Oct–Apr. Flight typical of heavier-bodied large *Pterodroma*: in light winds, flies with bursts of strong, slightly snappy wingbeats and low wheeling glides; arcs high and powerfully in strong winds.

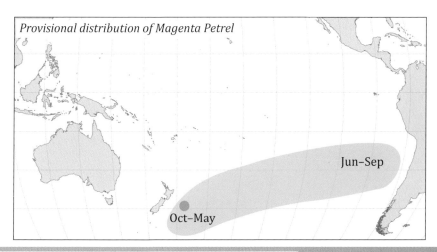

Provisional distribution of Magenta Petrel

Jun–Sep

Oct–May

very rare; size, shape, and flight suggest Great-winged Petrel, but ventral plumage distinctive; note white undertail coverts

Magenta Petrel (Taiko) *Pterodroma magentae* 39.5–42cm, WS 102–108cm
Breeds late Nov–early May on Chathams, New Zealand; very rare, with <50 pairs. At-sea range poorly known, but in non-breeding season occurs e. in subtropical S Pacific to waters off Pitcairn and Juan Fernandez Is. Wing molt probably Mar–Sep. Habits much like White-headed Petrel, with which non-breeding birds may associate loosely. Named not for the color, but for the ship *Magenta*, on whose circumnavigation of the world the type specimen was collected.

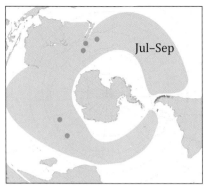

Jul–Sep

White-headed Petrel

large, distinctive, rather heavyset gadfly with white head, pale tail, contrasting dark underwings

gray on neck sides variable, rarely forming collar

White-headed Petrel *Pterodroma lessonii* 43–45.5cm, WS 102–109cm
Breeds late Nov–early Jun on subantarcic islands from Crozets e. to Antipodes. Ranges widely in subantarctic waters of Indian and Pacific Oceans, s. locally (mainly Dec–Mar) to 65°S, n. locally (mainly Jul–Sep) to around 25°S in subtropical waters; uncommon to rare in S Atlantic. Wing molt mainly Apr–Sep. Flight typical of heavier-bodied large *Pterodroma*: in light winds, flies with bursts of strong snappy wingbeats and low wheeling glides; arcs high and powerfully in strong winds.

Soft-plumaged Petrel

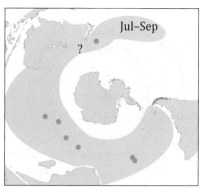

Jul–Sep
?

medium-size, distinctive stocky gadfly with gray neck collar, contrasting dark underwings; appreciably larger and fatter than Cookilaria

fresh plumage

collar variable; often appears dark-hooded

worn plumage

Soft-plumaged Petrel (light morph) *Pterodroma mollis* 35.5–37cm, WS 84–92cm; also see dark morph on p. 139
Breeds mainly Dec–May on Gough and Tristan group in S Atlantic, and from Prince Edwards e. to Antipodes. Ranges in subantarctic and subtropical waters, mainly 30–55°S; n. locally (mainly Jun–Sep) to around 25°S in Indian Ocean and Cen Pacific. Wing molt mainly Mar–Sep. Flight buoyant and easy in calm to light winds, when often stays fairly low; wheels steeply in strong winds. Indian Ocean birds have been described as race *dubia,* averaging darker and browner above than Atlantic birds, with average heavier breast band; critical study needed.

136

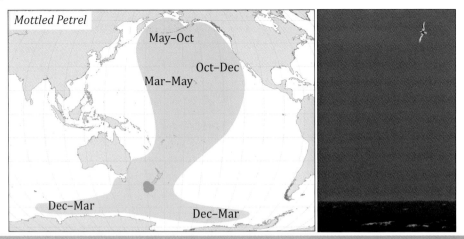

Mottled Petrel

May–Oct

Oct–Dec

Mar–May

Dec–Mar

Dec–Mar

medium-size, distinctive stocky gadfly; note white underwings with thick black bar, dark body contrasting with white vent; appreciably larger and fatter than Cookilaria

silvery-gray trailing edge

fresh plumage

worn plumage

Mottled Petrel *Pterodroma inexpectata* 32–36cm, WS 84–92cm

Breeds Dec–May in s. New Zealand; ranges Nov–May around s. New Zealand and (mainly Dec–Mar) s. to pack ice and antarctic waters. Non-breeding range (mainly May–Oct; some imms. year-round) in N Pacific and Bering Sea; migrates quickly across Cen Pacific, mainly Mar–May and Oct–Nov. Wing molt mainly May–Aug (adults), Jan–Jul (1st-years). In calm to light winds, flight typically low, with long low glides interspersed with bursts of quick wing-beats; in high winds, wheels strongly and steeply, at times towering very high above the sea.

DARK-BODIED GADFLY PETRELS

These comprise 15+ species (10+ in genus *Pterodroma*, 1 in *Aphrodroma*, 2 in *Pseudobulweria*, 2+ in *Bulweria*) of small to large gadfly petrels found in all oceans. Until recently, the genera *Aphrodroma* and *Pseudobulweria* were often subsumed into *Pterodroma*. Most *Pterodroma* occur in subtropical waters; *Aphrodroma* in subantarctic waters; and *Pseudobulweria* and *Bulweria* mainly in tropical waters.

For ID, besides location and habitat pay attention to general size (often reflected in flight manner), overall structure (especially tail length and shape), bill size, and any underwing patterns. As with other seabirds, species of cooler and windier latitudes tend to have heavier bodies and narrower wings (such as Murphy's Petrel), whereas those of warmer and calmer latitudes tend to have lighter bodies and broader wings (such as Henderson Petrel); these structural differences are reflected in subtly distinctive different flight manners (see pp. 21–22). Four *Pterodroma* species are polymorphic; light morphs are treated with white-bodied gadflies (see p. 107).

For ID purposes dark-bodied gadflies can be considered in 3 groups: southern-breeding *Pterodroma* and *Aphrodroma* (below); subtropical and tropical *Pterodroma* (p. 138); and the tropical genera *Pseudobulweria* and *Bulweria* (p. 138).

Southern-breeding

Kerguelen
p. 139

Great-winged complex
pp. 140–141

Soft-plumaged (dark morph), p. 139

138

Subtropical and Tropical *Pterodroma*

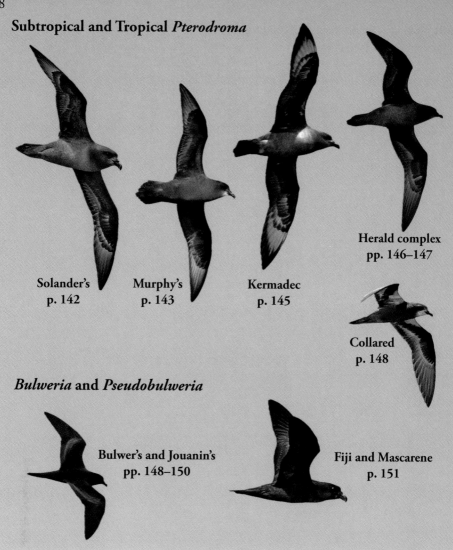

Solander's
p. 142

Murphy's
p. 143

Kermadec
p. 145

Herald complex
pp. 146–147

Collared
p. 148

Bulweria and *Pseudobulweria*

Bulwer's and Jouanin's
pp. 148–150

Fiji and Mascarene
p. 151

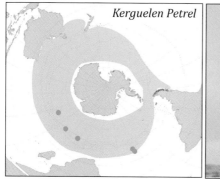

Kerguelen Petrel

Soft-plumaged Petrel (dark morph) *Pterodroma mollis* 35.5–37cm, WS 84–92cm; see light morph and map on p. 135
Dark morph rare in Atlantic (<0.5% of birds), uncommon in Indian Ocean (about 2% of birds). Species breeds mainly Dec–May from Tristan group in S Atlantic e. to Antipodes, New Zealand; ranges in subantarctic and subtropical waters, mainly 30–55°S, n. locally (mainly Jun–Sep) to around 25°N in Indian Ocean and Cen Pacific.

Soft-plumaged (dark morph)

variably dark below; can be dark-faced; also cf. Murphy's Petrel (p. 143)

chestier and 'curvier' than rather 'linear' Kerguelen

Kerguelen Petrel

towering, high-level glides diagnostic

worn plumage browner overall

leading edge silvery

in some lights, underwing and dark hood can suggest dark Soft-plumaged Petrel

medium-size, steely-gray petrel with narrow angular wings, dark hood, big eyes

Kerguelen Petrel *Aphrodroma (Lugensa) brevirostris* 33–35.5cm, WS 88–90cm
Breeds Oct–Feb on subantarctic islands from Gough and Inaccessible e. to Kerguelen. Circumpolar range in subantarctic and antarctic waters, mainly 45–65°S, n. locally (mainly May–Sep) to 35°S; locally common in S Atlantic and S Indian Oceans; uncommon in Pacific. Wing molt mainly Dec–Jun. In light winds usually wheels fairly low, with bursts of quick stiff wingbeats; in moderate to strong winds flight spectacular, with steeply rising climbs and prolonged level glides high above the sea before sweeping down and then up again steeply; at other times, flight more 'normal' and *Pterodroma*-like, with high wheeling arcs that lack prolonged high-level glides.

Great-winged Petrel (*Pterodroma macroptera*) Complex

Comprises 2 taxa of large dark gadfly petrels, traditionally combined as Great-winged Petrel. Slightly larger, stouter-billed, and paler-faced taxon *gouldi* now usually treated as separate species, Gray-faced Petrel, but field ID not always possible unless classic examples are encountered.

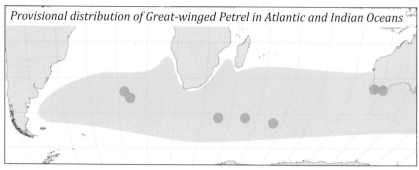

Provisional distribution of Great-winged Petrel in Atlantic and Indian Oceans

large, dark brown gadfly with pale chin, dark eye patch; cf. Gray-faced Petrel

averages less contrasting dark hood than Gray-faced Petrel

no white wing flashes but can reflect silvery

bill less stout than Gray-faced Petrel

whitish usually limited to chin, but can have pale face

Great-winged Petrel *Pterodroma macroptera* 42–44.5cm, WS 104–111cm
Breeds late May–Nov in S Atlantic on Gough and Tristan group, and in S Indian Ocean from Prince Edwards e. to SW Australia. Ranges from subtropical S Atlantic e. to SE Australia, mainly 35–55°S (scarce in SW Atlantic). Wing molt mainly Aug–Mar. Flight typical of large subtropical *Pterodroma*: in light winds, low wheeling glides interspersed with bursts of strong, slightly snappy wingbeats; arcs high and powerfully in strong winds.

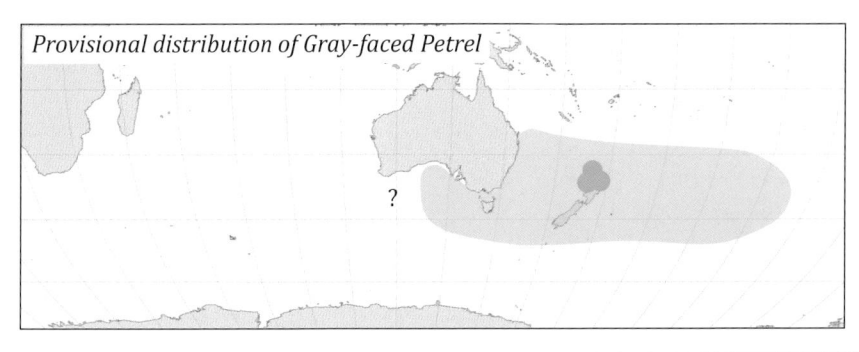

Provisional distribution of Gray-faced Petrel

?

large, dark brown gadfly with variable whitish 'blaze' around base of very stout bill

no white wing flashes
but can reflect silvery

pale face reduced
on some birds

Gray-faced Petrel *Pterodroma [macroptera] gouldi* 42–45cm, WS 105–113cm
Breeds late Jun–Jan around n. New Zealand, including mainland. Ranges in subtropical SW
Pacific, mainly 30–50°S and w. (mainly Feb–May) to S Australia; details of at-sea distribution
clouded by plumage variation in this and Great-winged Petrel. Wing molt mainly Oct–Apr.
Habits much as Great-winged, but may scavenge more frequently at fishing vessels, when often
found with similar-sized Flesh-footed Shearwaters and Parkinson's Petrels.

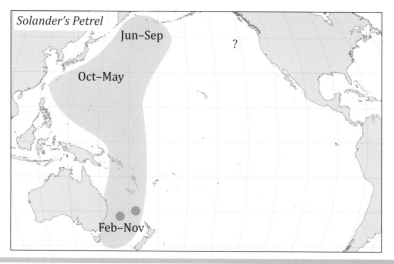

large, with long wings, big bill, double white underwing flashes, steely-gray upperparts

dark hooded
from below

pale face most extensive
on lores and forehead

Solander's (Providence) Petrel *Pterodroma solandri* 43–46cm, WS 100–107cm; also see p. 144

Breeds May–Nov on Lord Howe; a few pairs also on Phillip I. Ranges Feb–Nov in Tasman Sea region; non-breeding range mainly in subtropical NW Pacific (Oct–May, imms. year-round), n. locally to around 55°N. Wing molt mainly Sep–Mar. In calm to light winds often stays fairly low, buoyant glides interspersed with easy, powerful wingbeats; in strong winds wheels high, in long-wavelength arcs. Nests in burrows, but visits colonies during day. Cf. Kermadec Petrel.

143

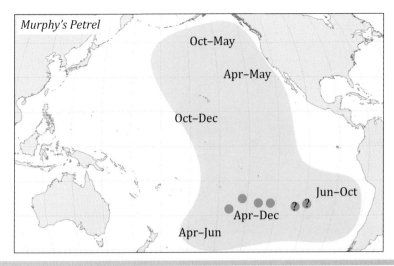

Murphy's Petrel

Oct–May

Apr–May

Oct–Dec

Jun–Oct

Apr–Dec

Apr–Jun

medium-size but stocky, with small bill, silvery underwing flashes, steely-gray upperparts

plumage tones vary
greatly with lighting

pale face most extensive
on chin and throat

Murphy's Petrel *Pterodroma ultima* 34.5–37cm, WS 89–97cm; also see pp. 128, 144
Breeds mainly Jun–Dec in Pitcairns; also s. Tuamotus, Australs, perhaps Easter I. and Salas y
Gómez. Ranges May–Dec in subtropical S-Cen and SE Pacific; non-breeding range mainly in
subtropical NE Pacific (Oct–May, imms. year-round), n. locally to around 50°N. Wing molt
mainly Oct–Apr. In calm to light winds often stays fairly low, buoyant glides interspersed with
fairly quick, snappy wingbeats; in high winds, flight strong and fast, often bounding high in
steep wheeling arcs. Nests on surface, visits colonies during day. See possible hybrids on p. 128.

Comparison of larger dark-bodied Pacific *Pterodroma*

In much of the tropical and subtropical Pacific, 4–5 species of large dark-bodied *Pterodroma* petrels potentially co-occur, and ID can be challenging (3–4 species breed alongside each other and may even hybridize; see p. 128). The main ID features are overall size and structure, bill size, underwing patterns, and plumage tones (beware that fresh dorsal plumage is grayer, worn plumage duller and browner); with some experience, flight manner can also be helpful.

Murphy's	Solander's	Kermadec	Herald/Henderson
medium; small bill; high wing-loading; gray-toned	large; big bill; gray-toned	large; broad-winged; brown-toned	medium; slender bill; low wing-loading; brown-toned

silvery flash

white narrows at leading edge

muted paler flash

dark-hooded

double white flashes

single or double white flashes

white wide at leading edge

white most extensive on chin of Murphy's, on lores of Solander's

dark shafts can reflect silvery

white shafts

medium-large, rather stocky gadfly with broad wings, rather short and broad tail, white primary shafts; plumage highly variable (see pp. 126, 128); cf. Solander's Petrel (p. 142)

underparts dark brown to pale brown; also see p. 128

white shafts

ashy-gray tones of fresh juv. soon fade to brownish

white shafts reduced on some birds; study needed

Kermadec Petrel (dark morph) *Pterodroma neglecta* 37–40cm, WS 97–106cm; also see pp. 118, 126, 128 and opposite
Breeds in subtropical S Pacific; ranges in subtropical and tropical Pacific, n. to around 40°N. Small numbers also breed Round I., SW Indian Ocean. Dark morph uncommon in W Pacific, fairly common in E Pacific. Nests on surface and visits colonies during day.

Herald Petrel (*Pterodroma heraldica*) Complex

This complex has been considered as a single species, including Trindade Petrel, which is now usually treated as a separate species. It has also been suggested that dark-morph 'Herald Petrels' breeding on Henderson I. represent a separate species, 'Henderson Petrel' (Brooke & Rowe 1996), which leaves the vexed questions of what a true dark-morph Herald Petrel looks like, where it occurs, and even, does it exist?

Until a satisfactory study is made of plumage variation within Henderson Petrel, this issue is even harder to resolve. For example, are birds with a ghosting of Herald's dark hood and underwing pattern (as shown to the right) simply paler extremes of 'Henderson Petrel' or might they be dark variations of Herald Petrel, or possibly even hybrids?

Photos of confirmed dark-morph Herald Petrel remain elusive, suggesting this form is rare or at least rather local. At-sea observations indicate that, unlike Henderson Petrel, some presumed dark-morph Heralds have white underwing primary flashes, like light-morph Herald, and a grayish ground color to the plumage (H. Shirihai, pers. comm.). Recent reports come from only a few breeding sites of Herald Petrel in French Polynesia, such as Ducie I. (H. Shirihai, pers. comm.). Further study is needed.

underparts pale to dark brown; underwing usually has paler primary flashes, sometimes a whitish median panel

Trindade Petrel (dark morph) *Pterodroma arminjoniana* 36–39cm, WS 94–102cm; also see pp. 117–118

Breeds year-round in S Atlantic on Trindade; also in SW Indian Ocean on Round I. Ranges widely in subtropical and tropical Atlantic and Indian Oceans. Complex hybridization with Kermadec Petrel and Herald Petrel reported on Round I. Dark morph fairly common. Range not known to overlap with Henderson/dark-morph Herald Petrels.

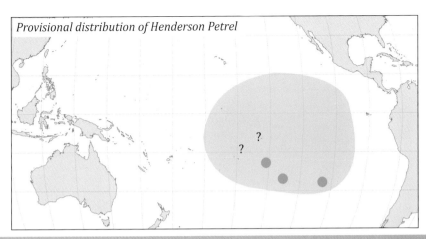

Provisional distribution of Henderson Petrel

medium-size, lightly built dark gadfly; plumage variation awaits elucidation; note weakly defined whitish leading edge to underwing, slender bill vs. Murphy's

no whitish patches, but can reflect silvery

plumage tones vary with light from cold to warm brown

Henderson Petrel *Pterodroma [heraldica] atrata* 34.5–37cm, WS 90–97cm; also see p. 144 Status clouded with respect to status of dark-morph Herald Petrel. Breeds (mainly May–Sep) on Henderson I., where common; also small numbers apparently on s. Tuamotus, Easter I., and perhaps elsewhere in E Polynesia. Henderson/dark Herald ranges in tropical and subtropical E Pacific, n. to around 15°N (mainly May–Oct). Nests on surface and visits colonies during day. Flight and habits like Herald Petrel. Also see possible hybrids on p. 128.

148

distinctive and attractive small petrel with dark body, white throat, bold underwing pattern

Collared Petrel (dark morph) *Pterodroma brevipes* 29–31cm, WS 67–73cm; also see p. 103
Breeds locally (mainly Mar–Aug) in tropical Southwest Pacific, from Vanuatu e. to Cooks.
Ranges in tropical W and Cen Pacific. Proportion of dark morphs varies regionally: dark
morphs perhaps 80–90% of population in n. Vanuatu, whence race *magnificens* ('Magnificent
Petrel') described recently (Bretagnolle & Shirihai 2010; but see Tennyson et al. 2012); else-
where, dark morphs usually comprise about 10–20% of population. Range map on p. 103.

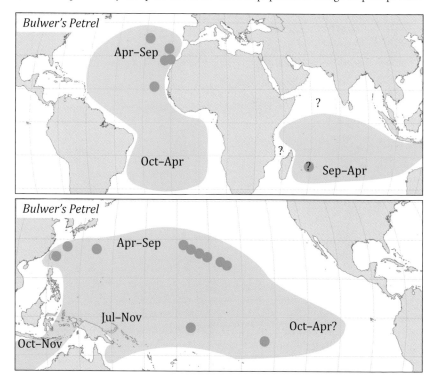

distinctive, small dark petrel with long tapered tail, pale upperwing panel; can be puzzling, and likely includes multiple cryptic species

Madeira, May

plumage tones and contrast of pale upperwing panel vary with lighting, plumage wear and fading

Hawaii, Apr

Marquesas, Sep

relatively stocky, small-billed

Indian Ocean, Dec

relatively large, long-billed

Japan, Jul

Bulwer's Petrel *Bulweria bulwerii* 27–29cm, WS 63–68cm
Widespread, fairly common; likely includes cryptic species. In Pacific, breeds May–Sep from s. Japan e. to Hawaii; and (mainly Oct–Mar?) from Phoenix e. to Marquesas; ranges in subtropical and tropical Pacific; also migrates w. into Indian Ocean (mainly Sep–Apr, imms. year-round). In Atlantic, breeds May–Sep from Azores s. to Canaries; Jan–Sep in Cape Verdes; ranges in tropical and subtropical Cen Atlantic. In Indian Ocean, presumed Bulwer's has bred since 1980s on Round I., and an enigmatic *Bulweria* occurs around the Comoros (see under Jouanin's Petrel). Usually flies low on crooked wings, tail held closed: buoyant weaving glides interspersed with fairly quick bowed wingbeats; in stronger winds can wheel higher but does not bank steeply and tends to 'hug' the water. Distinctive, but cf. larger dark storm-petrels, brown and black noddies.

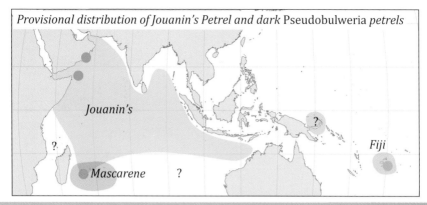

Provisional distribution of Jouanin's Petrel and dark Pseudobulweria petrels

Jouanin's

?

?

Mascarene   ?

Fiji

medium-size, thickset dark petrel with very stout bill, fairly long tapered tail

appreciably larger, stockier, and thicker-necked than Bulwer's Petrel, with a more massive bill and heavier, languid flight

upperwing typically rather plain, cf. Bulwer's

Jouanin's   Bulwer's

fresh plumage can show paler upperwing panels

Jouanin's Petrel *Bulweria fallax* 32–35.5cm, WS 76–80cm
Tropical Indian Ocean; locally fairly common. Breeds Jul–Dec in Arabian Sea. Ranges year-round in NW Indian Ocean (mainly 25°N–10°S; in small numbers s. to Réunion, e. to NW Australia); vagrant to Pacific (Hawaii). An undescribed Jouanin's-like petrel also occurs around the Comoros (Shirihai & Bretagnolle 2015b). Wing molt mainly Nov–Mar (adults), Sep–Jan (1st-years). Flight in calm to light winds unhurried, with easy, slightly springy wingbeats (emphasis on upstroke) and buoyant sailing glides on slightly arched wings; meanders lazily when foraging. In stronger winds wheels in low shallow arcs, suggesting a small, thickset Wedge-tailed Shearwater. Found singly or in loose aggregations; at times rests in flocks on the water.

poorly known, fairly small dark petrel with stout bill, tapered tail

Fiji Petrel *Pseudobulweria macgillivrayi* 27–30cm, WS 76–82cm; see map opposite
Tropical Southwest Pacific; very rare and poorly known. Small numbers presumably breed (Apr–Sep?) on Gau I., Fiji; at-sea range presumed in tropical W Pacific. Sightings since 2003 of a small dark *Pseudobulweria* around New Ireland may represent a disjunct population of Fiji Petrel or an undescribed taxon (Shirihai et al. 2009, Flood et al. 2017). In calm to light winds, flies with supple wingbeats interspersed with easy, low sailing glides; wingbeats quicker and less languid than much larger Tahiti Petrel, but distinct from snappier *Pterodroma* or quicker and stiffer Christmas Shearwater; flight more relaxed than quicker, jinking flight of smaller, longer-tailed Bulwer's Petrel.

medium-size dark petrel with blocky head, very stout bill, fairly broad tapered tail

some have buff hindneck streaks

chunkier than Jouanin's Petrel, with larger head, shorter and broader tail, different flight

Mascarene Petrel *Pseudobulweria aterrima* 31–35cm, WS 84–90cm; see map opposite
South Indian Ocean; rare. Breeds mainly Nov–Apr on Réunion. At-sea range presumably in tropical and subtropical Indian Ocean. In calm to light winds, flight rather languid: low sailing glides on slightly bowed wings interspersed with unhurried, supple wingbeats; probably wheels higher in moderate winds, but flight overall similar to other *Pseudobulweria*, unlike snappier, more dynamic flight of *Pterodroma* petrels. See Shirihai et al. (2014) for more information.

SHEARWATERS AND ALLIES (41+ species in 4 genera)

Varied assemblage of medium-large to fairly small petrels comprising the genera *Ardenna* (7+ species), *Calonectris* (4 species), *Procellaria* (5 species), and *Puffinus* (25+ species) Most diverse in subtropical and higher latitudes, but some species are tropical, and several are long-distance migrants. Larger species especially are often gregarious, and mixed-species assemblages can be found rafting and feeding. Unlike most gadfly petrels, several shearwaters and allies can be seen readily from shore; some larger species often follow ships and scavenge from fishing boats. Feed by snatching fish and squid near the surface, often by diving, and by scavenging. Nest in burrows and crevices, and mostly visit colonies at night.

ID of most species straightforward, at least when assumptions based on range are taken into account, but a few species notoriously similar. **For ID purposes**, we treat shearwaters and allies in 3 groups: **dark-bodied species**; **large white-bodied species**; and **small black-and-white shearwaters** (opposite).

Shearwater species often associate together when feeding and resting. The above feeding group off North Carolina comprises Audubon's and Cory's along with single Great and Sooty Shearwaters. Below, a raft of Black-venteds off southern California, among which are single Pink-footed and Flesh-footed Shearwaters, plus a Pomarine Jaeger.

Dark-bodied
pp. 154–165

Large White-bodied
pp. 166–175

Small Black-and-white
pp. 176–193

DARK-BODIED SHEARWATERS AND ALLIES

Comprise 2 smaller tropical shearwaters in genus *Puffinus*, 4 large shearwaters in mainly S Hemisphere genus *Ardenna* (formerly *Puffinus*), and 4 large 'black petrels' in S Hemisphere genus *Procellaria*. While subtle plumage tones can be helpful for ID (such as dark chocolate-brown vs. sooty gray-brown), under field conditions most ID relies on size and general structure (such as wing width, tail length and shape), flight manner, and bill size and pattern; underwing pattern also helpful for Sooty vs. Short-tailed Shearwaters, and head pattern for Spectacled vs. White-chinned Petrels. Dark-bodied gadfly petrels (pp. 137–151) typically have snappier wingbeats, more dynamic and controlled flight, thicker and wholly black bills, and different habits.

Taxonomy of Wedge-tailed Shearwater in need of critical study, cf. variation in bill pattern of dark morphs and opposite breeding seasons of N and S Hemisphere populations. Spectacled Petrel traditionally considered a race of White-chinned Petrel.

Dark-bodied Shearwaters

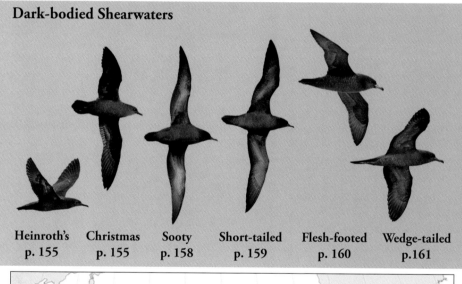

Heinroth's	Christmas	Sooty	Short-tailed	Flesh-footed	Wedge-tailed
p. 155	p. 155	p. 158	p. 159	p. 160	p.161

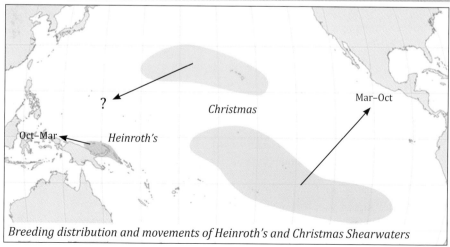

Breeding distribution and movements of Heinroth's and Christmas Shearwaters

very small, with long slender bill, pale eyes, variable whitish underwing patches; belly variably whitish on some birds but undertail coverts always dark

white-bellied extreme

Heinroth's Shearwater *Puffinus heinrothi* 28–30cm, WS 64–68cm
Equatorial Western Pacific; poorly known. Fairly common but local (breeds mainly Mar–Aug?) from ne. New Guinea e. to w. Solomons; ranges w. (Oct–Mar, at least) to Moluccas. Flight usually low to the water; loose quick wingbeats interspersed with buoyant glides on slightly arched wings. Found singly or in small groups, often in nearshore waters or channels between islands, feeding with terns, especially with noddies over schooling fish.

toes do not project past ample tail

coverts dark

angular in strong winds

can reflect silvery

dark chocolate-brown overall with slender black bill

with Wedge-tailed Shearwaters

Christmas Shearwater *Puffinus nativitatus* 33–38cm, WS 83–92cm
Tropical Central Pacific, 2 populations (cryptic species?); s. population averages slightly larger and longer-billed. Fairly common but rather local. Breeds Apr–Oct in Hawaii, mainly Oct–Mar from Phoenix e. to Easter I. Ranges w. to n. Micronesia (from Hawaii?); regular migrant Mar–Oct to Middle America (from Polynesia, based on wing-molt timing). Singly or in small groups, often with feeding flocks of other shearwaters, terns, boobies. Flight usually rather low, with quick stiff wingbeats and short glides, but in strong winds can wheel in low arcs.

Sooty Shearwater versus Short-tailed Shearwater

Separation of Sooty and Short-tailed Shearwaters is a common challenge in much of the SW Pacific and N Pacific, where both species range widely and can occur together. Away from the Pacific, Short-tailed is an exceptional vagrant and Sooty is the default option. Usually, one or the other species predominates in a given region (e.g., Short-tailed migrates through the tropical W Pacific to the Bering Sea, areas where Sooty is very rare or unknown). In areas where Sooty is commoner, if you wonder whether you're seeing a Short-tailed it's probably a small Sooty—a real Short-tailed tends to stand out by virtue of its structure and flight manner.

Sooty Shearwater (left, small-billed individual) and Short-tailed Shearwater (right, long-billed individual): note smaller size, steeper forehead, and smaller, finer bill of Short-tailed

Structure Both species have short tails, beyond which the toe tips often project in flight, so this is an unhelpful feature. Short-tailed averages smaller and appreciably lighter-bodied, with a shorter neck, more steeply domed forehead, and smaller, finer bill (Short-tailed used to be known as Slender-billed Shearwater, which is a more helpful name). Ironically, the short neck and small head projection of Short-tailed often make the tail projection behind the wings seem relatively long, versus a longer neck, more sloping head, and longer bill of Sooty, which makes for a longer, 'snoutier' projection forward of the wings. Sooty tends to glide with wings held out straighter, less crooked than Short-tailed, and its wing-tips often curl up (see opposite).

note straighter wings and longer head/bill projection of Sooty Shearwater versus crooked wings, shorter head/bill projection, smaller bill, and lighter body of Short-tailed Shearwater

Sooty   *Short-tailed*   *Sooty*   *Short-tailed*

Flight/Behavior Courtesy of its lighter body, Short-tailed has a more maneuverable and buoyant flight than Sooty, with quicker, snappier wingbeats that can suggest a gadfly petrel (a resemblance enhanced by the crooked wings), versus the stronger, deeper, and more fluid wingbeats of Sooty. Head-on, Short-tailed typically has arched wings that lack the swept-up wing-tips of Sooty. Off the US West Coast, Short-tailed seems more prone to follow boats, but Sooty does this also, perhaps mainly weaker immatures (such birds are lighter-bodied and smaller-billed than healthy adults, more likely to be mistaken for Short-tailed).

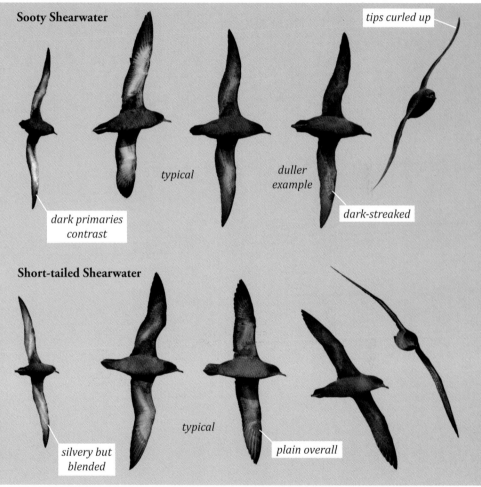

Sooty Shearwater

tips curled up

typical

duller example

dark primaries contrast

dark-streaked

Short-tailed Shearwater

typical

silvery but blended

plain overall

Plumage Both species show appreciable variation in plumage tones and underwing pattern, compounded by wear and, especially, lighting. Some Sooties have rather dull underwings, much like 'textbook' Short-tailed, and in bright light the underwings of many Short-taileds flash silvery white, suggesting 'textbook' Sooty. The pale underwing panel of Short-tailed tends to be more even in width and often blends into the primary bases; the pale underwing panel of Sooty tends to be narrower on the coverts and flares out of the primary coverts, which typically contrast with the darker primary bases (obviously this effect depends on lighting). The underwing primary coverts of Sooty typically have dark streaks; those of Short-tailed appear plain.

158

large, heavy-bodied, sooty-brown shearwater with narrow wings, slender grayish bill, variable silvery underwing flashes (see pp. 156–157)

dark streaks, cf. Short-tailed

toes often project

compare lean, post-migration juv. (left, Jun) with fattened, pre-migration adult completing tail molt (right, Sep)

with Pink-footed and Buller's Shearwaters

Sooty Shearwater *Ardenna grisea* 43–45.5cm, WS 97–106cm; also see pp. 156–157 Widespread; transequatorial migrant; generally common. Breeds Nov–Apr in SE Australia, New Zealand, S South America, and Falklands. Most Australia/New Zealand birds migrate n. Apr–Oct to N Pacific, e.g., common off US West Coast (where some imms. remain year-round); migration mainly tracks prevailing winds, thus largely avoids calm tropical areas of W Pacific (where Short-tailed Shearwater is a common migrant) and waters off Middle America. South American birds common year-round in Humboldt Current, n. to Peru, and also year-round off SW Africa; others migrate Apr–Oct into N Atlantic, where migration follows clockwise loop; thus commonest off NW Europe in Aug–Oct. Often in dense flocks (in Pacific, at times 10s of 1000s) and regularly seen from shore. Flies with quick, strong deep wingbeats and long low glides in calm, high steep wheeling when windy. Cf. very similar Short-tailed Shearwater. Adult wing molt fairly rapid, mainly May–Sep; 1st-year wing molt Jan–Jun in N Hemisphere, Nov–May in S Hemisphere.

fairly large, sooty-brown shearwater with rather small fine bill, typically muted pale underwing flashes (also see pp. 156–157)

primaries typically do not contrast with coverts, cf. Sooty Shearwater

often has pale chin

Apr–May migrants (1st-years?) can have fresh head and body plumage, worn wings and tail

rounded head and small bill can lend a 'cute' aspect, unlike Sooty

glides on arched wings

underwings can flash strongly silvery white in bright sun

with Matsudaira's Storm-Petrel

head typically more rounded than Sooty Shearwater

with Pink-footed Shearwater

Short-tailed Shearwater *Ardenna tenuirostris* 40.5–43cm, WS 91–99cm; see pp. 156–157
Pacific; transequatorial migrant; locally common. Breeds late Nov–Apr in SE Australia, ranging at sea s. to E Antarctica, at least occasionally (Mar–Apr) w. to vicinity of Bouvet I. Migrates n. late Mar–May through W Pacific to Aleutians and Bering Sea (some range into Arctic Ocean); adults migrate s. mainly Sep–Oct through Cen Pacific, imms. migrate s. Sep–Nov, ranging farther e. to waters off W US (where some birds remain Nov–Mar). Locally in large flocks (at times 10s of 1000s). Flies with snappy quick wingbeats and buoyant glides in calm; high steep wheeling when windy. Adult wing molt fairly rapid, May–Sep; 1st-year wing molt timing unknown.

variable pale reflection

large chocolate-brown shearwater with black-tipped pink bill, pink feet

bright pink bill, tipped black

feet pink, cf. Procellaria *petrels*

with single Gray-faced and Parkinson's Petrels

Flesh-footed Shearwater *Ardenna carneipes* 45–48cm, WS 109–116cm
Subtropical Pacific and Indian Oceans; transequatorial migrant; fairly common. Breeds Nov–
Apr from S Australia e. to n. New Zealand; also St. Paul I., Indian Ocean. Migrates n. mainly
Apr–Oct into Indian Ocean (nw. to Arabian Sea, rarely to SE Africa) and into NW Pacific off
Japan, with smaller numbers looping clockwise through NE Pacific off US West Coast (mainly
Aug–Oct). Typically flies with languid wingbeats and easy glides, but wheels high when windy;
often scavenges at fishing boats. Cf. Parkinson's Petrel, dark-morph Wedge-tailed Shearwater,
rare melanistic or dark-morph Pink-footed Shearwater. Adult wing molt Apr–Aug; 1st-year
wing molt Jan–Jun.

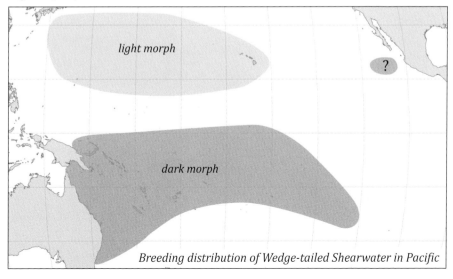

light morph

?

dark morph

Breeding distribution of Wedge-tailed Shearwater in Pacific

large but lightly built dark shearwater with small head, broad wings, long tapered tail, pinkish feet; note structure and flight manner

slender bill gray to pinkish, tipped darker

gray-billed type, cf. Sooty Shearwater

pinkish-billed, cf. Flesh-footed Shearwater

long tail projects past wing-tips

Wedge-tailed Shearwater (dark morph) *Ardenna pacifica* 43–47cm, WS 99–109cm
Tropical Pacific and Indian Oceans; see light morph, p. 174. Dark morph widespread and
locally common in tropical S Indian Ocean and tropical SW and S-Cen Pacific, uncommon in
tropical E Pacific. Breeds mainly Nov–Jun (season more protracted near equator), with some
movement (mainly Apr–Nov) n. to around 23°N in Pacific and into N Indian Ocean. Isolated
colony on San Benedicto, Mexico, reported to be mainly dark morph, breeds May–Nov; post-
breeding movements unknown. Often in flocks, feeding with Sooty Terns, noddies, gadfly
petrels, and boobies over dolphins, tuna. In calm, flight typically unhurried, with wings pressed
forward and slightly crooked; wingbeats shallow and easy, interspersed with buoyant glides;
wheels easily in strong winds, but generally in low arcs, not towering high like heavy-bodied
species. Wing molt of S Hemisphere breeders Apr–Sep (Sep–Apr in N Hemisphere breeders).

162

fairly large dark petrel with variable dark bill tip, blackish feet; note relatively small rounded head, long wings, dark chin

wings narrower than Westland

toes often project

should be distinguished with care from somewhat larger and stockier Westland Petrel

bill size varies with age and sex, pattern varies individually

bill tip often appears pale in bright light, cf. White-chinned

cf. head/bill proportions with Westland

longer wing projection than Westland Petrel

with Flesh-footed Shearwater (left)

Parkinson's (Black) Petrel *Procellaria parkinsoni* 41–46cm, WS 112–123cm
Pacific, warmer waters; transequatorial migrant; locally fairly common. Breeds Nov–May in n. New Zealand, ranging over adjacent waters, rarely w. to SE Australia; migrates mainly Mar–Oct to Cen E Pacific (where imms. occur year-round), from s. Mexico to n. Peru. Favors shelf-break waters; scavenges at fishing boats and over groups of cetaceans; often follows ships. Mainly found as singles or small groups, at times with Flesh-footed Shearwaters and larger, broader-winged White-chinned Petrels. In calm, flies with easy, smooth wingbeats and buoyant glides; in strong winds can wheel fairly high, with wings crooked, suggesting large gadfly petrel. Adult wing molt mainly Feb–Aug; 1st-year wing molt Dec–Apr.

large dark petrel with variable black bill tip, blackish feet; note large blocky head with relatively stout bill, dark chin

toes often project

bleached, molting (Oct–Dec)

should be distinguished with care from slightly smaller, more lightly built Parkinson's Petrel

bill size varies with age and sex, deepest on adult males; pattern varies individually

bigger, blockier head than Parkinson's

with Flesh-footed Shearwater (right)

Westland Petrel *Procellaria westlandica* 48–53cm, WS 135–145cm

South Pacific, cooler waters; locally fairly common. Breeds May–Dec on South I., New Zealand, ranging over adjacent waters and very rarely w. to SE Australia; migrates mainly Oct–Apr to SE Pacific (where imms. occur year-round), in Humboldt Current and fjords from n. Chile (rarely Peru) s. to Cape Horn region. Favors shelf and shelf-break waters, also inland passages and fjords; feeds mainly by scavenging, often at fishing boats with albatrosses, White-chinned and Pintado Petrels, etc.; often follows ships. Associates readily with groups of White-chinned Petrels. Flight not appreciably different from White-chinned Petrel, but appears heavy relative to large shearwaters; wheels confidently in strong winds. Adult wing molt mainly Sep–Mar.

large dark petrel with pale bill, blackish feet; note rounded head, small white chin patch (often not visible at sea)

pale tip, cf. Westland, Parkinson's

white chin more extensive on Indian Ocean breeders; chin wholly dark on some imms.

toes often project

fat-bodied, hump-backed

long wings, easy flight

narrow wings, spindle body

bill rarely has small dark tip

Giant-Petrels

White-chinned

Sooty Shearwater

White-chinned Petrel *Procellaria aequinoctialis* 50–57cm, WS 132–145cm
Southern Ocean; generally common. Breeds Nov–Apr on subantarctic islands from South Georgia e. to New Zealand. Ranges widely in s. oceans, mainly 45–65°S in breeding season, 20–45°S in non-breeding season, when mainly over shelf and shelf-break waters of s. South America (n. to Peru in Humboldt Current, where imms. occur year-round), S Africa, Australia, and New Zealand. Feeds mainly by scavenging, often at fishing boats with albatrosses, Pintado Petrels, etc.; commonly follows ships. Flight appears heavy relative to large shearwaters, with steady smooth wingbeats, easy glides; wheels confidently in strong winds. Adult wing molt mainly Feb–Aug; 1st-year wing molt Nov–May.

distinctive, large dark petrel with variable white 'spectacles,' dusky bill tip, blackish feet; toes often project well beyond tail tip

extensive white

reduced white

with Soft-plumaged Petrel

with storm-petrels

Spectacled Petrel *Procellaria conspicillata* 50–55cm, WS 130–140cm
South Atlantic; locally fairly common. Breeds Oct–Mar only on Inaccessible I. (where known as 'Ring-eye'); perhaps formerly on Amsterdam I., Indian Ocean. Ranges in subtropical S Atlantic, w. to n. Argentina and s. Brazil, rarely e. to South Africa and into S Indian Ocean. Feeds mainly by scavenging, often at fishing boats; associates readily with groups of White-chinned Petrels; often follows ships. Flight not appreciably different from White-chinned Petrel, but appears heavy relative to large shearwaters; wheels confidently in strong winds. Adult wing molt mainly Mar–Aug; presumed 1st-year wing molt Nov–Apr.

LARGE WHITE-BODIED SHEARWATERS AND ALLIES

Comprise 1 large petrel in S Hemisphere genus *Procellaria,* 4 large shearwaters in N Hemisphere genus *Calonectris,* and 4 large shearwaters in largely S Hemisphere genus *Ardenna* (formerly *Puffinus*). Main ID features within large white-bodied shearwaters and allies are head and bill patterns, underwing pattern, overall structure (especially tail length and shape, wing width). General color and pattern of upperparts also useful for some species, and flight manner can be helpful, mainly with experience. Small black-and-white shearwaters (p. 176) typically have quicker wingbeats and more hurried-looking flight, although size of swimming birds can be difficult to judge. Larger white-bodied gadfly petrels (p. 107) typically have snappier wingbeats, more dynamic and controlled flight, thicker black bills, and different habits.

Cory's Shearwater complex traditionally treated as a single species, but now usually as 3 species. Wedge-tailed Shearwater in need of critical study, may include cryptic species.

Atlantic

Great
p. 171

Cory's
p. 170

Scopoli's
p. 168

Cape Verde
p. 169

Pacific

Buller's
p. 173

Pink-footed
p. 172

Wedge-tailed
p. 174

Streaked
p. 175

distinctive large petrel with gray head and upperparts; white underparts contrast with dark underwings; bill pale gray-green, legs dusky pinkish

dark undertail coverts

toes often project

often looks dark-capped

with Westland (swimming) and White-chinned Petrels

Gray Petrel *Procellaria cinerea* 48–51cm, WS 125–135cm
Southern Ocean; locally fairly common. Breeds Mar–Oct on islands near Subtropical Convergence, from Inaccessible and Gough e. to Antipodes, New Zealand. Ranges in subtropical and subantarctic waters (mainly 30–60°S) from S Atlantic e. to SW Pacific, rarely in E Pacific and s. Humboldt Current. Feeds by scavenging over cetaceans and at fishing boats; often follows ships. In calm, flies with rather stiff, slightly hurried wingbeats and short glides; wheels high and steeply in strong winds. Wing molt mainly Oct–Mar. Cf. smaller Atlantic Petrel, Great Shearwater.

Cory's Shearwater (*Calonectris diomedea*) **Complex**

Here considered as 3 species, which have all been considered conspecific under the name Cory's Shearwater (see map opposite for breeding ranges). All are transequatorial migrants, with non-breeding ranges in warmer waters off E South America and W Africa. Males appreciably larger and bigger-billed than females; hence, large-billed male Scopoli's overlaps small female Cory's.

In calm, flight generally unhurried, with languid wingbeats, easy buoyant glides; in strong winds, *Calonectris* wheel easily, sailing high but not as steeply as heavy-bodied *Ardenna* species such as Great Shearwater, which also have stiffer wingbeats, less crooked wings. Often in flocks. Sometimes scavenge at fishing boats, but more often feed over dolphins and tuna, frequently with mixed-species feeding flocks of other shearwaters, terns, and gadfly petrels.

large shearwater with gray-brown upperparts, extensively white underwings, yellowish bill with dark subterminal band

long white 'tongue' on outer primary

from Cory's Shearwater by lighter build, smaller head, shallower bill, extensive white underwing-tip

with Cory's (right)

small head often accentuates big bill

with Great, 3 Cory's (at back), and Sooty

Scopoli's

Scopoli's Shearwater *Calonectris [diomedea] diomedea* 44–49cm, WS 110–121cm

Mediterranean and Atlantic; transequatorial migrant; locally common. Breeds May–Oct in Mediterranean (a few on s. France Atlantic coast); non-breeders uncommon May–Oct off E North America, mainly 30–40°N, and in Gulf of Mexico. Migrates s. Nov–Apr to S Atlantic, mainly off SW Africa, perhaps w. to Brazil, e. into W Indian Ocean. Adult wing molt Sep–Mar; 1st-year wing molt Aug–Jan. Habits: see introduction to Cory's Shearwater complex (above).

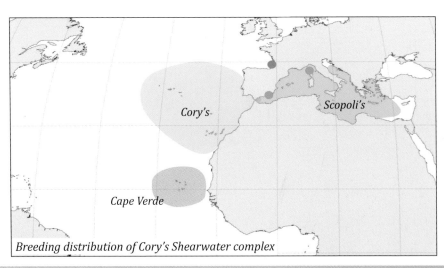

Breeding distribution of Cory's Shearwater complex

large shearwater with gray-brown upperparts, subtly darker cap, dusky pinkish bill with dark subterminal band

solidly dark underside

presumed male (left) and female

Cape Verde Shearwater *Calonectris edwardsii* 42–47cm, WS 101–112cm
Tropical Atlantic; transequatorial migrant; locally fairly common. Breeds Jun–Nov on Cape Verdes and ranges off W Africa; migrates s. Nov–May to waters off e. Brazil and (mainly Mar–May) s. to n. Argentina. Adult wing molt Oct–Mar; 1st-year wing molt probably Aug–Jan. Habits: see introduction to Cory's Shearwater complex (p. 168).

very large, broad-winged shearwater with gray-brown upperparts, clean white underparts, big yellowish bill with dark subterminal band

extensive dark wing-tip, cf. Scopoli's (p. 168)

maximum pale for presumed Cory's

with Great Shearwater (top)

with Audubon's Shearwater

with Black-capped Petrels and storm-petrels

Cory's Shearwater *Calonectris [diomedea] borealis* 48–56m, WS 113–124cm
Atlantic; transequatorial migrant; locally common. Breeds May–Oct in NE Atlantic, from Portugal and Azores s. to Canaries (a few in W Mediterranean); ranges over adjacent waters and in late summer–fall n. to Britain; non-breeders common May–Oct off E North America, mainly 30–40°N, fairly common in Gulf of Mexico. Migrates s. Nov–Apr to S Atlantic, mainly e. Brazil to n. Argentina, and SW Africa; some range into W Indian Ocean. Adult wing molt Sep–Mar; 1st-year wing molt Aug–Jan. Habits: see introduction to Cory's Shearwater complex (p. 168).

distinctive large shearwater with neat dark cap, dark-smudged underparts, slender dark bill

dark belly patch variable, can
be absent in worn plumage

juv.

juv. cap browner, white hindneck reduced

adult | *with Buller's Shearwater (left)*

Great Shearwater *Ardenna gravis* 45–49cm, WS 108–116cm
Atlantic; transequatorial migrant; locally common. Breeds Nov–May from Tristan s. to Falklands, ranging mainly at 30–55°S, sw. to Cape Horn, e. to SW Africa. Migrates n. May–Nov to NW Atlantic, mainly 30–60°N, with some birds moving e. and s. through NE Atlantic mainly Aug–Oct. Vagrant to E Pacific, from Chile n. to US. Favors cooler waters over shelf, shelf break, and banks; can be seen from shore, mainly in windy conditions. Often scavenges at fishing boats. In calm, flies with fairly stiff wingbeats and short glides; in strong winds towers steeply with little flapping. Wingbeats stiffer and narrower wings held straighter than Cory's Shearwater. Adult wing molt fairly rapid, May–Aug; 1st-year wing molt Jan–Jun.

typical

dusky

dark

upperparts glossed gray when fresh,
dark brown when worn or in shade

large bulky shearwater with smudgy brown head sides, black-tipped pink bill,
variable dusky markings on white underparts (exceptionally all-dark)

with Wedge-tailed Shearwater (left)

with Flesh-footed Shearwater (at back)

very rare dark type grayer than Flesh-footed
Shearwater (p. 160), bill duller pinkish

Pink-footed Shearwater *Ardenna creatopus* 45–48cm, WS 110–118cm
Eastern Pacific; transequatorial migrant; fairly common to locally common. Breeds Dec–May
on Juan Fernandez and Mocha I., Chile, ranges in adjacent seas and Humboldt Current; most
migrate n. Mar–Nov to NE Pacific, from Alaska s. to California (where a few occur year-round),
but some remain year-round in Humboldt Current. Often feeds over cetaceans and scavenges
at fishing boats. Typically flies with languid wingbeats and easy glides, but can wheel high when
windy. Adult wing molt Apr–Aug; 1st-year wing molt Jan–Jun.

fresh *worn*

handsome, distinctive large shearwater with neat dark cap, snow-white underparts, striking upperwing pattern, long tapered tail

blends easily against gray seas

swimming bird can be confused with Manx and other small shearwaters

with Pink-footed Shearwater

Buller's Shearwater *Ardenna bulleri* 43–45.5cm, WS 97–104cm
Pacific; transequatorial migrant; fairly common to locally common. Breeds late Nov–Mar in n. New Zealand; adults range mainly over adjacent subtropical waters and w. to SE Australia, with non-breeding imms. ranging e. to Chile (mainly Jan–Apr). Migrates May–Nov to Cen N Pacific; adults return s. in Aug–Sep; imms. in Sep–Nov, ranging e. to waters off w. US. Often feeds along fronts, at times in flocks that wheel in synchronized 'ballets.' Flight typically buoyant and graceful, low to the water; in strong winds can sail high, but not steeply like gadfly petrels. Adult wing molt Mar–Aug; 1st-year wing molt likely Jan–Jun, but few data.

dusky (uncommon)

typical

variably dark-capped

worn

variable pale scaling above

fresh

large but lightly built shearwater with small head, broad wings, long tapered tail; plumage highly variable; see dark morph on p. 161

pinkish-billed

long tail projects past wing-tips

Pink-footed (right) bulkier and bigger-headed, with stouter pink bill, shorter tail, heavier flight

gray-billed

with Pink-footed Shearwater (front right)

Wedge-tailed Shearwater (light morph) *Ardenna pacifica* 43–47cm, WS 99–109cm
Mainly tropical North Pacific, locally common; see dark morph on p. 161. Light morph breeds May–Nov from s. Japan e. to Hawaii, perhaps a few in w. Mexico; small numbers breed Nov–May in W Australia. N. populations range s. to equator and, at least in Cen Pacific, s. to 10°S (mainly Nov–Apr); common migrant off Mexico and Cen America, Nov–Jun (smaller numbers Jul–Oct, when also n. to s. Gulf of California). Often in flocks, feeding with Sooty Terns, gadfly petrels, other shearwaters, and boobies over dolphins and tuna. In calm, flight typically unhurried, with wings pressed forward and slightly crooked; wingbeats shallow and easy, interspersed with buoyant glides on arched wings; wheels easily in strong winds, but generally in low arcs, not towering high like heavy-bodied species. Wing molt of N Hemisphere breeders Sep–Apr.

distinctive large shearwater with clean white underparts, variable white spots and streaks on face and crown, variable dark streaks on underprimary coverts

with Wedge-tailed Shearwater (right)

with Pink-footed Shearwaters, Buller's Shearwater, Western Gulls

Streaked Shearwater *Calonectris leucomelas* 45–52cm, WS 103–113cm
Western Pacific; locally common. Breeds May–Nov in subtropical NW Pacific, locally from Japan s. to se. China, ranges in adjacent seas, mainly over shelf and shelf-break waters. Migrant s. mainly Nov–Apr to tropical SW Pacific, from Philippines to N Australia, in smaller numbers to SE Australia; vagrant to N Indian Ocean and NE Pacific. Often in flocks, feeding with terns, boobies, and other shearwaters over dolphins and tuna; follows fishing boats. In calm, flight typically rather languid, with fairly loose wingbeats and low wheeling glides; in strong winds wheels easily, sailing high but not as steeply as heavy-bodied species such as Sooty Shearwater. Adult wing molt probably mainly Nov–Mar and1st-year wing molt Sep–Jan, but few data.

SMALL BLACK-AND-WHITE SHEARWATERS

A taxonomically vexed group of numerous species in the genus *Puffinus*, which formerly included large shearwaters now placed in the genus *Ardenna*. Manx is the only long-distance migrant in the group, and therefore distribution is a key feature in the ID of many species. The other main ID features are head and neck pattern, undertail-covert pattern, bill size, overall structure, and to a lesser extent underwing pattern, foot color, and general color tone of upperparts. Several species favor shelf and inshore waters and occur in small to large flocks; others range farther offshore and are more often encountered as singles. Flight is usually low to the water, with quick wingbeats and short glides.

Taxonomy especially unclear for several tropical taxa in the Indian and Pacific Oceans, where formally undescribed populations still occur; one species was described only in 2011. We have adopted an approach that provisionally recognizes several different populations as species, while acknowledging that changes will undoubtedly occur in this poorly understood group of tubenoses.

Atlantic, pp. 177–181

Indian tropical, pp. 182–183

Pacific tropical, pp. 184–186

Pacific subtropical, pp. 187–190

Southern Ocean/
New Zealand, pp. 190–193

Manx Shearwater (*Puffinus puffinus*) Complex

Here considered as 3 species, which have all been considered conspecific under the name Manx Shearwater; the 2 Mediterranean taxa were not widely considered species until the mid–late 1990s. Small population breeding on Menorca shows mixed characters of Yelkouan and Balearic, with plumage closer to Yelkouan; taxonomic status unresolved. See Gil-Velasco et al. (2015) for more detailed ID treatment of the Manx complex in a European context.

small but heavy-bodied with rather short tail (toes often project), white undertail coverts, whitish hook behind dark cheek

often shows small white 'saddlebags'

toes can create dark 'tail tip'

worn

fresh

white, unlike Balearic, Yelkouan

upperparts blackish when fresh, browner when worn and faded

with Black-vented Shearwater (right)

Manx Shearwater *Puffinus puffinus* 31–35cm, WS 75–84cm; also see p. 179
Atlantic; fairly common to locally common. Breeds Apr–early Oct in NE Atlantic (mainly British Isles, also n. to s. Iceland, s. to Canary Is.); since 1970s in NE North America; winters (Oct–Feb) in temperate S Atlantic, n. in small numbers to se. US. Recent colonist of E Pacific: small numbers summer in NE Pacific, migrant s. to California, scattered records from Mexico s. to Chile. Often in flocks, feeding and resting with other shearwaters (mainly Great and Sooty in much of Atlantic range); often seen from shore. In calm, flight low to the water, with bursts of quick stiff wingbeats and short glides; in strong winds, often wheels high and steeply, recalling Sooty Shearwater. Adult wing molt Sep–Mar; 1st-year wing molt mainly Aug–Dec.

bulkier and bigger billed than Manx; dark brown upperparts not cleanly demarcated from dirty whitish underparts; some birds mostly brownish below, cf. larger Sooty Shearwater

extensively dark 'armpits'

brown undertail coverts

Balearic Shearwater *Puffinus mauretanicus* 36–40cm, WS 82–89cm; also see p. 15
Western Mediterranean and Eastern North Atlantic. Breeds Mar–Jun on Balearic Is. in W Mediterranean; post-breeding dispersal Jul–Oct into Atlantic off NW Africa and W Europe, n. to s. UK. Often in flocks, and regularly seen from shore; associates readily with feeding and resting Manx and Yelkouan Shearwaters. Flight quick and typically low to the water, a little more fluttery, less powerful, than flight of trimmer, heavy-bodied Manx. Wing molt mainly May–Sep.

averages smaller, more lightly built, and smaller-billed than Balearic, with more contrasting whitish underparts; cf. Manx Shearwater

worn plumage, Aug

fresh plumage, Jan

variably dusky

diffuse contrast, cf. Manx

Yelkouan Shearwater *Puffinus yelkouan* 33–37cm, WS 75–83cm; also see p. 15
Mediterranean and Black Seas. Breeds Apr–Aug from s. France e. to Greece, ranges year-round into Black Sea and (mainly Jun–Oct) w. to Spain and Strait of Gibraltar; only very rarely known to exit out into Atlantic. Habits much like Balearic Shearwater, with which Yelkouan associates readily when feeding and resting. Wing molt mainly Jun–Oct.

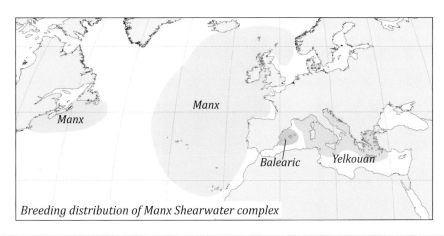

Breeding distribution of Manx Shearwater complex

Manx Shearwater versus Audubon's Shearwater

Manx and Audubon's Shearwaters co-occur in much of the W North Atlantic, where they are the only 2 regularly encountered small black-and-white shearwaters. Plumage differences are useful in ID, but an appreciation of structure and associated flight manner is also helpful. Manx is a rather heavy-bodied, narrow-winged, short-tailed species adapted to windier, cooler waters; Audubon's is a light-bodied, broader-winged, and longer-tailed species adapted to calmer tropical waters. Thus, Manx flies strongly, similar to other heavy-bodied species, such as Sooty Shearwater, whereas Audubon's has a more fluttery and buoyant flight, with short glides.

relative to Audubon's, Manx has stocky body, narrow wings, and narrow dark underwing margins; white undertail coverts of Manx offset black thigh patch, and toes often project past short tail

note lighter build, longer tail, and dark undertail coverts of Audubon's

Audubon's Shearwater (*Puffinus lherminieri*) Complex

Here considered as 3 species; Barolo long treated as an isolated race of Little Shearwater, and sometimes lumped with Boyd's Shearwater as Macaronesian Shearwater; Boyd's sometimes treated as a race of Audubon's. Several small shearwater taxa in Indian and Pacific Oceans historically have been treated as races of Audubon's Shearwater (but see Austin et al. 2004).

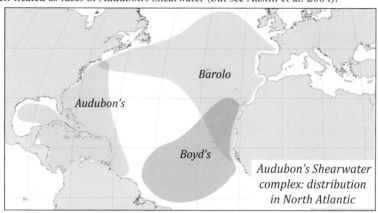

Barolo

Audubon's

Boyd's

Audubon's Shearwater complex: distribution in North Atlantic

small, rather long-tailed shearwater with dark undertail coverts, broad dark underwing margins, variable whitish spectacles

wing molt May–Oct, cf. Manx

sometimes shows small white 'saddlebags'

fresh upperparts slaty blackish, soon fading to show brown tones

Audubon's Shearwater *Puffinus lherminieri* 30–33cm, WS 65–74cm; also see p. 179
Tropical Western Atlantic; fairly common. Breeds Jan–Jul in Caribbean and Bermuda, ranges n. in warmer waters to e. US (mainly May–Oct), s. to N South America; disjunct (?) small population in Espírito Santo, Brazil. Often in small groups, associating readily with feeding and resting groups of other shearwaters (especially Cory's) and tropical terns; commonly feeds around mats of *Sargassum*, 'snorkeling' with its face below the surface. Not usually seen from shore except around nesting islands. In calm, flight typically low to the water with quick wingbeats, short buoyant glides; in strong winds can wheel fairly high in shallow arcs, not steeply.

very small and quick shearwater with variable white face, mostly white undertail coverts, extensively white underwings

fresh plumage has frosty upperwings, white tips to upperwing coverts

Barolo Shearwater *Puffinus baroli* 26–28cm, WS 58–61cm
Subtropical Eastern North Atlantic; uncommon. Breeds Jan–May on Azores, Madeira, and Canaries; ranges mainly in subtropical NE Atlantic, w. rarely to waters off e. Canada and ne. US (Aug–Sep). At sea, usually found as singles, often separate from other seabirds; near breeding islands, may be seen in small groups. Flight typically fast and low to the water, with hurried wingbeats and short glides; can wheel fairly high in strong winds. Wing molt mainly Mar–Aug.

averages smaller than Audubon's Shearwater, with smaller bill, but ID outside known range may not be possible with present knowledge

longer-tailed than Barolo; face averages duskier, like Audubon's

mostly dark, cf. Barolo

Boyd's Shearwater *Puffinus boydi* 28–30cm, WS 60–65cm
Tropical North Atlantic; locally fairly common. Breeds Jan–May on Cape Verdes (formerly Bermuda), ranges in tropical N Atlantic, s. to equatorial regions mainly May–Aug. Habits much like Audubon's Shearwater; around the nesting islands often feeds and rafts with Cape Verde Shearwaters. Adult wing molt mainly May–Aug; imm. wing molt likely earlier.

Indian Ocean tropical shearwaters. Taxonomy vexed, and undescribed taxa may exist; we consider at least 3 species are involved. All occur in small to fairly large groups, less often singly; feed in association with flocks of tropical terns (especially noddies, Bridled Tern), other shearwaters, and petrels. Flight typically fast and low, with quick wingbeats, short buoyant glides; can wheel fairly high in strong winds, but not steeply.

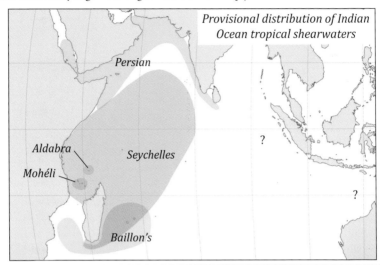

Provisional distribution of Indian Ocean tropical shearwaters

Persian

Aldabra

Mohéli

Seychelles

Baillon's

?

?

rather distinctive, with broad dark underwing margins, dark distal undertail coverts, rather long heavy bill; persicus *shown here*

underwing can be wholly dark

face pattern variable, affected by wear and bleaching

Persian (Arabian) Shearwater *Puffinus persicus* 31–33cm, WS 64–73cm
Tropical Northwest Indian Ocean; locally fairly common to common. 2 taxa: *persicus* breeds May–Oct in s. Oman (often seen from shore), ranges in NW Indian Ocean; *temptator* ('Mohéli Shearwater') breeds on Comoros and ranges at least in nearby waters (Shirihai & Bretagnolle 2015a). Birds found off NW Australia since Oct 2010 may be Persian Shearwaters (suggesting wider dispersal than usually recognized, or unknown populations) or an undescribed taxon.

'generic' small black-and-white shearwater, with dark undertail coverts; nicolae shown here

less dark than Persian Shearwater

fresh upperparts slaty blackish, fading to show brown tones

Seychelles Shearwater *Puffinus nicolae* 29–31cm, WS 63–70cm
Equatorial Indian Ocean; locally fairly common to common. 2 taxa: *nicolae* breeds year-round, on less than annual cycle (peaking Mar–Jul) in Seychelles, Maldives, Chagos Archipelago; slightly larger, heavier-billed *colstoni* breeds on Aldabra. Taxonomic relationships await elucidation.

contrasty, and distinctive in range: note white undertail coverts

fresh upperparts slaty blackish, fading to show brown tones

Baillon's (Mascarene) Shearwater *Puffinus bailloni* 28–31cm, WS 64–73cm
Tropical Southwest Indian Ocean; fairly common locally. Breeds Réunion (perhaps year-round, but mainly Sep–Mar) and Europa I., in s. Mozambique Channel; ranges in adjacent waters.

184

Pacific Ocean tropical shearwaters. Taxonomy vexed, and undescribed taxa may exist. Austin et al. (2004) lumped sundry Pacific and Indian Ocean taxa as a single catchall species 'Tropical Shearwater,' despite marked differences in structure, plumage, ecology, and biogeography. We prefer to emphasize differences and for Pacific populations provisionally follow Murphy (1927). Typically found in small groups or singly, mainly nearer shore late in day; often feed in association with flocks of tropical terns (especially noddies) and other seabirds. Flight typically fast and low with quick wingbeats, short buoyant glides; can wheel fairly high in strong winds, but usually not steeply.

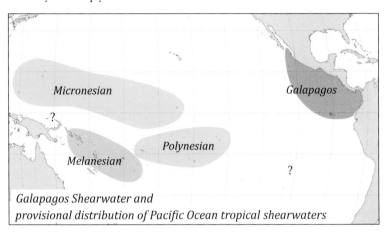

Galapagos Shearwater and
provisional distribution of Pacific Ocean tropical shearwaters

upperwing coverts tipped white in fresh plumage

averages larger and bigger-billed than Micronesian and Polynesian; blacker above, darkest on crown; undertail coverts dark

Melanesian Shearwater *Puffinus gunax* 30–33cm, WS 67–74cm
Equatorial Western Pacific; uncommon to locally fairly common. Breeds Vanuatu and probably elsewhere in Melanesia (perhaps se. to Tonga, w. to Solomons). Breeding and at-sea ranges await elucidation; may range e. at least to Tahiti.

very similar to Polynesian but averages smaller and more compact, with shorter bill

with Pacific Black Noddy

smallest tropical shearwater, with broad dark underwing margins, dark undertail coverts, variable dusky patches at sides of chest, variable white 'saddlebags'

Micronesian Shearwater *Puffinus dichrous* 28–30cm, WS 65–72cm
Tropical Western Pacific; fairly common but local. Breeds widely on tropical islands and atolls from Micronesia e. at least to Phoenix Is., perhaps s. to Solomons; ranges in adjacent tropical waters. Breeding and at-sea ranges await elucidation.

averages larger and longer-billed than Micronesian, but ID criteria require study; may more often visit colonies during daytime

upperparts browner and face can fade paler in worn plumage

Polynesian Shearwater *Puffinus [dichrous] polynesiae* 29–31cm, WS 65–73cm
Tropical South-Central Pacific; fairly common but local. Breeds from Samoa e. to Tahiti, Tuamotus, and Marquesas; ranges in tropical waters of S-Cen Pacific. Breeding and at-sea ranges await elucidation. Affinities of birds found recently at Easter I. unknown, likely this taxon.

186

distinctive in range: very small and rather compact, with clean-cut dark neck sides, dark undertail coverts, variable pale spectacles; underwings overall whitish or dark

with Wedge-tailed Shearwaters

light-winged

dark-winged

whitish tips lost with wear

light-winged types commoner overall

dark-winged types average darker-faced

Galapagos Shearwater *Puffinus subalaris* 28–31cm, WS 63–70cm; also see map, p. 184
Tropical Eastern Pacific. Breeds year-round on Galapagos Is. (breeding cycle averages 9 months);
ranges n. in warmer waters to Cen America and w. Mexico; rarely ranges to cooler waters off
mainland Ecuador. Favors shelf and shelf-break waters; often in flocks (locally in 1000s), associating readily with feeding and resting groups of other shearwaters (especially Wedge-tailed),
boobies, and terns. Light-winged types often seen flying around cliff faces during daytime, in
noisy pairs and small groups. Dark-winged and light-winged types may represent separate species and study is needed; see Howell (2012) for further comments, possible voice differences.

Pacific Ocean subtropical shearwaters. Unlike in tropical species, there is general agreement on species limits in subtropical taxa, with Bryan's Shearwater described as recently as 2011. Typically found in small groups or singly, mainly nearer shore late in the day; often feed in association with flocks of other shearwaters, terns, and gadfly petrels. Flight typically fast and low with quick wingbeats, short buoyant glides; can wheel fairly high in strong winds, but usually not as steeply as heavier-bodied species such as Manx.

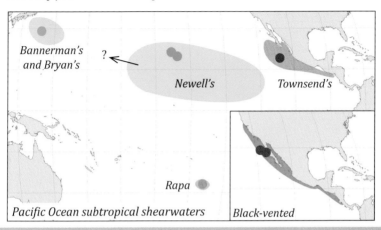

Bannerman's and Bryan's — ? — Newell's — Townsend's — Rapa — Pacific Ocean subtropical shearwaters — Black-vented

hindneck typically slightly paler than back; also note broad dark underwing margins, dark undertail coverts, relatively stout bill; often shows obvious white 'saddlebags'

white tips when fresh

Bannerman's (Bonin) Shearwater *Puffinus bannermani* 28–31cm, WS 70–76cm
Subtropical Northwest Pacific; uncommon to locally fairly common. Breeds Apr–Sep on Bonin and Volcano Is., ranges in subtropical NW Pacific. Wing molt mainly Jul–Nov. Face can bleach whitish in worn plumage, mainly Jul–Sep, cf. appreciably smaller Bryan's Shearwater (p. 189). Long tail and white saddlebags suggest Newell's Shearwater of Cen Pacific (p. 188), which has blacker head and neck contrasting strongly with white throat and notch behind cheeks.

contrasty black-and-white; no similar species in normal range

often has small
white teardrop

white 'saddlebags'
usually distinct

white tips in
fresh plumage

black distal, white
basal coverts

told from Townsend's by white 'hook' behind clean-cut black
cheeks, white basal undertail coverts, relatively longer tail

Newell's Shearwater *Puffinus newelli* 35–38cm, WS 77–85cm
Subtropical and tropical Central North Pacific (map, p. 187); fairly common locally. Breeds Jun–Oct in main Hawaiian Is.; ranges mainly e. and s. of Hawaii; vagrant (?) w. to Japan. Wing molt mainly Jul–Feb (mostly Oct–Feb for breeding adults).

blackish above, white below with dark undertail coverts;
cf. Black-vented Shearwater (which can be contrasty in strong sun)

white 'saddlebags'
usually distinct

dark

smudgier head and
neck sides than Newell's

face often blacker
than neck sides

Townsend's Shearwater *Puffinus auricularis* 32–35cm, WS 76–83cm
Subtropical and tropical Eastern Pacific (map, p. 187); rare. Breeds Jan–Jul on Socorro I. (formerly Clarion and San Benedicto Is.) in Revillagigedos, Mexico; ranges year-round to waters off w. Mexico, at least formerly s. to n. Cen America. Away from Socorro, found as singles or small groups, often with feeding flocks of other shearwaters, boobies, and terns. Direct flight stronger, less fluttery than smaller Galapagos Shearwater. Wing molt mainly late Apr–Nov.

NW Pacific; rare and poorly known, but distinctive in range: note very small size, rather long tail, white face, dark undertail coverts

Bryan's Shearwater *Puffinus bryani* 25–27cm, WS 56–60cm, also see p. 347
Subtropical Northwest Pacific (map, p. 187); rare and poorly known. Presumed winter breeder (Nov–Apr?) on Bonin Is. (Higashi-jima, at least); vagrant (Dec–Feb) to nw. Hawaiian Is. At-sea range presumed in NW Pacific, ranging slightly farther n. during at least Jul–Aug.

w. Mexico and California: note dark brown upperparts, variable smudgy head and neck sides, dark undertail coverts, rather long bill; cf. Townsend's and Manx Shearwaters

toes often project, unlike Townsend's

with Wedge-tailed Shearwater (behind); birds in tropics can bleach whitish on head

Black-vented Shearwater *Puffinus opisthomelas* 35–38cm, WS 78–86cm;
Eastern Pacific (map, p. 187). Breeds Mar–Aug off Pacific coast of Baja California Peninsula, Mexico (mainly Natividad I.); ranges n. (mainly Sep–Dec) to cen. California, s. (mainly Sep–Apr) to s. Mexico, rarely to s. Cen America; also Jun–Feb in Gulf of California. Favors shelf waters and often seen from shore, at times in flocks of 1000s; associates readily with other shearwaters, boobies, etc. Adult wing molt Jun–Nov; 1st-year wing molt Mar–Aug.

distinctive in limited range, with white face and undertail coverts; fresh plumage grayer above with white tips to wing coverts, worn plumage darker and browner above; see Shirihai et al. (2017) for further information

Rapa Shearwater *Puffinus myrtae* 31–33cm, WS 65–71cm
Subtropical South-Central Pacific (map, p. 187). Rare and local, perhaps <500 pairs; breeds mainly Jun–Nov on islets off Rapa I., s. French Polynesia. At-sea range unknown; adults return to colonies late Mar–May. Described in 1959 as a large, relatively long-tailed race of Little Shearwater; genetic studies suggest closer affinity to very different-looking Newell's Shearwater.

Fluttering Shearwater versus Hutton's Shearwater

Separation of Fluttering and Hutton's Shearwaters is a common challenge around New Zealand and Australia, where both species range widely. Usually, one or the other species predominates in a given region or season and often the 2 species segregate, but they can occur together.

Fluttering Shearwater

Hutton's Shearwater

Fluttering has whiter underwings; often distinct contrast between dark face and whitish throat; bill averages shorter, paler

Hutton's has duskier underwings; typically more extensive and smoother dark hood; bill averages finer, darker

Fluttering

Hutton's

small dark wedge

large dark wedge

variable dark on neck sides; bill averages shorter and paler than Hutton's, underwings whiter; often shows white 'saddlebags'

dark-headed

typical

well-defined whitish throat

Fluttering Shearwater *Puffinus gavia* 33–36cm, WS 67–75cm
New Zealand and Southern Australia. Breeds Sep–Feb in n. New Zealand, ranges s. to s. New Zealand, e. to SE Australia (mainly Mar–Aug, but some year-round). Often seen from shore, at times in flocks of 100s; associates with feeding and rafting groups of other shearwaters. Flight typically low and quick, with hurried wingbeats and short glides (but no more fluttery than many other small shearwaters). Wing molt mainly Nov–Apr, cf. Hutton's Shearwater.

dark brown overall with white belly and undertail coverts, slender dark bill

typically lacks white 'saddlebags'

duskier than Fluttering

small, diffuse whitish chin patch

Hutton's Shearwater *Puffinus huttoni* 34–37cm, WS 69–77cm
New Zealand and Australia. Breeds Nov–Apr in s. New Zealand, ranges to n. New Zealand, and e. to SE Australia (year-round) and W Australia (where molting Apr–Aug). Breeds in mountains above Kaikoura, South Island, and flocks of 100s or 1000s often seen in nearby waters. Elsewhere, more often found in small groups or singly; associates with feeding and rafting groups of other shearwaters. Habits much like Fluttering Shearwater. Wing molt mainly Feb–Aug.

192

Little Shearwater (*Puffinus assimilis*) Complex

Group of 5 very small Southern Hemisphere taxa with distribution centered around Australia and New Zealand; 1 species more widespread in subantarctic waters. Presently treated as 2 species (Little and Subantarctic Shearwaters), but no critical study has been made of relationships among Little Shearwater populations. Little Shearwater formerly included Barolo Shearwater of North Atlantic and Rapa Shearwater of Polynesia.

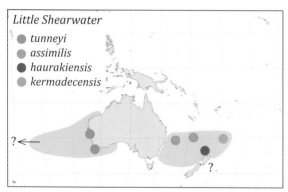

Little Shearwater
- *tunneyi*
- *assimilis*
- *haurakiensis*
- *kermadecensis*

very small and 'cute,' with white face, small bill, extensively white underwings

Western Australia

Tasman Sea

worn plumage

silvery flight feathers

fresh plumage

white face reduced on some birds, but still tends to look beady-eyed

Little Shearwater *Puffinus assimilis* 26.5–29.5cm, WS 59–66cm
Subtropical Southeast Indian Ocean e. to New Zealand. 4 taxa: breeds Jun–Dec in W Australia (*tunneyi*), Tasman Sea (*assimilis*), n. New Zealand (*haurakiensis*), and Kermadecs (*kermadecensis*); ranges in nearby subtropical waters, perhaps w. to Cen Indian Ocean; vagrant to South Africa. The 4 taxa (cryptic species?) differ slightly in size and plumage, *tunneyi* averages smallest, *haurakiensis* largest and biggest-billed. Found singly or in small groups, often not with other seabirds. Flight typically low with hurried wingbeats, short glides. Wing molt presumed mainly Oct–Feb. Cf. Subantarctic Shearwater.

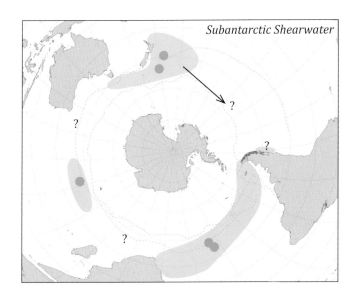

Subantarctic Shearwater

? ? ? ?

averages larger, stockier, and bigger-billed than Little, with grayish face

Little   Subantarctic   Manx

coverts tipped white in fresh plumage

with Broad-billed Prion (right)

Subantarctic Shearwater *Puffinus elegans* 28–30cm, WS 63–69cm
Subantarctic oceans. Breeds Sep–Feb on Gough and Tristan group in S Atlantic (ranges w. to s. Argentina, e. to South Africa), Amsterdam/St. Paul in Indian Ocean, and on Chathams and Antipodes, New Zealand; perhaps also near Chiloé I., Chile. Ranges in subantarctic oceans; away from breeding islands, usually seen as singles or small groups, often separate from other seabirds. Flight fast, with quick wingbeats, usually low to the water; can bank high in strong winds, but not as steeply as Manx Shearwater. Wing molt presumed mainly Jan–May.

ALBATROSSES (24 species in 4 genera)

Iconic, very large, long-winged seabirds characteristic of the windy Southern Hemisphere, with 3 species also breeding in N Pacific; absent (except as vagrants) from N Atlantic. Often follow ships; feed on fish and squid, mostly by scavenging. Ages differ slightly to strikingly; most species resemble adult in 3–10 years. Males average larger, broader-headed, and bigger-billed than females; also age-related sex differences in plumage of great albatrosses and probably also Steller's Albatross. Wing molts during non-breeding periods, often protracted and with complex patterns that assist in ageing. Nest colonially, often on remote islands. At sea, found singly or in foraging and ship-following groups that can involve several species. Usually silent except in interactions, when can give brays and whistles.

For ID purposes can be viewed as 4 groups: **short-tailed albatrosses** of N and E-Cen Pacific (4 species, genus *Phoebastria*); **great albatrosses** of S Hemisphere; (7 species, genus *Diomedea*); **mollymawks** of S Hemisphere (11 species, genus *Thalassarche*); and **sooty albatrosses** of S Hemisphere (2 species, genus *Phoebetria*). While some species are distinctive, ID of other species often not possible in the field given poor understanding of age and sex variation.

Short-tailed Albatrosses pp. 195–198	Great Albatrosses pp. 199–215	Mollymawks pp. 216–229	Sooty Albatrosses pp. 230–231

SHORT-TAILED ALBATROSSES (4 species in 1 genus)

Relatively small albatrosses of N and E-Cen Pacific, with relatively short tails (feet often project in flight); unlike other albatross species, molt outer 3 primaries every year. Ages differ strikingly only in Steller's Albatross, sexes mostly similar. For ID check overall plumage patterns, bill size and color.

striking and basically unmistakable: dark overall (fine wavy markings on body visible at close range) with creamy head and neck, long ochre-yellow bill

adults

feet often project in flight but can be pulled in

adult

Galapagos (Waved) Albatross *Phoebastria irrorata* 80–90cm, WS 220–250cm

Tropical Eastern Pacific; uncommon. Breeds Apr–Dec on Española I., Galapagos; a few pairs also on Isla de la Plata, off coast of Ecuador. Ranges in Humboldt Current of s. Ecuador and Peru, rare and irregular s. to n. Chile, exceptional n. to s. Cen America. Adult wing molt Dec–Apr. Juv. fledges Nov–Dec, resembles adult but lacks strong butterscotch wash on hindneck.

striking, rather gull-like albatross, distinctive in N Pacific range: note white head and body, dull pinkish bill; black underwing markings highly variable

juv. upperparts average browner than adult's

juvs.

adults

most underwings lie between these extremes, regardless of age

juv. has whiter cheeks than adult

with Black-footed Albatross

Laysan Albatross *Phoebastria immutabilis* 71–79cm, WS 195–215cm

North Pacific; fairly common to locally common. Breeds Nov–Jul, mainly in Hawaii, with smaller numbers on islands off s. Japan and nw. Mexico. Ranges at sea widely in N Pacific, mainly n. of 20°N, with an overall more northerly distribution than Black-footed Albatross. General northward shift of at-sea population in summer–fall (reaches s. Bering Sea mainly Jul–Oct); southward shift in winter (most frequent off W Coast of US Oct–Apr, plus northward dispersal to California Current of juvs. from Mexico during Aug–Oct). Adult wing molt mainly Jul–Oct, imm. and non-breeder wing molt Apr–Oct. Juv. fledges Jun–Jul, starts head and body molt Oct–Dec, with first wing molt Jul–Sep, about 12–14 months after fledging.

distinctive, dark sooty-brown albatross with narrow whitish 'bridle'; bill dark gray to pinkish with darker tip; adults develop variable white on tail coverts

adults

subadult

imms.

juv. has uniformly fresh brown plumage

adult

Black-footed Albatross *Phoebastria nigripes* 71–82cm, WS 200–220cm

North Pacific; fairly common to locally common. Breeds Nov–Jul, mainly in Hawaii, with smaller numbers on islands off s. Japan, and 1–2 pairs off nw. Mexico. Ranges at sea widely in N Pacific, mainly n. of 20°N, with an overall more southerly distribution than Laysan Albatross. Occurs year-round in California Current off W Coast of US, with largest numbers Apr–Sep; small numbers reach s. Bering Sea mainly Sep–Oct. Adult wing molt mainly Jun–Sep, imm. and non-breeder wing molt Apr–Oct. Juv. fledges Jul, starts head and body molt Oct–Dec, with first wing molt Jul–Sep, about 12–14 months after fledging.

198

distinctive, large-bodied N Pacific albatross with huge, bubblegum-pink bill tipped pale bluish; progression of complex age/sex plumages awaits elucidation

imms.

adult

1st-cycle

adult

imm. with Black-footed Albatross (behind)

adult

Steller's (Short-tailed) Albatross *Phoebastria albatrus* 80–90cm, WS 220–240cm
North Pacific; rare to locally uncommon. Breeds late Oct to mid-Jun on islands s. of Japan (mainly Torishima); 1–2 pairs have bred in nw. Hawaiian Is. since 2010. Ranges at sea widely in N Pacific, mainly n. of 30°N. Ranges n. to Aleutians and Bering Sea mainly May–Oct, when can be locally 'fairly common' at some fishing grounds; southward shift in winter, when rare but increasing off W Coast of US (recorded year-round, mainly Oct–Apr). Adult wing molt mainly Jun–Sep, imm. and non-breeder wing molt Apr–Sep. Juv. fledges Jun, starts head and body molt Oct–Dec, with first wing molt Jun–Sep, about 12–15 months after fledging.

GREAT ALBATROSSES (7 species in 1 genus)

Huge and very long-winged, with massive pink bills, mostly white underwings. Formerly considered as 2 species (Wandering and Royal), but Wandering now usually considered as 4–5 species, Royal as 2. Breed Nov/Feb to Nov/Feb depending on species, then take a year off to molt; outer 3 primaries molted every other cycle. Age/sex variation complex and poorly understood. For ID check overall plumage patterns (especially head, scapulars, upperwing, tail) and bill pattern.

MOLT AND AGE/SEX PLUMAGES IN GREAT ALBATROSSES

Within both wandering and royal albatrosses, southern-breeding taxa are whiter overall than northern-breeding taxa and males develop white plumage more quickly than females. At sea, darker-plumaged birds (mainly immatures and females) tend to forage north of whiter birds (mainly adult males)—think whiter birds nearer Antarctica, the white continent.

Great albatrosses can be aged in the field up to 4 or 5 years by wing molt patterns; knowing age can help with ID of different taxa (and sexes); wing molt occurs mainly during Feb–Nov.

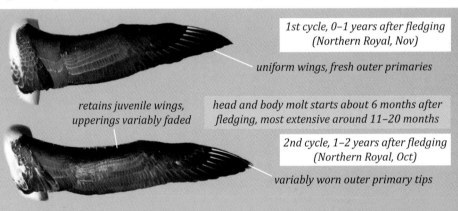

1st cycle, 0–1 years after fledging (Northern Royal, Nov)

uniform wings, fresh outer primaries

retains juvenile wings, upperings variably faded

head and body molt starts about 6 months after fledging, most extensive around 11–20 months

2nd cycle, 1–2 years after fledging (Northern Royal, Oct)

variably worn outer primary tips

coverts mixed generation, mottled

3rd-cycle molt 27–33 months after fledging includes outer primaries, tail, head, body

3rd cycle, 2–3 years after fledging (Southern Royal, Nov)

outer 3 primaries fresher, blacker than retained juv. middle primaries (contrast can be subtle)

1 or more inner primaries can be replaced in 3rd- and 4th-cycle molts

4th-cycle molt 39–45 months after fledging includes middle primaries, tail, head, body

4th cycle, 3–4 years after fledging (Northern Royal, Dec)

fresher, blacker   outer 3 primaries relatively faded, worn

block of retained juv secondaries, most of which will be replaced in 5th-cycle molt

Great Albatrosses—Wandering versus Royal

While the traditional 2 species of great albatrosses are now usually treated as 6–7 species, a common concern for many observers remains separating the whiter plumages of Wandering taxa (male Snowy, Gough, and Gibson's) from Southern Royal. Much of the time, ID comes down to the pattern and contrast of the black/white upperwing markings: Royal rarely if ever has extensive white on the middle section of the wing, and the whitest birds are male Wandering. The tail of Southern Royal is clean white or with only a few lacey black distal tail markings; older Wanderers can have clean white tails or with only a few black streaks, and even a fairly broad black tail tip can be surprisingly difficult to discern against the sea.

At close range, the bill of Royal shows diagnostic dark cutting edges, or 'lips.' Royals do not have the pinkish or tawny neck patches shown by some Wanderers. These patches appear to be staining from food solution, blown back from the nostrils, and are seen mainly on males, which have broader heads than females; Royal's nostrils are angled differently, and its narrower head is not prone to staining.

dark lips

pink bill color of both varies greatly in intensity; averages brighter on Wandering

Southern Royal (behind) has more sloping, 'serpentine' head profile vs. blockier head of Wandering (in front, presumed Gibson's)

more extensive white, coarsely spotted black

less extensive white, like snow-dusted bricks and filigree

Wandering

Southern Royal

Wandering

narrow dark trailing edge, often broken

often some black (hard to see)

white more extensive

coarsely spotted dark/white border

Southern Royal

wider dark trailing edge

white tail

'softer' and neater dark/white border

broader white back

Wandering

Southern Royal

narrow dark

stain diagnostic when present

wider dark

'snoutier' head and bill

coarser, spotted dark/white border

neater, 'frostier' dark/white border

202

Wandering Albatross (*Diomedea exulans*) Complex

Here considered as 5 species, 3 of which have been described formally since 1983. Species ID is mostly presumed by location, in combination with some plumage characters, but at-sea ranges of different taxa poorly known (all taxa combined on map below). Plumage differences between sexes develop within 2–3 years (pp. 204–207) and birds usually return to the breeding islands around 5 years of age, in subadult plumage. Plumage can continue to whiten through 20 years or older, and a range of typical 'adult' (breeding-age) plumages is shown opposite.

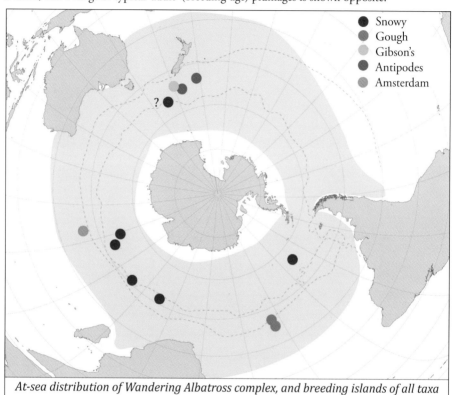

- Snowy
- Gough
- Gibson's
- Antipodes
- Amsterdam

At-sea distribution of Wandering Albatross complex, and breeding islands of all taxa

nesting pair of Snowy Wanderers at South Georgia, whiter male on the right

Wandering Albatrosses—Typical Breeding ('Adult') Plumages
(see map opposite for color spot key)

Wandering Albatross—Snowy immatures

fresh 1st-cycle
(Jan; sexes alike)

2nd-cycle
females
(Feb–Mar)

3rd-cycle
female (Mar)

late 1st-cycle
male (Nov)

2nd-cycle males
(Feb–Apr)

3rd-cycle males
(Mar–Apr);
many subadult females
similar but upper-
wings solidly blackish

4th-cycle males
(Mar–Apr)

PLUMAGE PROGRESSION IN WANDERING ALBATROSS COMPLEX

Information presented here is provisional, and much remains to be elucidated. Age of birds shown confirmed by wing molt patterns (p. 199); sex and species inferred by bill size, plumage, and location. Juveniles of all taxa look similar, with brown body and white face (see p. 208); belly starts to fade paler within 6 months when molt starts on scapulars, head, neck, and breast; molt then progresses through upperparts and underparts; first wing molt (outer 2–4 primaries) occurs in 3rd cycle, around 2.5 years after fledging. Male Snowy whitens most quickly, female Antipodes most slowly, with other taxa intermediate and varying with sex and individually. Immature refers to birds 1–5 years after fledging, subadult to birds about 5–10 years.

Wandering Albatross—Gough immatures

faded 1st-cycle
(Apr; sexes alike)

3rd-cycle
female (Apr)

4th-cycle females
(Mar–Apr)

5th-cycle
female (Mar)

2nd-cycle male
(Mar)

3rd-cycle male
(Apr)

5th-cycle male
(Apr)

Gough whitens more slowly than Snowy, with 3rd/5th-cycle males retaining a dusky breast band and often traces of a dark cap; 2nd/3rd-cycle females resemble imm. Antipodes or adult Amsterdam, some even having dark lips and a greenish bill tip similar to Amsterdam; by 5th cycle, females resemble imm. or subadult female Gibson's but may develop a white head earlier. Subadults and adults not separable from Snowy or Gibson's on present knowledge.

Wandering Albatross—Gibson's immatures

3rd-cycle female
(Dec)

late 1st-cycle
(Nov)

2nd-cycle females
(Mar–May)

6th-cycle female
(May)

late 1st-cycle
male (Dec)

2nd-cycle
male (Apr)

3rd-cycle
male (Nov)

4th-cycle
male (Dec)

5th-cycle
male (Jan)

Gibson's whitens more slowly than Snowy, loses the freckled bonnet later, and adults tend to have coarser and more extensive dark barring than adult Snowy; male attains mostly white scapulars by 3rd/4th cycle and female by 5th/6th cycle, unlike mostly dark scapulars of Antipodes. Subadults and adults not readily separated from Snowy or Gough on present knowledge.

Wandering Albatross—Antipodes immatures

late 1st-cycle (Nov)

4th-cycle female (Nov)

3rd-cycle females (Feb–Mar)

2nd-cycle male (Feb)

4th-cycle males (Feb–Mar)

3rd-cycle male (Feb)

5th-cycle male (Feb)

whitening of back and development of cap varies appreciably between individuals of the same age; note extensively dark scapulars versus Gibson's Albatross

The most distinctive Wanderer. Antipodes whitens more slowly than Gibson's, and typically all plumages have solidly dark upperwings and tail; even adult males retain a neatly defined dark cap (cap messier, more diffuse on subadult female Gibson's). 3rd/4th-cycle females resemble adult Amsterdam and imm. female Gough. 3rd/5th-cycle males resemble corresponding ages of female Gibson's but note dark scapulars of Antipodes (mottled to mostly white on Gibson's).

208

circumpolar; largest and longest-winged wanderer; complex age/sex plumages (see p. 204); adults and subadults much like Gough and Gibson's; ID usually inferred by range

subadult female

younger adult female

younger adult males (older adult females similar, but average more black in tail)

older adult male

juv. (all Wandering taxa similar)

adult male

Snowy Wandering Albatross *Diomedea [exulans] exulans* 115–122cm, WS 290–350cm
Southern oceans. Breeds Dec/Jan–Dec/Jan locally on subantarctic islands from South Georgia
e. to Indian Ocean; Macquarie I. birds perhaps this taxon or mixed with Gibson's. At-sea range
circumpolar, mainly 40–60°S, locally father s. in summer. Uncommon to locally fairly common;
population 7500 pairs/year. Also see pp. 200–204.

South Atlantic; ID usually inferred by range; imm. female can have dark lips and greenish bill tip like Amsterdam (see p. 205); older males much like Gibson's and Snowy

duskier bonnet but cleaner white rump than imm. male

subadult female

adult female

younger adult male (oldest adult females similar?)

older adult males

Gough (Tristan) Wandering Albatross *Diomedea [exulans] dabbenena* 110–117cm, WS 275–330cm

South Atlantic. Breeds Dec/Jan–Dec/Jan on Gough; a few pairs on Inaccessible. Ranges at sea in S Atlantic (mainly 30–50°S, locally farther n. in winter) and into S Indian Ocean, at least occasionally e. to Australia. Uncommon; population 1500 pairs/year. Also see pp. 202–203, 205.

210

New Zealand and Australia; plumage highly variable (also see p. 106); resembles Snowy and Gough but male averages coarser, more extensive dark barring; ID usually inferred by range

scapulars mostly white, cf. Antipodes

subadult male (older adult female similar?)

subadult/younger adult females

whitest males much like whitest male Snowy

adult female; note smaller bill than male

'piano-key' tail typical of Gibson's

adult male

male

subadult female (9th-cycle)

adult male

Gibson's Wandering Albatross *Diomedea [exulans] gibsoni* 110–117cm, WS 280–335cm Southwest Pacific. Breeds Jan–Jan in New Zealand, primarily on Auckland Is. Ranges in SW and S-Cen Pacific (mainly 35–55°S, farther n. in winter), w. to Australia. Uncommon to locally fairly common; population 7200 pairs/year. Sometimes lumped with Antipodes Wanderer, the combined species known as New Zealand (Wandering) Albatross. Also see pp. 202–203, 206.

South Pacific; upperwings and tail typically all-dark, scapulars extensively dark; adult has neat blackish cap; female also has variable dark bonnet; see imms. on p. 207

older adult females

adult male

adult males

oldest adults may have a few white spots on elbow

subadult female

adult male

Antipodes Wandering Albatross *Diomedea [exulans] antipodensis* 110–117cm, WS 280–335cm South Pacific. Breeds Jan–Jan in New Zealand, primarily on Antipodes, a few on Campbell Is. Ranges in Pacific (mainly 30–55°S) from SE Australia e. to Humboldt Current of cen. and s. Chile. Uncommon to locally fairly common; population 5000 pairs/year. Also see pp. 202–203, 207.

Indian Ocean; very rare; even adult males resemble immatures of other Wandering taxa; at close range note dark lips and greenish to orangey bill tip (cf. imm. Gough Wanderer)

bill markings less distinct on immatures

younger adult/female

4th-cycle

older adult/male

nestling (6–7 months after hatching; all Wandering taxa similar)

all plumages have dark upperwings and tail, variable dark bonnet and back

Amsterdam Wandering Albatross *Diomedea [exulans] amsterdamensis* 110–117cm, WS 280–335cm
Indian Ocean, with breeding population only about 15 pairs/year. Breeds Feb–Feb on Amsterdam I. Ranges in S Indian Ocean, e. to S Australia; very rarely seen (or at least identified) away from breeding island. Also see pp. 202–203. Often known simply as Amsterdam Albatross.

Royal Albatross (*Diomedea epomophora*) Complex

Here considered as 2 species, both of which breed only in New Zealand. Note that wing molt patterns (p. 199) can help with ageing and thus potentially with species ID; e.g., a 3rd- or 4th-cycle bird with solidly black upperwings is unlikely to be Southern, which by that age should show some white mottling on the elbow, especially if male.

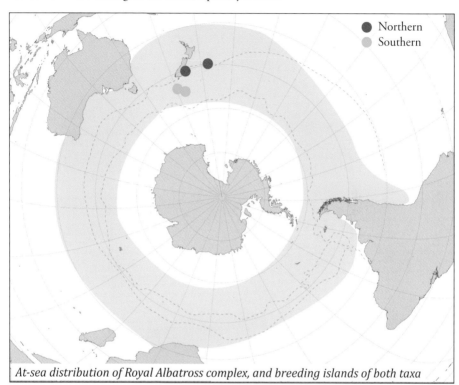

At-sea distribution of Royal Albatross complex, and breeding islands of both taxa

subadult Southern Royals displaying at Campbell Island

circumpolar; all ages have blackish upperwings contrasting with white back; scapulars wholly to mostly dark; tail white or with small black distal markings

often shows white upperwing spots during molt

black wedge, all ages

1st-cycle

some adults (oldest males?) have faint white speckling

Northern

Southern

head-on, leading edge of wing mostly black

1st-cycle

adult

Northern Royal Albatross *Diomedea [epomophora] sanfordi* 110–120cm, WS 290–340cm
Southern oceans. Breeds Nov–Nov in New Zealand, primarily on Chatham Is., a few pairs on main South Island, where occasionally hybridizes with Southern Royal. Ranges in s. oceans, especially Humboldt Current of Chile; favors shelf waters and occurs mostly to n. of Southern Royal. Royals accompany ships, but less habitually than Wanderers; often relatively aloof when scavenging at fishing boats. Uncommon to locally fairly common; population 2000 pairs/year.

215

circumpolar; upperwings and scapulars become whiter with age; imm. from Northern Royal by white leading edge to wing; also see p. 201, cf. Wandering Albatross complex

1st–2nd cycle, black wedge

1st-cycle (male?)

3rd-cycle and older, little black

narrow white leading edge

scapulars extensively white

2nd-cycle

3rd-cycle

adult

mostly dark scapulars, but whitish mottling on elbow

1st-cycle

adult

Southern Royal Albatross *Diomedea [epomophora] epomophora* 112–122cm, WS 295–350cm; also see pp. 200–201
Southern oceans. Breeds Nov–Nov primarily on Campbell I., New Zealand; also small numbers on Auckland Is. Ranges in s. oceans, especially shelf waters of Falklands and s. Argentina; occurs mostly to s. of Northern Royal, but the 2 species readily associate together. Habits much like Northern Royal. Uncommon to locally fairly common; population 7800 pairs/year.

216

MOLLYMAWKS (11 species in 1 genus)

Rather small to fairly large albatrosses of the Southern Hemisphere. Breed colonially, building mud cup nests. Bill patterns vary with age and species, often colorful on adults. For ID note head, bill, and underwing patterns; species ID not always possible, especially for imms. Molt outer 3 primaries every other year.

Black-browed complex
p. 218–219, 221

Gray-headed
pp. 220–221

Chatham
p. 225

Salvin's
p. 224

Shy complex
pp. 224–227

Buller's complex
pp. 222–223

Yellow-nosed complex
pp. 228–229

MOLT AND AGE IN MOLLYMAWKS

By virtue of wing molt patterns, in combination with bill and plumage patterns, mollymawks can be aged in the field up to 3–5 years, when adult-like appearance is attained. Most species fledge Apr/May wearing uniform 1st-cycle (juvenile) plumage (Auckland Shy and both Buller's Albatrosses fledge later, Jul–Sep). Some head and body molt can start within 5–6 months, and by 18 months birds have fresh head, body, and tail feathers contrasting with worn upperwings (sometimes a few new coverts), the outer primary tips often frayed.

Subsequent molts include head, body, and tail feathers, plus some primaries and secondaries, which are molted in 2 phases: 3rd-cycle molt starts with outer primaries (phase 1 molt) about 19–23 months after fledging (Dec–Apr in most species), followed by head, body, and tail mainly Apr–Sep; 4th-cycle molt involves middle primaries (phase 2) at about 31–34 months (Dec–Mar in most species). Subsequent molts alternate outer (and some inner/middle) primaries in 5th, 7th, and so on cycles (phase 1) with middle (and some inner) primaries in 6th, 8th, and so on cycles (phase 2). 5th-cycle and later wing molts occur mainly during Mar–Oct, although in adult Southern Buller's primary molt can continue into Nov or later.

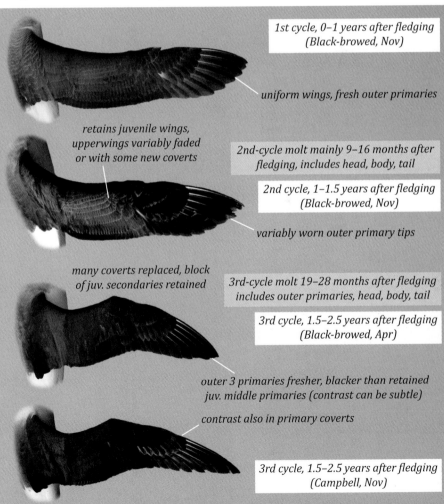

1st cycle, 0–1 years after fledging
(Black-browed, Nov)

uniform wings, fresh outer primaries

retains juvenile wings, upperwings variably faded or with some new coverts

2nd-cycle molt mainly 9–16 months after fledging, includes head, body, tail

2nd cycle, 1–1.5 years after fledging
(Black-browed, Nov)

variably worn outer primary tips

many coverts replaced, block of juv. secondaries retained

3rd-cycle molt 19–28 months after fledging includes outer primaries, head, body, tail

3rd cycle, 1.5–2.5 years after fledging
(Black-browed, Apr)

outer 3 primaries fresher, blacker than retained juv. middle primaries (contrast can be subtle)

contrast also in primary coverts

3rd cycle, 1.5–2.5 years after fledging
(Campbell, Nov)

circumpolar; all plumages white-headed; adult has mostly orange bill; imm. has dark underwing contrasting with white body; cf. p. 221 and imm. Shy Albatross (p. 226)

2nd-cycle

3rd-cycle

4th-cycle

1st-cycle

adult has clean orange bill with darker tip

imms. with imm. Salvin's Albatross (right)

adult

Black-browed Albatross *Thalassarche [melanophris] melanophris* 79–86cm, WS 205–230cm Circumpolar; fairly common to locally common. Breeds late Sep–Apr on subantarctic islands from s. Chile and Falklands e. to New Zealand. Ranges widely in s. oceans, mainly 30–60°S, n. (mainly May–Aug) to Peru, s. Brazil, and Namibia. Most numerous in S Atlantic; often seen from shore in s. South America. Regular vagrant to N Atlantic.

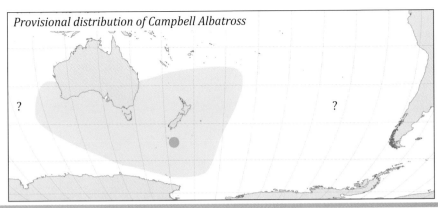

Provisional distribution of Campbell Albatross

? ?

safely told from Black-browed by pale eyes (can be surprisingly hard to see), which develop in 2nd cycle; adult averages thicker black underwing margins, but much overlap in pattern

3rd-cycle

adults

note smudgy face, pale 'honey eyes'

1st-cycle Campbell/Black-browed

adult

Campbell Albatross *Thalassarche [melanophris] impavida* 78–85cm, WS 200–225cm
Split from Black-browed Albatross. New Zealand and Australia; locally fairly common. Breeds late Sep–Apr on Campbell I., New Zealand. Ranges in SW Pacific (mainly 30–55°S), w. to Australia; in summer ranges s. to n. Ross Sea, in winter imms. rarely reach tropical Cen Pacific.

circumpolar, fairly small, thick-necked albatross; adult distinctive in range (but cf. Buller's Albatross, mainly Pacific); imm. can be confused with imm. Black-browed (see opposite)

4th-cycle

fresh 2nd-cycle

3rd-cycle

5th-cycle

thick black leading edge

narrower yellow bill edges than Buller's (pp. 222–223)

adults

hindneck often paler than head

1st-cycle

Gray-headed Albatross *Thalassarche chrysostoma* 79–86cm, WS 205–230cm
Circumpolar; uncommon to locally fairly common; pairs breed every 2 years. Breeds late Sep–May on subantarctic islands from s. Chile and South Georgia e. to New Zealand. Ranges widely in colder S Ocean, mainly 45–60°S; occurs s. to pack ice in summer, n. rarely to 35°S in mid-winter. Adult distinctive in range, but cf. Buller's Albatross (typically n. of Gray-headed range).

Immature Black-browed Albatross versus Gray-headed Albatross

Black-browed and Gray-headed albatrosses commonly occur together throughout the Southern Ocean and are similar in size, shape, and underwing patterns. Adults are readily separated (white head or gray head, plus bill pattern), but imm. plumages can be very similar. Although Gray-headed fledges in a distinctive gray-hooded and white-faced juv. plumage, molt and fading in 2nd–4th plumage cycles produces a whiter-headed appearance with a partial grayish collar or neck ring, much like late 1st-cycle and 2nd-cycle plumages of Black-browed.

For the most part, ID comes down to bill color and pattern: Gray-headed has a rather uniform blackish bill, sometimes with traces of a paler ridge; Black-browed has a dark grayish or dusky pinkish bill with a blacker tip often offset by a narrow pale subterminal line.

dusky bill with darker tip

Black-browed

early 2nd-cycle (Apr)

black bill, no darker tip

Gray-headed

3rd-cycle (Apr)

2nd-cycle (Nov)

Gray-headed usually looks stockier, thicker-necked than Black-browed

paler, mottled

darker, more solid

Black-browed

3rd-cycle (Apr)

3rd-cycle bill often paler, more orangey than this; note black tip

Gray-headed

3rd-cycle (Apr)

222

Buller's are rather small gray-hooded mollymawks; all ages have similar underwing pattern, cf. Shy Albatross complex; imm. S and N Buller's not known to be separable (study needed)

2nd-cycle

1st-cycle

thicker black than Shy complex

adult

3rd-cycle

4th-cycle

imm. with imm. Salvin's (right)

adult

bill pale with neat black lines, dark subterminal band

1st-cycle

adult

Southern Buller's Albatross *Thalassarche [bulleri] bulleri* 76–84cm, WS 198–225cm
New Zealand to Chile; uncommon to locally fairly common. Breeds Jan–Sep on Snares and Solanders. Ranges in S Pacific (mainly 30–55°S), e. to Humboldt Current of cen. and s. Chile, w. to SE Australia; vagrant to SW Atlantic. Juvs. fresh in Sep–Nov. vs. Jun–Aug in Northern Buller's. Cf. adult Gray-headed Albatross of subantarctic waters (p. 220).

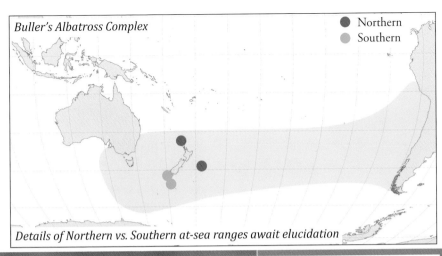

Buller's Albatross Complex

● Northern
● Southern

Details of Northern vs. Southern at-sea ranges await elucidation

adult averages darker hood, smaller white cap, and 'sterner' face than Southern Buller's; imm. N and S Buller's not known to be separable; note underwing pattern vs. Shy complex

adult Northern

averages broader, more squared

yellow averages narrower, sharper

adult Southern

averages more tapered

yellow averages wider, more diffuse

Northern Buller's Albatross *Thalassarche [bulleri] platei* 76–84cm, WS 198–225cm
New Zealand to Chile; uncommon to locally fairly common. Breeds Nov–Jun on Chathams, with a few pairs on Three Kings. Ranges in S Pacific (mainly 30–50°S), e. to Humboldt Current from cen. Chile n. to s. Peru; may range w. to SE Australia. Juv. fresh Jun–Aug, vs. Sep–Nov for juv. Southern Buller's. Cf. adult Gray-headed Albatross of subantarctic waters (p. 220).

Shy Albatross Complex

Here considered as 4 species, all breeding in New Zealand and SE Australia (see map, p. 227).
Relatively large and broad-winged mollymawks, with distinctive, extensively white underwings.

> *large gray-hooded mollymawk: adult has dusky bill with pale yellowish edges, black distal spot; imm. bill dull, dark grayish to pinkish gray with black tip or distal band*

all members of Shy complex have dark notch at base of underwing

2nd-cycle

1st-cycle

adult

extensive dark underwing tip, cf. Shy Albatrosses

3rd-cycle

ashy-gray hood with paler forecrown

1st-cycle

adult

Salvin's Albatross *Thalassarche salvini* 87–96cm, WS 235–255cm; also see p. 233

New Zealand to Chile; fairly common to locally common. Breeds Sep–Apr mainly on Bounties; small numbers on Snares and Crozets. Ranges at sea (mainly 30–60°S) in S Pacific, e. to Humboldt Current of Chile and Peru; small numbers w. to Australia and S Indian Ocean.

distinctive, gray-hooded mollymawk: adult has steely blue-gray hood, bright orange-yellow bill; yellowish bill tones apparent in 1st cycle, and hood darker than Salvin's Albatross

adult

imm. crown can fade to whitish

1st-cycle

2nd-cycle

adult

messier than adult, still narrower than Buller's

1st-cycle with 1st-cycle Salvin's (left)

2nd-cycle

1st-cycle

adult

Chatham Albatross *Thalassarche eremita* 86–95cm, WS 230–250cm; also see p. 233
New Zealand to Chile; uncommon. Breeds Sep–Apr on Pyramid Rock in Chathams. Ranges at sea (mainly 30–45°S) in S Pacific, e. to Humboldt Current of cen. Chile, rarely n. to Peru; vagrant w. to SE Australia.

largest mollymawk; adult has white neck, smoky-gray cheeks, bill lacks yellow base typical of adult Tasmanian Shy; imm. has paler bill than Salvin's, white primary bases below

1st/2nd-cycle

4th-cycle

narrower than imm. Salvin's

3rd-cycle (Apr)

3rd-cycle (Nov)

whitish bases, cf. Salvin's

adult

2nd-cycle (Nov)

head and neck pattern suggests imm. of smaller Black-browed; note paler bill, underwing pattern

1st-cycle

adult

Auckland Shy Albatross *Thalassarche [cauta] steadi* 90–100cm, WS 240–265cm
New Zealand to Indian Ocean; fairly common to locally common. Breeds Nov–Aug, mainly in Auckland Is.; small numbers on Antipodes. Ranges (mainly 30–60°S) from New Zealand w. to S Africa, with small numbers into S Atlantic. Shy Albatross (taxon unidentified) occurs as vagrant to Humboldt Current region. Juvs. fresh in Aug–Sep. Also known as White-capped Albatross.

Main breeding distribution and non-breeding dispersal directions of Shy Albatross complex

● Chatham
◑ Salvin's
○ Auckland Shy
● Tasmanian Shy

adult Auckland Shy

lacks yellow base

yellow stain on 'lips' averages stronger than Tasmanian

adult Tasmanian Shy

yellow base (not always present)

averges smaller and shorter-billed than Auckland Shy, but only separable if 'classic' adult Tasmanian is seen, with yellow base to culmen; imms. not known to be separable, but juv. Tasmanian fresh in Apr–Jun vs. Aug–Sep in Auckland; molt timings need study

Tasmanian Shy Albatross *Thalassarche [cauta] cauta* 87–96cm, WS 230–250cm
Australia to Indian Ocean; fairly common to locally common. Breeds Sep–Apr around Tasmania. Ranges (mainly 30–50°S, locally farther n. in winter) from Australia w. to S Africa, with a few into S Atlantic. Shy Albatross (taxon unidentified) occurs as vagrant to Humboldt Current region. Juvs. fresh in Apr–Jun. Also known simply as Shy Albatross.

small, rather lightly built albatross with relatively slender bill; black bill develops yellow ridge in 2nd/3rd cycle; cf. very similar Indian Yellow-nosed Albatross

1st-cycle

imm. head can fade whitish, with beady black eye like Indian

messier than adult

adult has pearly-gray hood, white forecrown

4th-cycle

juv.

adult

yellow at base averages blunter than Indian

note dark eye patch, cf. Indian Yellow-nosed

Atlantic (Western) Yellow-nosed Albatross *Thalassarche [chlororhynchus] chlororhynchus*
70–76cm, WS 188–215cm
South Atlantic; fairly common to locally common. Breeds Sep–Apr on Gough and Tristan group. Ranges in S Atlantic (mainly 30–45°S, n. locally to 20°S in winter), w. to Argentina and Brazil, e. to S Africa; vagrant e. to Australia, and regular vagrant to N Atlantic.

very similar to Atlantic Yellow-nosed Albatross; adult Indian has whitish hindneck, paler gray clouding on cheeks, beady dark eye; beware that apparent gray tones of head and neck vary greatly with plumage wear and lighting

4th-cycle

adults

3rd-cycle

lacks dark eye patch of Atlantic

averages more sharply pointed than Atlantic

early 2nd-cycle   *adult*

Indian (Eastern) Yellow-nosed Albatross *Thalassarche [chlororhynchus] carteri* 70–76cm, WS 188–215cm
Southern Indian Ocean; fairly common to locally common. Breeds Sep–Apr from Prince Edwards e. to Amsterdam/St. Paul. Ranges in S Indian Ocean (mainly 30–50°S, n. locally to 25°S in winter), w. to S Africa, e. to Australia, rarely New Zealand.

SOOTY ALBATROSSES (2 species in 1 genus)

Southern Hemisphere. Spectacular, dark-plumaged albatrosses with angular wings, long tapered tails. Breed in small groups or scattered pairs. For species ID note bill patterns, plumage contrast between head and body, back and upperwings.

chocolate-brown overall with darker face; yellow stripe on side of bill develops in 2nd cycle; faded 1st/2nd-cycles can be mistaken for Light-mantled Sooty of colder southern waters

often looks smaller-headed and broader-tailed than Light-mantled Sooty

adult

1st/2nd-cycle

faded imm. can have pale mantle but messy, often mottled brown

4th-cycle

Sooty Albatross *Phoebetria fusca* 86–91cm, WS 204–225cm

South Atlantic and Southern Indian Ocean; uncommon to locally fairly common; pairs breed every 2 years. Breeds Oct–May in S Atlantic on Gough and Tristan group, in S Indian Ocean from Prince Edwards e. to Amsterdam/St. Paul. Ranges in subtropical S Atlantic and S Indian Oceans, mainly 35–55°S; locally s. into subantarctic waters of Indian Ocean and e. to S Australia. At nesting islands can be located by loud *PEE-ar* calls, much like Light-mantled Sooty.

dark hood contrasts with paler body; pale mantle sharply demarcated from dark wings, but contrast varies with wear and lighting; pale blue stripe on side of bill develops in 2nd cycle

adult

2nd/3rd-cycle

1st-cycle

plumage tones and contrast very light dependent

with chick

Light-mantled Sooty Albatross *Phoebetria palpebrata* 89–93cm, WS 208–232cm
Circumpolar; uncommon to locally fairly common; pairs breed every 2 years. Breeds Oct–early Jun on subantarctic islands from South Georgia e. to New Zealand. Ranges widely in colder southern oceans, mainly 45–65°S; occurs s. to pack ice in summer, n. rarely to 40°S in mid-winter (mainly imms.). At nesting islands can be located by loud *PEE-ar* calls given by birds from nest sites, often as other birds sail over in synchronized display flights.

STORM-PETRELS (45+ species in 8 genera)

Small to very small tubenoses found over most of the world's oceans. Comprise 2 families, combined here for ID purposes: 18+ southern storm-petrels (family Oceanitidae) in 5 genera, 27+ northern storm-petrels (family Hydrobatidae) in 3 genera. Southern storm-petrels have short-armed, relatively broad wings well suited for gliding, and relatively long legs and big feet often used to kick off from the sea surface; several species are strikingly patterned. Northern storm-petrels differ from southern storm-petrels in having longer-armed, more crooked, and relatively narrower wings, and shorter legs and smaller feet, which are not habitually used to kick off from the sea surface; plumage patterns are more conservative than those of southern taxa.

Ages and sexes appear similar. Wing molt occurs mainly in non-breeding periods, but timing differs between 1st-years and adults, which can be helpful for ID of cryptic species. Feed by picking from near the surface, shallow diving, and scavenging; all species attracted to fish oil chum slicks. Some species gregarious, feeding and rafting in small flocks; at times, northern storm-petrels occur in assemblages of 1000s, with several species mixed together. Flight generally low over the water, but manner varies with behavior (see below). Most storm-petrels nest colonially, usually on islands or in other predator-free environments, sometimes in huge numbers. Nests typically are hidden in burrows and crevices, and most taxa visit colonies at night to avoid predators such as gulls and skuas. Voices are largely unmusical rattles, chuckles, moans, and whistles, which can be useful for ID at night on nesting grounds.

For ID purposes, storm-petrels can be divided into 3 groups: **white-rumped** (22+ species in 4 genera), **white-bodied** (15+ species in 5 genera), and **dark** (11 species in 3 genera). Taxonomy vexed in several groups, and species ID frequently challenging, sometimes not possible beyond assumption based on location or on timing of wing molt.

Perhaps more so than with other seabirds, flight manner (which often reflects structure) can be very helpful for ID of storm-petrel species, and it is far easier to see than details of plumage or bill shape. Beware, though, that flight manner can vary appreciably within a species depending on behavior (transiting, feeding, or being flushed or freaked out by a boat) and factors such as wind speed and flight direction relative to wind direction. Given similar conditions, however, different species often fly quite differently, which in mixed-species flocks may be better appreciated with the naked eye than by trying to focus on individual birds through the narrow view of binoculars.

233

White-rumped, pp. 234–253

White-bodied, pp. 254–267

Dark, pp. 268–279 (also pp. 262–263)

WHITE-RUMPED STORM-PETRELS (22+ species in 4 genera)

Very small to medium-size storm-petrels in the northern genera *Hydrobates* (5 species, including *Oceanodroma*), *Thalobata* (10+ species), and *Halocyptena* (2 species), plus the southern genus *Oceanites* (4+ species). Some authors lump all northern species into genus *Hydrobates*, a retrograde move that overlooks distinct structural, biogeographic, ecological, and genetic differences comparable to those in southern storm-petrels, which comprise multiple genera.

Plumage appears predominantly blackish with an obvious white 'rump' patch (actually the uppertail coverts); some species have variable whitish belly patches, but usually these are not striking, unlike the white on white-bodied species.

Most diverse in subtropical and tropical latitudes, but a few also in Arctic and antarctic waters; some species are long-distance migrants. Can be considered in terms of Atlantic and Pacific species, with Wilson's Storm-Petrel also occurring as a migrant in the Indian Ocean. Species ID among some cryptic groups often not possible at sea other than by assumption based on range, although timing of adult wing molt helpful in some cases.

Atlantic

European complex
pp. 235–236

Wilson's
pp. 250–251

Leach's
p. 238–240

Band-rumped complex
p. 243–246

Pacific

Leach's complex
pp. 237–242

Band-rumped complex
pp. 242–247

Wedge-rumped complex
pp. 248–249

Wilson's complex
pp. 250–253

European Storm-Petrel

(*Hydrobates pelagicus*) **Complex**

Comprises 2 taxa here treated as cryptic species: **British Storm-Petrel** *H. pelagicus* breeding in NE Atlantic and wintering in S Atlantic; and **Mediterranean Storm-Petrel** *H. melitensis* breeding and resident in Mediterranean.

Mediterranean averages slightly larger, stouter-billed, and blacker overall than British, with earlier molt timing; also differs from British in voice and genetics, but perhaps not safely separable in the field. See Robb et al. (2008) for more information. Species accounts on following page.

European Storm-Petrel Complex

Apr–Oct

May–Aug

British

Mediterranean year-round

Oct–Mar

small, with slightly rounded tail, white underwing stripe, rather plain upperwings

short legs, cf. Wilson's Storm-Petrel

sunny

overcast

white underwing stripe variable

as on all storm-petrels, plumage tones vary with lighting and wear

British Storm-Petrel *Hydrobates [pelagicus] pelagicus* 15–17cm, WS 35–37cm
Breeds late May/early Jul–Sep/Oct in NE Atlantic (mainly British Isles), from Norway and s. Iceland s. to Canaries; ranges Apr–Oct in NE Atlantic, with small numbers of imms. reaching NW Atlantic off E North America (May–Aug). Non-breeding range (Oct–Mar) largely in S Atlantic off W Africa, with migration mainly Mar–May and Sep–Oct; some may winter in Mediterranean. Adult wing molt starts Aug/Oct, completes Feb/Apr, may be interrupted during migration; imm. wing molt mainly Jun–Nov. Flight usually rapid, rather fluttery, and jinking; quick deep wingbeats and brief glides in light winds, more frequent sailing and shearing in strong winds; often follows in boat wakes. Patters and alights on water with wings raised.

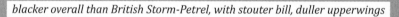

blacker overall than British Storm-Petrel, with stouter bill, duller upperwings

plumage blackish, even in strong sun

Mediterranean Storm-Petrel *Hydrobates [pelagicus] melitensis* 15–17cm, WS 35–37cm
Breeds mainly May–Aug in W and Cen Mediterranean, from se. Spain e. to Malta; also very local in Adriatic and Aegean Seas. Appears to remain in Mediterranean year-round, with only a handful of Atlantic records. Molt not well known, but adult wing molt starts late Jun/Jul and may complete by Nov/Dec. Habits much like British Storm-Petrel.

Leach's Storm-Petrel (*Hydrobates leucorhous*) **Complex** (also see pp. 272–273)
Comprises 3 cryptic species formerly placed in genus *Oceanodroma*: Leach's Storm-Petrel *H. leucorhous*, breeding in N Pacific and N Atlantic; Townsend's Storm-Petrel *H. socorroensis*, breeding in summer in nw. Mexico, and Ainley's Storm-Petrel *H. cheimomnestes*, breeding in winter in nw. Mexico. ID criteria still evolving (see Howell et al. 2010 and Howell 2012 for further information). Leach's and Townsend's are polymorphic, the dark-rumped form of Leach's often being known as Chapman's Storm-Petrel (see dark storm-petrels, pp. 272–273).

Provisional Pacific distribution of Leach's Storm-Petrel complex; also see p. 272

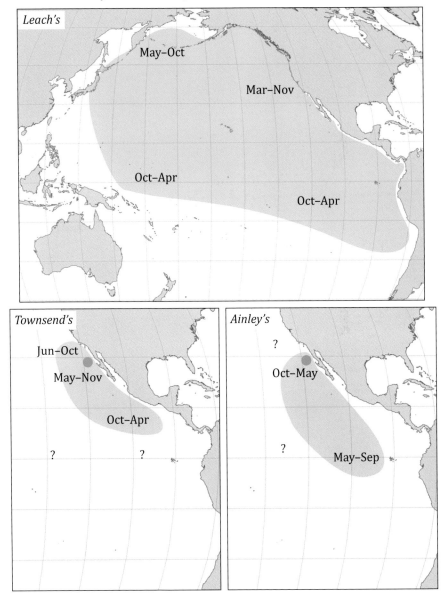

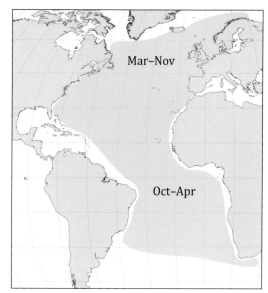

Atlantic distribution of Leach's Storm-Petrel

Leach's versus Townsend's and Ainley's Storm-Petrels

Comparison of Leach's Storm-Petrel (left) and Townsend's Storm-Petrel (right): Townsend's is slightly smaller, more compact, and blacker overall, with a finer bill, bolder white rump patch, and shorter, less deeply forked tail.

Leach's versus Townsend's and Ainley's Storm-Petrels

These 3 species co-occur in the E Pacific, mainly off Mexico, and ID criteria are nascent. Compounding the problem, Leach's breeding along the West Coast of the US average smaller than northern Leach's (Alaska and N Atlantic birds) and have shorter, slightly blunter wings plus more extensive white on the rump sides than n. birds. Images in the species accounts (pp. 240–241) show the 3 species, but an overview of differences is given here, particularly with respect to variation in rump pattern (see scoring system in figure at bottom of page).

Northern Leach's are largest, with relatively long pointed wings and typical rump scores of 1–2.5 (mainly 1.5–2.5); many have a 'textbook' dusky median line in the white, but many don't and are solidly white-rumped. **West Coast Leach's** average slightly smaller with typical rump scores of 1–3 (mainly 1–2.5), where they start to grade into the dark-rumped **Chapman's** race of Leach's (p. 272; rump score 2.5–5, mainly 4–5), which breeds in nw. Mexico.

Townsend's Storm-Petrel is smallest (usually appreciable when seen alongside Leach's; see opposite), darker and blacker overall than Leach's and Ainley's, with rump scores spanning 1–5 (but mainly bimodal, 1–2 and 4–5; see dark-rumped birds on p. 273). Townsend's has blunter wings, a shorter tail, and a relatively longer white rump patch than Leach's, which combine to suggest a wedge-rumped storm-petrel.

Ainley's Storm-Petrel is virtually unknown at sea but is overall similar in size to West Coast Leach's and has a rump score of 2–4 (mainly 2–3), often with messy, smudged dusky streaks (infrequent in Leach's, but matched by some birds).

Because Ainley's nests in winter its **wing molt timing** is reversed from that of the summer-breeding Leach's and Townsend's. Adult storm-petrels have protracted wing molts such that the inner primaries are several months older than outers, which can show as a cline in wear from browner and slightly faded inner primaries to darker and fresher outer primaries, unlike the uniformly grown feathers of a juvenile, which first show wear and fade on the exposed outer primaries. Although subtle, this feature can be seen in good images and help establish whether an adult or near-adult comes from a winter- or summer-breeding population.

Notwithstanding the foregoing, many Leach's-type storm-petrels seen in the E Pacific are best left unidentified to species until ID criteria can be refined.

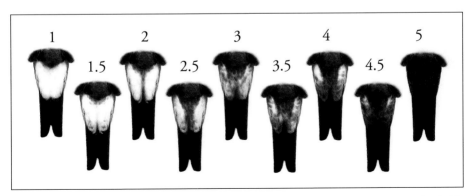

Scoring system for uppertail-covert patterns in Leach's Storm-Petrel complex. In the field, scores 1–2 usually appear as white-rumped, 3 as 'intermediate,' and 4–5 as dark-rumped. Extent of rump patches and depth of tail forks shown here are not intended to convey any taxonomic significance. © Ian Lewington.

240

medium-size, with forked tail, bold pale upperwing bands, variable rump pattern (see p. 245)

typical Northern type (see p. 239)

Atlantic dark extreme

white on sides averages more on W Coast types (see p. 239)

uniform fresh wings

wing molt

December birds, cf. Ainley's

shows little or no white on water

juv.

adult

Leach's Storm-Petrel (white-rumped) *Hydrobates leucorhous* 17.5–21.5cm, WS 44–49.5cm; also see pp. 237–239, 242, 272

Common and widespread, offshore. In **Pacific**, breeds May/Jun–Aug/early Nov from Commanders s. to n. Japan, from Aleutians s. to Baja California, Mexico. Ranges Mar–Nov in N Pacific, mainly beyond continental shelf. Non-breeding range (mainly Oct–Apr; imms. year-round) largely in tropical and equatorial waters, mainly 20°N–20°S. In **Atlantic**, breeds mid-May/mid-Jul to Sep/Nov, from Atlantic Canada s. to New England, and from Norway and s. Iceland s. to n. British Isles; small population breeds Oct–Mar in South Africa. Ranges Mar–Nov in N Atlantic, mainly beyond continental shelf. Non-breeding range (mainly Oct–Apr; imms. year-round) largely in tropical and equatorial waters, mainly 20°N–30°S.

Adult wing molt starts Aug/Oct, completes Feb/Apr; imm. wing molt starts May/Jul, completes Oct/Dec. Typical flight rather erratic and bounding, with springy wingbeats (emphasis on upstroke) and buoyant glides on slightly arched wings; in calm to light winds can forage in leisurely manner, with rather languid floppy wingbeats much like Band-rumped in same conditions; transiting flight stronger, with deeper, jerky wingbeats and at times prolonged wheeling glides when flying across the wind. Usually does not accompany vessels.

slightly smaller, more compact, and finer-billed than Leach's, with shorter tail, longer white rump

averages darker than Leach's, with more muted pale upperwing band

Townsend's Storm-Petrel (white-rumped) *Hydrobates socorroensis* 16.5–17.5cm, WS 41–45cm; also see pp. 237–239, 242, 273

Breeds late May/Jun–Oct/Nov on islets off s. end of Guadalupe I., Mexico; uncommon to locally fairly common. Ranges May–Nov w. of Baja California Peninsula, and n. Jun–Oct to s. California, mainly over pelagic waters beyond continental shelf. Non-breeding range (mainly Oct–Apr; imms. likely year-round) in E Pacific, mainly 10–20°N. Adult wing molt probably starts Sep/Nov, completes Feb/Apr; imm. wing molt likely starts Jun/Jul, completes Oct/Dec. Flight similar to Leach's but often more direct, with fairly clipped deep wingbeats, overall steadier and less bounding than the more confident and more erratic flight of Leach's.

averages smaller and stouter-billed than Leach's, slightly larger and bulkier than Townsend's; best told by wing molt timing, seasonal plumage wear (see p. 239)

smudgy dark rump streaks typical

wear cline from older brown inner to fresher dark outer primaries, cf. p. 239

December adults shown

Ainley's Storm-Petrel *Hydrobates cheimomnestes* 17.5–19cm, WS 42–46cm; also see pp. 237–239

Breeds mainly Nov/Dec–Apr/May on islets off s. end of Guadalupe I., Mexico; uncommon to locally fairly common. Probably ranges Oct–May over waters w. of Baja California Peninsula; non-breeding range poorly known; recorded May–Jun s. to waters w. of Galapagos. Adult wing molt mainly Mar–Oct; imm. wing molt not known, perhaps mainly Nov–Jun. Flight manner unknown; likely similar to Leach's, perhaps less bounding and erratic.

242

Leach's Storm-Petrel complex versus Band-rumped Storm-Petrel complex

Different members of these 2 complexes co-occur widely in both the Atlantic and Pacific, and ID can be very challenging. Width and shape of rump band, tail shape, and boldness and extent of pale upperwing bands are the best clues, in combination with flight manner. Potential flight manner and behavioral differences within Band-rumps await elucidation, but all Band-rumps typically fly differently from Leach's, although the two can appear very similar when foraging in calm or light winds, as often occurs in tropical regions. In general, Leach's has a more erratic and bounding flight, with springy wingbeats that emphasize the upstroke; it glides on slightly arched wings but usually not for prolonged periods in light winds. By contrast, Band-rumped has a more predictable flight, with more supple, less jerky wingbeats that emphasize the downstoke; it glides buoyantly on slightly cupped wings, often for prolonged periods. Details of bill structure (stouter on Band-rumped, relatively slender on Leach's) can often be seen in digital images.

Leach's complex

Band-rumped complex

North Atlantic

Leach's

bold pale band to edge of wing

tail tip notched to squared

Grant's

white wraps around

forked tail, crooked wings

narrow white band

little white

blue-gray hood

many spring-summer birds in obvious wing molt

Pacific Band-rumps average smaller than Atlantic, often with more distinct tail notch

Tropical Eastern Pacific

Townsend's

Darwin's

forked tail

notched tail

stout bill

narrow white band

upperwing bands on s. Pacific Leach's complex often duller than n. birds, and white rump band wraps more to sides

Band-rumped Storm-Petrel (*Thalobata castro*) Complex

Comprises an undetermined number of often poorly known and mostly uncommon warm-water taxa whose relationships remain vexed. Traditionally, Band-rumps have been placed in genus *Oceanodroma*, but see Penhallurick & Wink (2004). Simply from specimens, 'Band-rumped Storm-Petrel' has been considered a monotypic species, but vocal and genetic work (plus small morphological differences) indicates several cryptic species are involved (see Bolton et al. 2008, Harris 1969, Robb et al. 2008, Smith et al. 2007). We prefer to emphasize differences and treat the different populations as potential species. Of the populations we consider here, 3 appear to be formally unnamed, and for some populations we do not have images (in such cases, short accounts summarize what little is known).

Field ID characters remain to be elucidated (timing of adult wing molt can be helpful for separating taxa that breed in different seasons), and we encourage observers to help fill gaps in our knowledge of this truly complex complex; see Howell (2012) for further information.

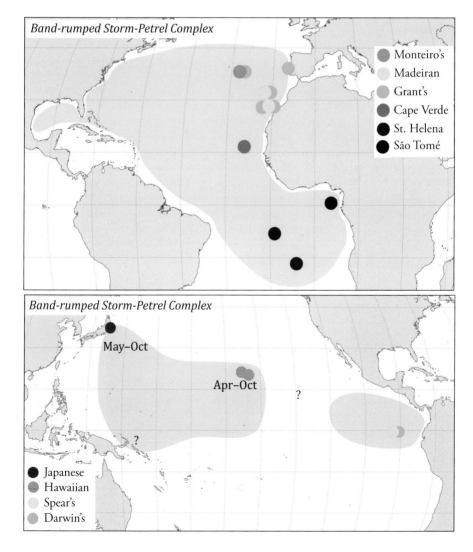

244

summer breeder; averages smaller, blacker, and more lightly built than Grant's Storm-Petrel; best told by wing molt timing, seasonal plumage wear

presumed Madeiran, North Carolina, May

May adults, Madeira

dusky median rump stripe may be more frequent than on Grant's and Monteiro's

Madeiran Storm-Petrel *Thalobata [castro] castro* 18.5–20.5cm, WS 42.5–48cm; see pp. 242–243
Fairly common summer breeder. Breeds Jun–Oct in E Atlantic from Madeira s. to Canaries; ranges in subtropical and tropical E Atlantic (details of at-sea range poorly known), with small numbers of imms. and non-breeders apparently in W Atlantic off e. US (mainly May–Aug). Adult wing molt mainly Oct–May, imm. wing molt may span Jun–Oct; study needed.
  Flies with fairly strong, unhurried wingbeats (emphasis on the downstroke, unlike Leach's) and buoyant sailing glides on slightly cupped wings; prolonged shearing glides and low weaving flight in light to moderate winds is distinct from more erratic, bounding flight of Leach's.

summer breeder; averages more compact than Grant's with average deeper tail notch; best told by wing molt timing, seasonal plumage wear

May adults, Azores

as in all Band-rumps, tail notch changes appreciably with angle of view and how much tail is spread

Monteiro's Storm-Petrel *Thalobata monteiroi* 19.5–21.5cm, WS 45–51cm; see pp. 242–243
Rare and local summer breeder; described in 2007. Breeds late May/Jun–Sep on Azores. At-sea distribution unknown, but may range w. into subtropical Atlantic. Adult wing molt starts Sep, likely ends Feb/Apr; imm. wing molt may span May–Sep; study needed.

winter breeder; averages larger and bulkier than Madeiran Storm-Petrel; best told by wing molt timing, seasonal plumage wear

May adults, North Carolina

wing molt

wing molt

wing molt

uniform fresh plumage

juv. North Carolina, Jun

wing molt

shows more white than Leach's

Grant's Storm-Petrel *Thalobata [castro]* undescribed 19.5–21.5cm, WS 45–51cm; see pp. 242–243 Relatively common and widespread winter breeder. Breeds Oct/early Dec–Feb/Apr in E Atlantic, from Portugal and Azores s. to Canaries; probably ranges Sep–Apr in subtropical and tropical E Atlantic; ranges May–Sep to W Atlantic and Gulf of Mexico. Adult wing molt Feb–Aug; imm. wing molt may span Sep–Apr, but study needed. Habits much like Madeiran Storm-Petrel, but in direct comparison of presumed Grant's and presumed Madeiran, the smaller, more lightly built Madeiran has a slightly quicker and more maneuverable flight.

Cape Verde Storm-Petrel *Thalobata jabejabe* 19–21cm, WS 43–49cm; see pp. 242–243 Locally fairly common. Breeds in Cape Verdes, with protracted or bimodal season, perhaps mainly Mar–Aug and Oct–Mar, but study needed. At-sea range poorly known; occurs at least over nearby waters and s. to around 7°N (R. L. Flood, pers. comm.). Wing molt may occur year-round. As with most Band-rumps, field ID criteria await elucidation and perhaps not safely identified in the field other than by presumption around breeding islands.

São Tomé Storm-Petrel *Thalobata [castro]* undescribed 20–22cm, WS 45.5–51.5cm; see pp. 242–243 Fairly common locally in Gulf of Guinea; presumably breeds (with protracted or bimodal season?) on São Tomé I. (Monteiro et al. 1997, R. L. Flood, pers. comm.). Relatively large and long billed with a relatively narrow white rump band (Harris 1969:97–100), which may make rather squared tail appear long and broad. Study needed.

246

St. Helena, Apr
fresh adults
cool season

often shows distinct
tail notch, extensive
white wrap-around

Ascension, Apr
possible juv.

relatively large, stocky, and stout-billed, but at-sea ID criteria await elucidation

St. Helena Storm-Petrel *Thalobata [castro] helena* 19.5–21.5cm, WS 45–51cm; see pp. 242–243
2 seasonal populations (cryptic species?), both uncommon: breeds mainly Oct/Nov–Mar/Apr
(warm season) and Apr–Sep (cool season) at St. Helena and Ascension; at both islands, visits
colonies during the daytime, at least in Mar–Apr. Ranges in equatorial and tropical S Atlantic,
where recorded from around the Equator s. to about 25°S. Adult wing molts probably span
mainly Mar–Sep and Sep–Mar; study needed.

*not known to be separable at sea from other Pacific populations
in Band-rumped complex, except by presumption based on range*

Japanese Storm-Petrel *Thalobata [castro] kumagai* 17.5–19.5cm, WS 44–49cm; see pp. 242–243
Rare and declining. Breeds Jun–Oct/Nov very locally in Japan (main colony 25,000 pairs in mid-
1960s; <50 pairs by 2010). At-sea distribution poorly known; likely ranges in subtropical and
tropical W Pacific; apparent pairs in courtship flights at sea in Solomons (Apr, pers. obs.) may
be migrants from Japan or perhaps local (undiscovered) breeders. Adult wing molt probably
spans Oct–Apr. Not known to be separable in the field from Hawaiian Storm-Petrel other than
by presumption around breeding islands, although white rump band of Japanese averages wider
(38.3mm vs. 32.5mm on Hawaiian; Harris 1969).

not known to be separable at sea from other Pacific populations
in Band-rumped complex, except by presumption based on range

Hawaiian Storm-Petrel *Thalobata [castro] cryptoleucura* 17.5–19.5cm, WS 44–49cm; see pp. 242–243
Uncommon. Breeds May/Jun–Oct/Nov locally in se. Hawaiian Is. At-sea distribution poorly known, but appears to range mainly over tropical and equatorial waters to s. and w. of Hawaii. Adult wing molt probably spans Oct–Apr.

from wedge-rumped storm-petrels (pp. 248–249) by narrow white rump band, easier
flight; Darwin's and Spear's separable by adult wing molt timing if age can be ascertained

molting, Nov
cf. adult Darwin's

age and taxon
unknown

fresh plumage, Nov
cf. juv. Darwin's

tail notch changes with angle of
view and how much tail is spread

Darwin's Storm-Petrel and **Spear's Storm-Petrel** *Thalobata [castro] bangsi* 17.5–19.5cm, WS 44–49cm; see pp. 242–243
Fairly common. Breed widely in Galapagos, with bimodal season: mainly May–Oct cool season (Darwin's) and Dec–May warm season (Spear's); details of population size and distribution for the 2 populations await elucidation. Type specimen of *bangsi* collected at sea, unassigned to a population; thus, one taxon remains to be named formally, but which one? Range year-round in equatorial and tropical E Pacific. Wing molt may occur year-round, but for adults likely spans Sep–Mar (Darwin's) and Apr–Oct (Spear's).

248

Wedge-rumped Storm-Petrel (*Halocyptena tethys*) Complex

Comprises 2 taxa treated here as species, given differences in size, morphology, and ecology greater than or equal to those of several other recently recognized cryptic species of storm-petrels: Galapagos Storm-Petrel *H. tethys*, breeding in Galapagos, and Peruvian Storm-Petrel *H. kelsalli*, breeding in Peru and Chile. Peruvian differs from Galapagos in smaller size but slightly deeper tail fork, and longer tail projection past shorter white rump patch. Like most storm-petrels, adults molt after breeding, but, unlike other northern storm-petrels, 1st-year *Halocyptena* (including Least and Black Storm-Petrels, pp. 274–275) may have an 'extra' (preformative) wing molt, within 4–9 months of fledging, before aligning with the adult schedule.

averages larger than Peruvian, but with shallower tail notch, shorter tail projection past white rump wedge; size similar to Townsend's Storm-Petrel

with Lowe's Storm-Petrel (behind)

like other Halocyptena, *Wedge-rumps have big feet and a relatively stout bill*

Galapagos Storm-Petrel *Halocyptena [tethys] tethys* 15–16.5cm, WS 36–40cm
Breeds locally (mainly May–Sep) on at least 3 islands in n. Galapagos (where visits colony during day): Roca Redonda, Genovesa, and Pitt. Ranges in tropical and subtropical E Pacific, n. to Mexico, s. to Peru and perhaps n. Chile, favoring waters >100km from land, thus farther offshore than Peruvian Storm-Petrel, but the 2 taxa overlap widely (from at least cen. Peru n. to Mexico). Adult and subadult wing molt presumably spans Oct–Apr; other birds molting Apr–Sep are likely 1st-years.

In calm to light winds, flies with strong deep wingbeats and short glides, often with an overall weaving or slightly jerky progression; travels much faster than the weak fluttery Lowe's Storm-Petrels behind a boat in the Galapagos. When flying across moderate winds can sail easily, recalling Leach's Storm-Petrel, with short bursts of flapping and banking glides on slightly arched wings. Feeds with legs and big feet dangling, pattering on the surface.

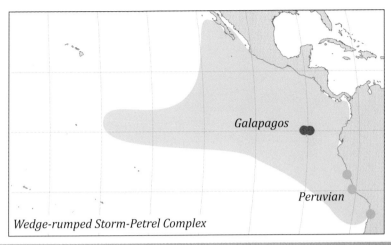

Wedge-rumped Storm-Petrel Complex

averages smaller than Galapagos Storm-Petrel, with deeper tail notch, shorter white rump wedge; size similar to Least Storm-Petrel

rump can show faint dividing line

longer tail projection than Galapagos

notch reduced on spread tail

with Least Storm-Petrel (left)

Peruvian Storm-Petrel *Halocyptena [tethys] kelsalli* 14.5–15.5cm, WS 33–37cm
Breeds (mainly Mar–Aug?) on inshore islands in cen. Peru, and (Nov–Apr?) in Atacama Desert of n. Chile (discovered 2017; F. Schmitt, pers. comm.); ranges in tropical and subtropical E Pacific, n. to Mexico, favoring waters <400km from land; thus more inshore than Galapagos Storm-Petrel, but the 2 taxa overlap widely. Wing molt likely occurs year-round, with bimodal peaks. Flight and habits similar to Galapagos, with strong deep wingbeats and short glides, but overall a little weaker and more like similar-size Least Storm-Petrel (with which Peruvian often associates), whereas Galapagos flight is stronger, more likely to be mistaken for Leach's.

Wilson's Storm-Petrel (*Oceanites oceanicus*) Complex

Comprises the genus *Oceanites*, traditionally considered as 2 species: widespread Wilson's Storm-Petrel (*O. oceanicus*), and smaller White-vented (or Elliot's) Storm-Petrel (*O. gracilis*) of the northern Humboldt Current and Galapagos. However, 6 taxa described in the genus and species limits remain vexed. We provisionally recognize the following taxa: Wilson's Storm-Petrel *O. [oceanicus] oceanicus* of Antarctica and subantarctic islands; Fuegian Storm-Petrel *O. [oceanicus] chilensis* of cen. and s. Chile (and Falklands?); Elliot's Storm-Petrel *O. [gracilis] gracilis* of Peru and n. Chile; and Lowe's Storm-Petrel *O. [gracilis] lowei* of the Galapagos. Status of Pincoya Storm-Petrel *O. [chilensis] pincoyae*, described recently from s. Chile, remains to be elucidated (see Howell & Schmitt 2016). In addition, race *exasperatus* of Wilson's has been described from Antarctic continent, averaging slightly larger than birds breeding on subantarctic islands, but not distinguishable in the field and here lumped into *oceanicus*. Wing molt timings not well understood for most taxa; adults molt after breeding, but 1st-year Wilson's has an 'extra' (preformative) wing molt, within 4–9 months of fledging, before adopting adult schedule; unclear if other *Oceanites* taxa have this added molt.

'small' relative to Leach's and Band-rumped, with shorter wings, weaker and fluttery flight, long legs; larger than European, with long legs, less hurried flight

many birds in Northern Hemisphere are molting

underwing lacks white markings

as in other members of Wilson's complex, toes usually project past tail tip, but can be pulled in

Wilson's Storm-Petrel *Oceanites [oceanicus] oceanicus* 18.5–20cm, WS 38–42cm

Widespread, transequatorial migrant. Breeds Dec–Mar around Antarctic continent (mainly on Antarctic Peninsula, where abundant), and locally on subantarctic islands in S Atlantic and S Indian Oceans. Migrates n. into Atlantic, Indian, and Pacific Oceans in non-breeding season (mainly May–Oct): common in N Atlantic (mainly 30–55°N), uncommon to rare in Pacific (mainly 30–45°N) and Indian Oceans. Migrations mainly mid-Mar to May and Sep–Nov, often in a broadly clockwise loop through N Pacific and N Atlantic (thus, commoner in e. ocean basins during Jul–Oct). May occur (rarely?) in Humboldt Current, but status there confounded by presence of Fuegian Storm-Petrel. Adult and subadult wing molt mainly Mar–Sep; 1st-year wing molt mainly Jul–Jan, starts only 4–5 months after fledging.

Transiting flight usually low and direct, with fluttery, swallow-like wingbeats and short glides; in strong winds can bank and sail long distances with little or no flapping, and also kicks off the water one-footed. Feeding birds hover and flutter with long legs dangling, seeming to dance on the surface. Often follows boats, and gathers in flocks of 10s or 100s when feeding and rafting.

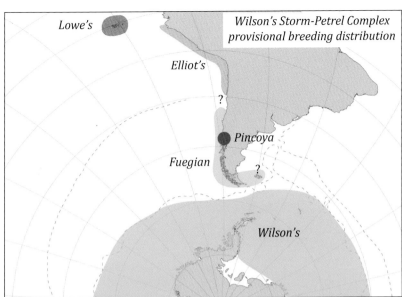

The transequatorial migrations of Wilson's Storm-Petrels take them from icebergs around Antarctica (below) to pattering around Sargassum in cobalt-blue tropical waters (above; with Leach's Storm-Petrel, the short-legged upper bird, right of center)

252

slightly smaller than Wilson's, with variable whitish tips to underwing coverts, often some whitish on belly; well-marked birds resemble poorly marked Elliot's

toe webbing yellow, as in other members of Wilson's complex, but difficult to see in field

Elliot's Storm-Petrel (far left) clearly smaller in direct comparison

Fuegian Storm-Petrel *Oceanites [oceanicus] chilensis* 16–18cm, WS 34–38cm; see pp. 250–251 Common in s. and cen. Chile, where can be seen from shore; ranges n. (mainly Apr–Nov) to Peru and very rarely n. to Gulf of Panama. Breeds Dec–Mar in s. Chile, and perhaps n. locally to cen. Chile. Falkland breeders also appear to be this taxon, perhaps ranging in S Atlantic e. to SW Africa, rarely May–Aug to N Atlantic. Adult and subadult wing molt mainly Feb–Jul; imm. wing molt may span Dec–Apr; study needed. Flight and habits like Wilson's Storm-Petrel.

averages more white on underwing, belly, and upperwing than Fuegian; poorly marked birds may be inseparable from Fuegian; study needed

reduced white, or Fuegian?

extensive white

Pincoya Storm-Petrel *Oceanites [chilensis] pincoyae* 16–17.5cm, WS 34–37cm; see pp. 250–251 Described in 2013, but taxonomic status unclear. Fairly common in vicinity of Chiloé I., Chile (breeding grounds unknown; presumed to breed Nov/Dec–Feb/Mar). 'Classic' whiter examples distinctive, but separation of darker birds from Fuegian Storm-Petrel remains problematic (Howell & Schmitt 2016). Wing molt timing probably similar to northern-breeding Fuegian. Flight and habits like Fuegian and Wilson's Storm-Petrels (contra Harrison et al. 2013).

averages larger than Elliot's, with less extensive white on belly, but highly variable;
not safely distinguished in the field on present knowledge, but no known range overlap

white belly patch variable;
best seen as a bird banks away

Lowe's Storm-Petrel *Oceanites [gracilis] galapagoensis* 14–16cm, WS 35–39cm; see pp. 250–251
Common and breeds (presumably) in Galapagos Is., though nest has never been found. Based
on specimens, breeding season likely spans Jun–Dec. Ranges over adjacent waters, but details of
at-sea distribution poorly known. Flight and habits like Wilson's Storm-Petrel; typical flight low
and fluttery, or swallow-like; often follows and accompanies boats and patters in the wake.

averages smaller than Lowe's, with more extensive white on belly, but highly variable;
not safely distinguished in the field on present knowledge, but no known range overlap

as in other members of Wilson's complex,
white below averages more extensive on juvs.

from above, plumage not
safely told from Fuegian

juv. white belly patch variable,
often hard to see

Elliot's Storm-Petrel *Oceanites [gracilis] gracilis* 13.5–14.5cm, WS 31–35cm; see pp. 250–251
Common in Humboldt Current of Peru and n. Chile, where can be seen from shore; ranges
over nearshore waters, not usually far offshore, and occurs n. rarely to Ecuador. Breeds (season-
ality poorly known, perhaps bimodal, Nov–Apr and May–Oct) in Atacama Desert of s. Peru
and n. Chile. Flight and habits like Lowe's Storm-Petrel.

254

WHITE-BODIED STORM-PETRELS (15+ species in 5 genera)

Varied assemblage of small to large storm-petrels comprising the southern genera *Garrodia* (1 species), *Fregetta* (8 species), *Nesofregetta* (1 species), and *Pelagodroma* (4+ species), plus the northern Hornby's Storm-Petrel (placed provisionally in *Hydrobates*, formerly *Oceanodroma,* but yet to be examined in genetic studies).

Plumage often boldly patterned, with predominantly white body and dark head or head and neck markings; several species white-rumped (if seen only from above, could be mistaken for white-rumped storm-petrels).

Most diverse in subtropical and subantarctic southern latitudes; a few species are long-distance migrants. Can be considered in terms of species found in the Pacific Ocean and those in the Atlantic and Indian Oceans. Species ID best based on a combination of structure (including leg length), flight manner, plumage patterns, and tail shape, but ID among some cryptic groups not possible at sea other than by inference based on range.

Pacific

Gray-backed
p. 256

Streaked complex
pp. 256–257

White-bellied complex
pp. 258–262

Polynesian, p. 263

White-faced complex
pp. 264–266

Hornby's, p. 267

Atlantic and Indian Oceans

Gray-backed, p. 256

White-faced complex
pp. 264–266

White-bellied complex
pp. 258–260

The attractive little Gray-backed Storm-Petrel often feeds around mats of kelp, which offer a good focal point when seeking this rather local and easily overlooked species.

distinctive small storm-petrel with gray rump and black-tipped tail; from below, black 'pinhead' contrasts with white body

Gray-backed Storm-Petrel *Garrodia nereis* 17–18cm, WS 36–39cm; also see p. 255
Southern Hemisphere; rather local in cooler waters; uncommon to fairly common. Breeds Oct/
Dec–Apr in S Atlantic on Falklands, South Georgia, and Gough; and locally on subantarctic
islands from Indian Ocean e. to New Zealand (including Chathams). Ranges locally (mainly
40–55°S) in subantarctic waters of Atlantic and Indian Oceans and around New Zealand;
occurs regularly (mainly Apr–Oct) n. to S Australia, very rarely to Cape Horn and South Africa.
Wing molt mainly Feb–Aug. Flight typically fast and fluttery, fairly direct and low to the water
with hurried wingbeats and only brief glides; feeds while pattering, often around mats of kelp.

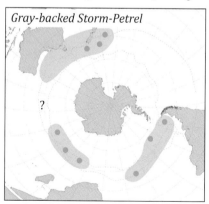

Gray-backed Storm-Petrel

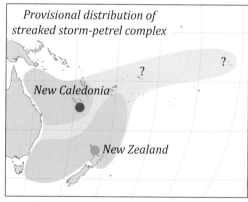

Provisional distribution of streaked storm-petrel complex

New Caledonia

New Zealand

Streaked Storm-Petrel (*Fregetta maoriana*) Complex

Comprises at least 2 poorly known and rather local taxa, allied to the white-bellied complex
(indeed, at any distance, streaked birds often appear simply white-bellied in the field): New
Zealand Storm-Petrel *F. maoriana* (rediscovered 2003); and 'New Caledonia Storm-Petrel' (perhaps formally undescribed and discovered 2008, but see p. 349). Enigmatic single old specimens
of streaked storm-petrels exist from Samoa and the Marquesas, but their affinities remain vexed
(Cibois et al. 2015). We await with interest further developments in this complex.

appreciably larger, rangier, and longer-billed than Wilson's and New Zealand Storm-Petrels

white underwing panel smaller than New Zealand Storm-Petrel; belly streaking variable

New Caledonia Storm-Petrel *Fregetta* undescribed? 21–23cm, WS 43–47cm; see p. 349
Presumed to breed New Caledonia; uncommon. Ranges in Coral Sea w. to E Australia, perhaps elsewhere in tropical W (and Cen?) S Pacific. No data on wing molt. Flight similar to New Zealand Storm-Petrel but stronger, less fluttery, with easier sailing glides on bigger wings; feeds by pattering with legs dangling.

size similar to Wilson's Storm-Petrel; belly streaking variable

white underwing panel more extensive than larger New Caledonia Storm-Petrel

New Zealand Storm-Petrel *Fregetta maoriana* 17.5–19cm, WS 38–41cm
Breeds Feb–Jul in n. New Zealand; uncommon. At-sea distribution poorly known; ranges at sea around n. New Zealand; also recorded w. to SE Australia (Mar–Jun) and ne. to Fiji (May). Wing molt probably spans May–Oct. Flight recalls Wilson's Storm-Petrel: usually rather low, fast, and direct, with fluttery wingbeats and only brief glides, but in strong winds can sail in low wheeling arcs and sometimes kicks off with one foot; feeds by pattering with legs dangling.

White-bellied Storm-Petrel (*Fregetta grallaria*) Complex

Traditionally considered to comprise 2 widespread Southern Hemisphere species: subantarctic-breeding Black-bellied Storm-Petrel (*F. tropica*) and subtropical White-bellied Storm-Petrel (*F. grallaria*), but situation more complex and still unresolved (e.g., Robertson et al. 2016). We provisionally treat the following 6 taxa as species: Black-bellied Storm-Petrel *F. tropica*; Gough Storm-Petrel *F. [tropica] 'leucogaster'*; Inaccessible Storm-Petrel *F. [grallaria] 'melanoleuca'*; Tasman Storm-Petrel *F. [grallaria] grallaria*; Titan Storm-Petrel *F. [grallaria] titan*; and Juan Fernandez Storm-Petrel *F. [grallaria] segethi* (see maps below and opposite). Some populations (Tasman, and perhaps Inaccessible) are polymorphic, with darker morphs covered on p. 262.

Field ID characters to check include extent of black hood, foot projection beyond tail tip (beware, even long-legged taxa can fly with legs pulled in and thus show no projection), extent and pattern of any dark belly and vent markings, and underwing pattern. Flight of all taxa similar and often eye-catching (below, a Black-bellied Storm-Petrel), as birds put one foot in the water, slicing up lines of spray, and at times splash belly-down on the surface.

Titan Storm-Petrel on nest, above ground

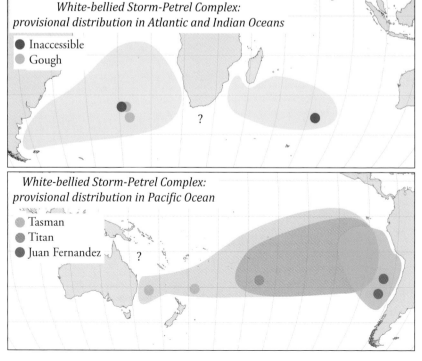

White-bellied Storm-Petrel Complex: provisional distribution in Atlantic and Indian Oceans

● Inaccessible
● Gough

?

White-bellied Storm-Petrel Complex: provisional distribution in Pacific Ocean

● Tasman
● Titan
● Juan Fernandez

?

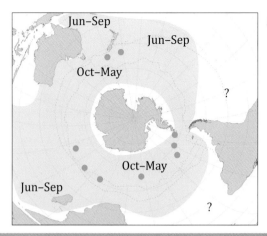

Jun–Sep

Jun–Sep

Oct–May

?

Oct–May

Jun–Sep

?

Black-bellied Storm-Petrel

black belly stripe variable (can be absent, at least in New Zealand region); black hood more extensive than on white-bellied storm-petrels; toes often project past tail tip

extensive dark on primary coverts

worn plumage

fresh plumage

very rarely lacks black belly stripe

even a broad black belly stripe can be hard to see in profile

Black-bellied Storm-Petrel *Fregetta tropica* 19.5–21cm, WS 42–46cm
Breeds Dec/Jan–Apr on subantarctic islands from South Shetlands e. to New Zealand. Ranges Oct–May in Southern Ocean (mainly 45–60°S). Moves n. in non-breeding season (mainly Jun–Sep) to subtropical and tropical waters of W Indian Ocean, SW Pacific, and S Atlantic. N range limits in Atlantic and E Pacific unclear: small numbers found n. to 35°N in W Atlantic (late spring–summer) and to 30°N in Canary Current of E Atlantic (autumn); vagrant n. to Peru. Wing molt probably spans Mar–Oct. Habits much like other white-bellied storm-petrels; flight often eye-catching (see photo opposite), but in light winds flight can be fairly direct with stiff fluttery wingbeats and short glides recalling Wilson's, although wingbeats a little looser.

Gough   Inaccessible

Gough has slightly more extensive
black hood, some have white chin

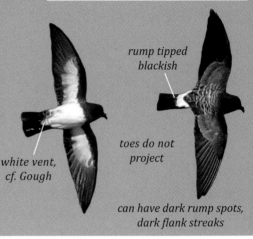

shorter-legged than Gough Storm-Petrel,
white from belly projects into vent

rump tipped
blackish

toes do not
project

white vent,
cf. Gough

can have dark rump spots,
dark flank streaks

Inaccessible Storm-Petrel *Fregetta [grallaria] 'leucogaster'* 21–22cm, WS 44–47cm; see p. 258
Breeds (mainly Dec/Jan–Apr/May?) on Inaccessible and Nightingale, in Tristan group; fairly
common. Ranges in S Atlantic, perhaps mainly 10–45°S, but at-sea range not well known
relative to Gough Storm-Petrel. Birds attributed to this taxon also breed at St. Paul in Indian
Ocean, where uncommon, and range in subtropical SW Indian Ocean. Flight and habits much
as other white-bellied storm-petrels. Some Atlantic birds, at least, can have mostly dusky rump.

slightly smaller than Inaccessible, but longer-legged;
toes often project past tail tip (can be pulled in)

can have dark rump spots, but
longest rump feathers white at tip

fresh plumage

black vent,
cf. Inaccessible

averages more dark
than Inaccessible

some have whitish chin patch,
lacking on Inaccessible

worn plumage

Gough Storm-Petrel *Fregetta [tropica] 'melanoleuca'* 19–20cm, WS 41–43cm; see p. 258
Breeds (mainly Dec/Jan–Apr/May?) on Gough (declining) and Tristan group (fairly common).
Ranges in S Atlantic, perhaps mainly 30–50°S, but at-sea distribution not well known relative to
Inaccessible Storm-Petrel. Flight and habits much like other white-bellied storm-petrels.

very large (size close to Polynesian Storm-Petrel) with relatively long stout bill, but plumage much like Juan Fernandez Storm-Petrel

adult, Mar

big bill

fresh plumage, Sep, likely juv.

white tips to fresh upperparts widest on juv., can look silvery in bright light

Titan Storm-Petrel *Fregetta [grallaria] titan* 23–25cm, WS 46.5–49.5cm; see p. 258 Breeds (mainly Jan–Jul?) on islets off Rapa; rare, with population <500 pairs. Ranges e. (mainly May–Nov?) to tropical E Pacific, where overlaps range of Tasman and Juan Fernandez Storm-Petrels. Wing molt probably Jun–Dec. Habits at sea similar to other white-bellied storm-petrels but flight stronger, less fluttery, wingbeats a little more measured. Visits colonies in daylight and, unlike all other storm-petrels, nests above ground (see photo, p. 258).

smallest Pacific white-bellied storm-petrel, not safely distinguished at sea from Tasman Storm-Petrel

heavily worn plumage

flanks can have dark streaks

dangling legs appear to project past tail tip

slightly worn plumage

as on Titan and Tasman, toes do not project past tail tip

juv., Oct

Juan Fernandez Storm-Petrel *Fregetta [grallaria] segethi* 18–19.5cm, WS 41–45cm; see p. 258 Breeds (mainly Dec–Jun?) on Juan Fernandez and Desventuradas, Chile. Ranges year-round in tropical and subtropical E Pacific, mostly in pelagic waters beyond Humboldt Current. Wing molt mainly May–Oct. Flight and habits much like other white-bellied storm-petrels.

smaller black hood and less black on underprimary coverts than Black-bellied; not safely told from Juan Fernandez Storm-Petrel unless darker morphs are seen

often has variable dark streaking below, mainly on flanks

Tasman Storm-Petrel *Fregetta [grallaria] grallaria* 19–21cm, WS 42–46cm; see p. 258 Breeds mainly Jan–Jun on Lord Howe and Kermadecs. Ranges e. (mainly May–Nov?) to equatorial and tropical Cen and E Pacific, where overlaps range of Titan and Juan Fernandez Storm-Petrels. Wing molt mainly May–Nov. Flight and habits much like other white-bellied storm-petrels. Flanks and sometimes belly streaked dusky; streaked birds can resemble New Zealand Storm-Petrel but have a less extensive black hood, no toe projection past tail tip. Darkest birds have dusky belly and rump; usually some white present but hard to see in the field, and such birds can appear wholly dark.

typical darker morphs of Tasman Storm-Petrel

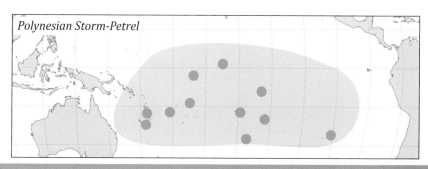

Polynesian Storm-Petrel

very large and ostensibly unmistakable, with big wings, long broad tail, big feet; note broad black neck ring, white throat strap, sailing and splashing flight

deeply notched tail, white rump band

narrow pale upperwing band

variable dark markings below on some birds; rarely can be wholly dark

steps and splashes on the surface to veer direction

Polynesian Storm-Petrel *Nesofregetta fuliginosa* 23–25cm, WS 51–54cm
Breeds locally (year-round at some sites) in equatorial and tropical S Pacific, from New Caledonia e. to Salas y Gómez; uncommon to locally fairly common. Ranges in generally low density across tropical Pacific, w. to Coral Sea and n. to around 10°N in Cen Pacific. Light morph can have variable dark streaking on underparts; wholly dark morph rare, known from Phoenix Is. and single old specimen from Samoa. Flight recalls a giant white-faced storm-petrel: in calm to light winds flies with shallow, rather fluttery wingbeats and easy sailing glides on broad, flat wings, legs often dangled and feet kicked and splashed in the surface; in moderate winds can sail across the wind in low wheeling arcs, with little flapping.

White-faced Storm-Petrel (*Pelagodroma marina*) Complex

No modern taxonomic study has been conducted on this complex, but given morphological variation and biogeographic distribution, it seems likely that cryptic species are involved. We recognize 4 groups, which may comprise up to 6 cryptic species: Cramp's Storm-Petrel *P. [m.] hypoleuca* (including Bourne's Storm-Petrel *P. [m.] eadesi*); Latham's Storm-Petrel *P. [m.] marina* (including Maori Storm-Petrel *P. [m.] maoriana*); Australian Storm-Petrel *P. [m.] dulciae*; and Kermadec Storm-Petrel *P. [m.] albiclunis* (see maps below). Field separation criteria for some groups require study, but southernmost taxa (*marina, maoriana*) are darker than other populations, with longer and more deeply forked tails, but shorter legs.

Most taxa are locally fairly common to common. White-faced storm-petrels feed singly or in fairly dense aggregations, usually not mixing with other species of storm-petrels except when attracted to chum slicks. Flight manner distinctive, even at long range, and similar in all taxa: transiting flight in calm to light winds often steady, low, and fairly direct, with shallow fluttery wingbeats and short sailing glides on flat wings, legs held dangling. Birds often kick the sea surface to veer direction with a jerky, scything rhythm. Foraging birds characteristically hop along with a progression of two-footed kicks and short sailing glides; they patter with wings fluttered stiffly, legs dangling. Feeding groups can suggest an animated field of ping-pong balls.

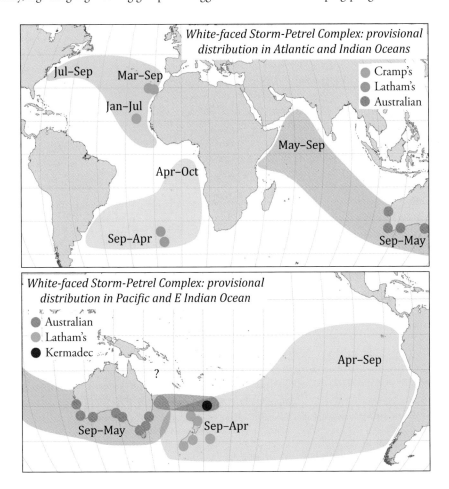

White-faced Storm-Petrel Complex: provisional distribution in Atlantic and Indian Oceans

Jul–Sep
Mar–Sep
Jan–Jul
● Cramp's
● Latham's
● Australian
May–Sep
Apr–Oct
Sep–Apr
Sep–May

White-faced Storm-Petrel Complex: provisional distribution in Pacific and E Indian Ocean

● Australian
● Latham's
● Kermadec
?
Apr–Sep
Sep–May
Sep–Apr

distinctive in N Atlantic range; eadesi *averages whiter-faced and longer-billed than* hypoleuca, *but rarely separable at sea; note wing molt timings, which need study for imms.*

*adults (*hypoleuca*)*

juvs. (presumed eadesi*)*

on all white-faced storm-petrels, color tone of upperparts can change appreciably with lighting

Cramp's Storm-Petrel *Pelagodroma [marina] hypoleuca* 20–22cm, WS 42–46cm
Race *hypoleuca* breeds mainly Apr–Aug on Canaries and Selvagens; locally common. At-sea distribution poorly known; presumably ranges in subtropical N Atlantic. Adult wing molt mainly Sep–Dec. Race *eadesi* breeds mainly Jan–Jul in Cape Verdes; locally fairly common. Ranges (year-round?) in tropical E Atlantic. Adult wing molt mainly Jul–Oct. Birds found Jul–Sep in W Atlantic off e. US usually attributed to *eadesi*, but also may include *hypoleuca*.

uncommon and local; note white rump, squared tail, small gray neck patches

Kermadec Storm-Petrel *Pelagodroma [marina] albiclunis* 20–22cm, WS 42–46cm
Breeds Aug–Dec on Kermadecs; uncommon. At-sea distribution poorly known; reported w. to Tasman Sea off E Australia. Much like Australian Storm-Petrel (p. 266) but rump white (pale gray rump of other white-faced taxa can fade to whitish, but not strikingly white when fresh), gray neck patches smaller. Adult wing molt likely spans Dec–Apr; study needed.

slightly smaller and paler than Latham's Storm-Petrel, with shorter, overall squared tail

rump may fade whitish in worn plumage,
cf. Kermadec Storm-Petrel (p. 265)

dark flank streaks more frequent
than on other white-faced taxa

Australian Storm-Petrel *Pelagodroma [marina] dulciae* 20–22cm, WS 42–46cm; see p. 264
Breeds mainly Oct–Mar in S Australia; locally common. Ranges Sep–May off S Australia, rarely
e. to New Zealand waters. Non-breeding range (May–Sep) mainly in NW Indian Ocean. Adult
wing molt mainly Mar–Aug. Habits much like other white-faced storm-petrels; see p. 264.

common and widespread white-faced storm-petrel; note relatively
long, distinctly notched tail and large dark gray neck patches

paler in worn
plumage

black mask averages deeper than
Australian Storm-Petrel

tail rounded
when spread

Latham's Storm-Petrel *Pelagodroma [marina] marina* 21–23cm, WS 43–47cm; see p. 264
Race *marina* breeds Oct–Mar on Gough and Tristan group; ranges in subtropical and tropical S
Atlantic (mainly 20–40°S), with non-breeding range (Apr–Oct) n. into equatorial waters. Race
maoriana breeds Oct–Mar in New Zealand; ranges Sep–May in subtropical SW Pacific; non-
breeding range (Apr–Sep) mainly in equatorial and tropical SE Pacific. Locally common. Adult
wing molt mainly Mar–Aug. Habits much like other white-faced storm-petrels; see p. 264.

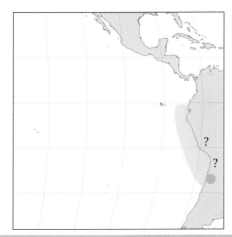

Hornby's Storm-Petrel

large, boldly patterned, and unmistakable storm-petrel of Humboldt Current

tail molt completing

note black cap and collar, dark underwings

Hornby's (Ringed) Storm-Petrel *Hydrobates hornbyi* 20–22cm, WS 48–51cm
Breeds (mainly Jan–Jul?) in Atacama Desert of n. Chile (first nest site discovered 2017; Barros et al. 2018) and perhaps Peru. Ranges off Peru and n. Chile (mostly 5–25°S), irregularly (Aug–Jan) n. to s. Ecuador; occurs mainly around and beyond the shelf break, not usually nearshore; locally fairly common. Adult wing molt mainly Jun–Dec, imm. wing molt mainly Mar–Sep. Associates readily with other storm-petrels, at times in rafts of 100s with Markham's, Black, and Peruvian Storm-Petrels. In calm to light winds, flight fairly steady and direct, with strong supple wingbeats and short glides; in stronger winds can bank and wheel in shallow arcs.

DARK STORM-PETRELS (11 species in 3 genera)

A group of very small to large northern storm-petrels comprising 8 species of *Hydrobates* (formerly *Oceanodroma*) and 2 species of *Halocyptena*, plus 1 southern species, Tasman Storm-Petrel (*Fregetta*). Polynesian Storm-Petrel also has a rare dark morph (see p. 263). All breed in the Pacific, with 2 migrating to the Indian Ocean and 1 of those occurring rarely in the Atlantic. Leach's and Townsend's are polymorphic (white-rumped forms on pp. 240–241), as is Tasman (p. 262).

Plumage dark overall, typically with variably paler upperwing bands, but lacking any bold white patches on rump or body. Most diverse in subtropical and temperate latitudes; a few species are long-distance migrants. Northern species are often gregarious, rafting locally and seasonally in groups of 1000s, when multiple species can occur together.

Can be considered in terms of Western Pacific and Eastern Pacific species. Species ID best based on a combination of size, structure (including bill shape, leg length), flight manner, plumage, and tail shape.

Western Pacific (and Indian Ocean)

Fork-tailed, p. 270

Tristram's, p. 277

Swinhoe's, p. 279
(also Indian Ocean and Atlantic)

Matsudaira's, p. 278
(also Indian Ocean)

Tasman, p. 262

Eastern Pacific

Fork-tailed, p. 270

Ashy, p. 271

Leach's complex
pp. 272–273

Least, p. 274

Black, p. 275

Markham's, p. 276

Dark storm-petrels gather locally and seasonally in large rafts, at times numbering 10,000 or more birds. This group in central California comprises mainly Ashy and Black Storm-Petrels—although other species are easily overlooked in these masses, which usually flush well before there is a chance to look through them carefully.

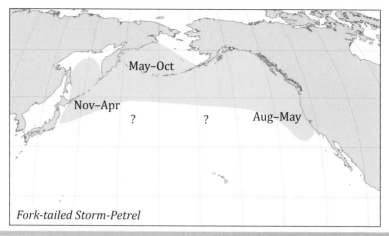

Fork-tailed Storm-Petrel

distinctive, heavy-bodied, dove-gray storm-petrel with black mask, black wing-linings

n. breeders average larger and paler, with whiter undertail coverts

with Ashy Storm-Petrels

Fork-tailed Storm-Petrel *Hydrobates furcatus* 20.5–24cm, WS 43–52cm
Breeds (mainly Apr–Aug in s. of range, Jun–Oct in n.) from s. Bering Sea s. to n. Japan and n. California; locally common. Ranges Mar–Oct in cooler shelf and shelf-break waters (mainly 45–55°N), moving s. and offshore Aug–May (mainly 35–50°N). Adult wing molt starts Jul/Sep, completes Dec/Apr; imm. wing molt spans May–Oct. Can be found in rafts of 100s, even 1000s, at times with other storm-petrel species. In calm to moderate winds, flight usually low and direct or slightly weaving with fairly quick, stiff, slightly fluttery wingbeats and short glides; in strong winds can whip around easily and wheel in fairly steep arcs, banking and sailing like a small gadfly petrel. Scavenges readily at fishing boats with fulmars, albatrosses, gulls, etc.

Ashy Storm-Petrel

medium-size, with long, deeply forked tail, fine bill; also see p. 273

strong steely-gray bloom
to fresh upperparts; worn
plumage much browner

heavily worn

pale underwing stripe variable, diagnostic when distinct

many late summer–fall birds
in obvious wing and tail molt

Ashy Storm-Petrel *Hydrobates homochroa* 18.5–19.5cm, WS 40–45cm; also see p. 273
California Current endemic; locally common. Breeds mainly late Apr–Nov from cen. California
s. to nw. Mexico. Ranges year-round off California and n. Baja California (where uncommon),
favoring shelf-break waters in summer–fall, more offshore waters in winter–spring. Adult wing
molt starts Aug/Sep, completes Jan/Mar; imm. wing molt spans May–Oct. Occurs locally in
rafts of 1000s in late summer–fall, often with other storm-petrel species (but rarely with Leach's,
which occurs farther offshore). In light to moderate winds, flight rather even-tempered and
direct with fairly steady, at times slightly fluttery wingbeats and short glides; in stronger winds
can bank and sail in low wheeling arcs. Feeds by pattering briefly or alighting on surface.

Leach's Storm-Petrel *(Hydrobates leucorhous)* **Complex** (also see pp. 237–241)
Comprises 3 cryptic, variably polymorphic species, 2 of which can be wholly dark-rumped:
Townsend's Storm-Petrel *H. socorroensis,* and the Chapman's race of Leach's Storm-Petrel *H. l.
chapmani,* both of which breed in summer in nw. Mexico.

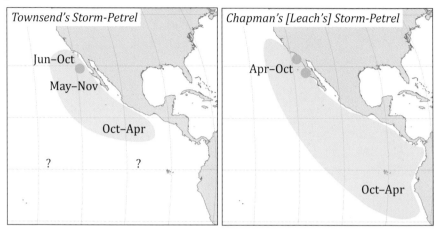

Townsend's Storm-Petrel

Jun–Oct
May–Nov
Oct–Apr
?   ?

Chapman's [Leach's] Storm-Petrel

Apr–Oct
Oct–Apr

*averages larger and longer-tailed than Townsend's, with more-pointed wings, deeper
tail fork, but many birds not safely identified at sea beyond 'dark Leach's complex'*

wing molt
(Dec)

Chapman's [Leach's] Storm-Petrel *Hydrobates leucorhous chapmani* 17.5–19.5cm, WS
44–48cm; also see p. 239–240
Breeds May–Oct on Coronados and San Benitos, and probably in small numbers n. to s. California, where intergrades with white-rumped Leach's; locally common. Ranges Apr–Oct off Baja
California and s. California, mainly over pelagic waters beyond the shelf break; non-breeding
range in tropical E Pacific (mainly 15°N–10°S; imms. year-round). Adult wing molt starts Aug/
Oct, completes Feb/Apr, imm. wing molt probably spans May–Dec. Habits much like Leach's
Storm-Petrel (p. 240) but flight averages a little weaker, less bounding, and thus more likely to
be confused with Ashy and Townsend's Storm-Petrels.

averages smaller, more compact than Chapman's with shorter tail, shallower tail fork

overcast skies

as on all storm-petrels, plumage
tones vary with lighting and wear

evening sun

Townsend's Storm-Petrel (dark-rumped) *Hydrobates socorroensis* 16.5–17.5cm, WS
41–45cm; also see pp. 239–241
Breeds May–Nov at Guadalupe I.; locally fairly common. Ranges May–Nov off Baja California and n. mainly Jun–Oct to s. California; favors pelagic waters beyond the continental shelf.
Non-breeding range (mainly Oct–Apr; imms. likely year-round) in subtropical and tropical E
Pacific, mainly 10–20°N. Adult wing molt probably starts Sep/Oct, completes Feb/Apr; imm.
wing molt likely starts Jun/Jul, completes Oct/Dec. Flight similar to Chapman's but often
steadier and less bounding, with deeper, fairly clipped wingbeats.

Ashy Storm-Petrel versus Chapman's [Leach's] Storm-Petrel

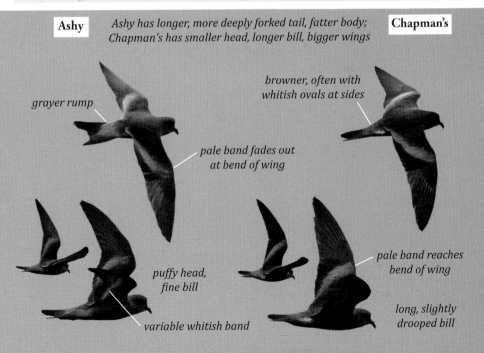

Ashy   Ashy has longer, more deeply forked tail, fatter body;   **Chapman's**
Chapman's has smaller head, longer bill, bigger wings

grayer rump

browner, often with
whitish ovals at sides

pale band fades out
at bend of wing

puffy head,
fine bill

pale band reaches
bend of wing

variable whitish band

long, slightly
drooped bill

tiny dark storm-petrel with tapered tail, fast flight; beware Ashy Storm-Petrel in tail molt

pale upperwing band usually rather dull

despite small size, like other Halocyptena *has big feet and relatively stout bill*

tail shorter in molt, can look 'sawn-off'

Least Storm-Petrel *Halocyptena microsoma* 13.5–15cm, WS 32–36cm
Breeds May/Jun–Aug/Sep in n. Gulf of California and late Jun/Jul–Sep/Oct on San Benitos; locally common. Variable numbers move n. Aug–Oct to s. California. Non-breeding range (mainly Oct–Apr, imms. year-round) in tropical E Pacific from Mexico to n. Peru. Favors inshore and shelf waters, uncommon far offshore. Adult wing molt spans Aug–May, 1st-year wing molt Mar–Sep. Often associates with Black and Wedge-rumped Storm-Petrels. Flight typically quick, often with a slightly side-to-side rocking cadence; wingbeats deep and slightly clipped (like a miniature Black Storm-Petrel) with little or no gliding; often dangles legs when feeding.

Black Storm-Petrel versus Markham's Storm-Petrel

These large dark storm-petrels co-occur in the tropical Eastern Pacific, although Black prefers inshore waters, Markham's warmer offshore waters. Traditionally they have been considered similar, yet they are distinct in structure and behavior and are placed in different genera.

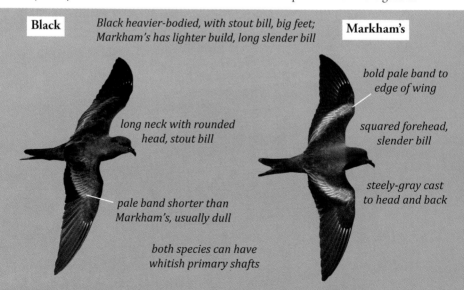

Black

Black heavier-bodied, with stout bill, big feet; Markham's has lighter build, long slender bill

Markham's

bold pale band to edge of wing

long neck with rounded head, stout bill

squared forehead, slender bill

steely-gray cast to head and back

pale band shorter than Markham's, usually dull

both species can have whitish primary shafts

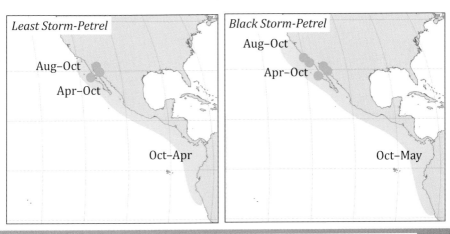

Least Storm-Petrel

Aug–Oct

Apr–Oct

Oct–Apr

Black Storm-Petrel

Aug–Oct

Apr–Oct

Oct–May

large dark storm-petrel with stout bill, big feet; big wings often make tail seem short

often holds head slightly raised, legs dangling

big feet

pale band does not reach edge of wing

sooty-brown plumage lacks steely-gray tones

Black Storm-Petrel *Halocyptena melania* 21.5–23cm, WS 50–55cm
Breeds mid-May/Jun–Aug/Oct in s. California and nw. Mexico; Apr–Aug in n. Gulf of California; locally common. Variable numbers move n. Aug–Oct to cen. California, rarely farther n. Non-breeding range (mainly Oct–May, imms. year-round) in tropical E Pacific from Mexico to Peru. Favors inshore and shelf waters, uncommon far offshore. Adult wing molt spans Aug–Apr, 1st-year wing molt May–Sep. Often with congeneric Least and Wedge-rumped Storm-Petrels off Middle America, and rafting with Ashy Storm-Petrels off cen. California. Flight typically powerful and unhurried, deep languid wingbeats interspersed with easy sailing glides; in strong winds, can wheel in fairly high arcs, similar to Leach's Storm-Petrel.

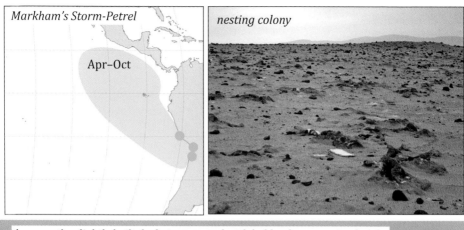

Markham's Storm-Petrel

Apr–Oct

nesting colony

large, rather lightly built dark storm-petrel with bold pale upperwing bands, long slender bill; deeply forked tail not contrastingly darker than rump

small feet rarely visible, cf. Black Storm-Petrel

often has white primary shafts

glides on arched wings

Markham's Storm-Petrel *Hydrobates markhami* 21–23cm, WS 49–54cm; also see p. 274
Breeds in Atacama Desert, mainly Jul–Feb in s. Peru and n. Chile; also Oct–May in Chile (status of seasonal populations unclear); locally common. Ranges year-round off Peru and n. Chile (mainly 5–25°S), mostly in pelagic waters past the cooler inshore zone, and thus only limited overlap with more nearshore Black Storm-Petrel. Ranges n. Apr–Oct to warmer waters well off Middle America. Wing molt may occur year-round. Flight generally fairly low and rather buoyant, with supple, fairly shallow wingbeats and easy glides on slightly arched wings; flight recalls Leach's in calm conditions, rather than very different typical flight of Black Storm-Petrel.

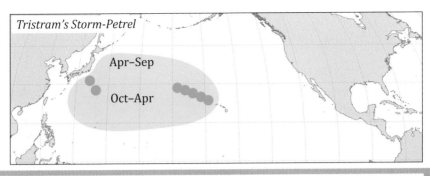

Tristram's Storm-Petrel

Apr–Sep

Oct–Apr

very large, heavy-bodied dark storm-petrel with deeply forked tail, bold pale upperwing bands, variably paler rump band; steely-gray sheen to head and back in fresh plumage

dark primary shafts can reflect silvery

fresh juv. Jul

'average' bill

Tristram's Storm-Petrel *Hydrobates tristrami* 24.5–27 cm, WS 52–57 cm
Breeds Dec–Jun on Bonins, Izu Is., and nw. Hawaiian Is.; locally fairly common. Ranges in subtropical NW Pacific, mostly 15–40°N. Adult wing molt mainly May–Oct; imm. wing molt likely Mar–Sep. Flight rather heavy-bodied, not buoyant, and can suggest a giant Fork-tailed Storm-Petrel: in light winds, flight rather low and direct with fairly quick, stiff wingbeats and short glides; in moderate to strong winds, sails and wheels easily on slightly crooked wings and can arc quite high and steeply, recalling a small gadfly petrel. Foraging birds often patter briefly and alight to feed, wings held slightly raised.

278

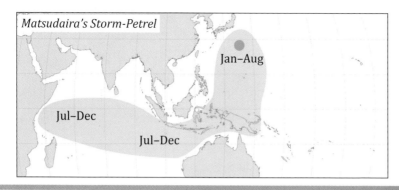

Matsudaira's Storm-Petrel

Jan–Aug

Jul–Dec

Jul–Dec

large, light-bodied, rather rangy dark storm-petrel with big wings, long forked tail, bold white primary flash, variable pale upperwing bands, relatively long bill

big wings, accentuated by long narrow tail, often create small-headed look

Matsudaira's Storm-Petrel *Hydrobates matsudairae* 24–26.5cm, WS 53–56cm
Breeds Jan–Jul on Volcano Is., possibly also on Bonins; ranges Jan–Aug in tropical W Pacific, migrating s. and w. to tropical Indian Ocean for non-breeding season (mainly Jul–Dec, imms. year-round). Status unclear in some non-breeding areas because of confusion with Swinhoe's Storm-Petrel. Adult wing molt mainly Jul–Dec; imm. wing molt may span Apr–Sep. Flight rather languid and often buoyant, sailing easily on broad, slightly cupped wings, long tail often held mostly closed (tip sometimes flexes); wingbeats typically measured and supple. In moderate to strong winds flies with prolonged, low-wavelength wheeling glides, unlike steeper wheeling of heavy-bodied Tristram's. Often follows ships. Foraging birds patter briefly and alight to feed, wings held slightly raised.

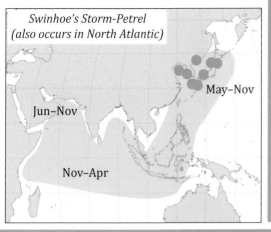

Swinhoe's Storm-Petrel
(also occurs in North Atlantic)

May–Nov

Jun–Nov

Nov–Apr

even in North Atlantic, some Leach's
(as above) can appear dark-rumped
in the field; note crooked wings (held
out straighter on Swinhoe's), flight
manner, lack of white primary shafts

medium-size, rather compact dark storm-petrel with forked tail, variable
white primary flash and pale upperwing bands, relatively stout bill

heavily worn
adult, Sep–Oct

1st-year completing
wing molt, Oct

Swinhoe's Storm-Petrel *Hydrobates monorhis* 18–20cm, WS 45–50cm
Breeds May–Nov on islands in Sea of Japan and Yellow Sea; locally fairly common. Ranges Apr–
Nov in tropical W Pacific, migrating s. and w. to tropical Indian Ocean for non-breeding season
(mainly Nov–Apr; imms. year-round); migrants regular off Singapore Apr–May and Sep–Nov.
Status unclear in some non-breeding areas because of confusion with Matsudaira's Storm-Petrel.
Rare presumed resident in N Atlantic, perhaps breeding on Macaronesian Is. Adult wing molt
mainly Oct–Apr; imm. wing molt likely spans Jun–Dec. Flight typically unhurried or languid,
recalling Band-rumped rather than Leach's; slightly stiff, loping wingbeats often suggest a larger
bird. Glides fairly buoyantly on slightly cupped wings, and wheels easily in moderate to strong
winds. Foraging birds often patter briefly, wings held slightly raised.

TROPICBIRDS (5 species in 1 genus)

Small family of spectacular, plunge-diving tropical seabirds. Overall white plumage and bright-colored bills suggest large terns, but tropicbirds differ in plumage patterns, tail shape, and behavior. ID at sea, especially for immatures, can be challenging when birds are high overhead (as is often the case), but with good views ID is relatively straightforward, and birds are often curious around boats.

Ages differ, with adult appearance attained in 2–3 years; sexes look alike. Wing molt mainly in non-breeding periods, and proceeds in 2–3 waves within the primaries. Feed by plunge diving, often from a fair height, entering the water with a tall splash that can suggest a whale blow. Tend to be sparsely distributed at sea, in ones and twos, and often apart from mixed-species feeding flocks; spend much time sitting on the water. Nest on the ground, on ledges, and in crevices, on predator-free islands and in steep cliffs. Aerial courtship flights of pairs or small groups are a conspicuous feature of nesting areas. Voices are largely unmusical chatters, screeches, and clucks, mainly uttered around breeding grounds or in interactions.

Red-tailed Tropicbird
p. 281

White-tailed Tropicbird Complex
pp. 282–283

Red-billed Tropicbird Complex
pp. 284–285

2nd-cycle

adult

juv.

adult has red bill, wire-like tail streamers

juv. has short tail tipped black, small black spots in wing-tip

largest tropicbird, with relatively broad wings, translucent white primaries; red tail streamers can be hard to see

adult with chick

juv. has dark gray bill, heavy black barring above

Red-tailed Tropicbird *Phaethon rubricauda* 43–48cm (+ streamers), WS 101–121cm Indo-Pacific. Breeds from tropical S Indian Ocean e. to Cen Pacific, locally in E Pacific off Mexico and Chile. Ranges widely in tropical waters, often far out to sea, and into subtropical N and E Pacific. Nests on ground under bushes and rubble, also on cliff ledges. Flight less hurried than other tropicbirds, and soars more readily on rather broad wings. Display flight involves pairs hovering fairly high overhead into the wind, one bird above the other before switching positions with a cycling progression; varied honking clucks can suggest geese. 2nd-cycle has orange-red bill; whitish to pinkish tail streamers shorter, less wire-like than adult.

White-tailed Tropicbird (*Phaethon lepturus*) Complex

Treated here as 2 species: Catesby's Tropicbird of Caribbean region, and widespread Yellow-billed Tropicbird, which may comprise further cryptic species. Smallest tropicbirds, with rather buoyant and graceful flight; wingbeats less hurried than larger species. Adults have long white tail streamers, bold black upperwing bar. Tail streamers, and sometimes much of plumage, can be suffused tawny or pinkish, most pronounced in some birds at Christmas Island, Indian Ocean. Nest typically in crevices in cliffs and among boulders.

juv. bill pinkish to yellowish, often tipped dark, back sparsely barred, short tail has small black subterminal spots

2nd-cycle has yellow to yellow-orange bill, scattered black bars above

longer than juv. Red-billed

white, cf. Red-billed

adult has orange bill, no black bars on back

overhead from Red-billed by broader white primary tips, translucent primary coverts

translucent

Catesby's Tropicbird *Phaethon [lepturus] catesbyi* 43–47cm (+ streamers), WS 93–103cm North Atlantic. Fairly common breeder locally on Bermuda and widely in Caribbean; ranges at sea in tropical N Atlantic, regularly May–Sep to waters off Mid-Atlantic US, and storm-driven to Atlantic Canada; vagrant to E Atlantic. Clucks and yelps lower than Yellow-billed.

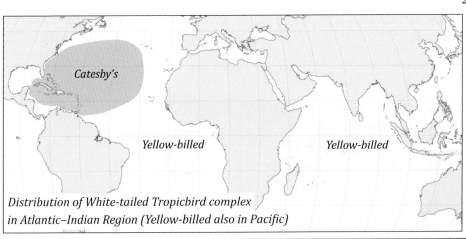

Distribution of White-tailed Tropicbird complex
in Atlantic–Indian Region (Yellow-billed also in Pacific)

Yellow-billed Tropicbird *Phaethon lepturus* 37–41cm (+ streamers), WS 86–95cm
Widespread. Breeds tropical S Atlantic; from tropical Indian Ocean e. to Cen Pacific; and in E
Pacific on Easter I. and Desventuradas, Chile. Ranges widely in tropical waters, often far out to
sea. Plumage progression parallels Catesby's. Sharp clucks and yelps, mainly in interactions.

284

Red-billed Tropicbird (*Phaethon aethereus*) Complex

Treated here as 2 species: Red-billed Tropicbird of tropical Atlantic and Eastern Pacific, Arabian Tropicbird of Northwest Indian Ocean. Medium-size tropicbirds with long white tail streamers; all ages have blackish barring on upperparts, black wedge on primary coverts. Nest typically in crevices in cliffs and among boulders.

adults

heavy-bodied tropicbird with barred upperparts, long black mask

opaque

narrow white tips, cf. Catesby's

adults

diagnostic black wedge, cf. Catesby's and Yellow-billed

juv. has yellowish bill, short tail tipped black

older 1st-cycle

adult has solidly bright red bill

from white-tailed tropicbirds by longer black mask, heavier bill

Red-billed Tropicbird *Phaethon aethereus* 43–50cm (+ streamers), WS 97–110cm
Americas and Atlantic. Breeds locally in E Pacific from nw. Mexico s. to n. Chile, and on Galapagos; in Atlantic region locally from Caribbean s. to Brazil, and on Cape Verdes, Ascension, and St. Helena. Ranges mainly over shelf waters and not as far out to sea as Red-tailed and white-tailed tropicbirds; regular n. in summer–fall to s. California and in spring–fall n. to e. US. Screechy and rasping chatters mainly given in aerial chases near nesting grounds.

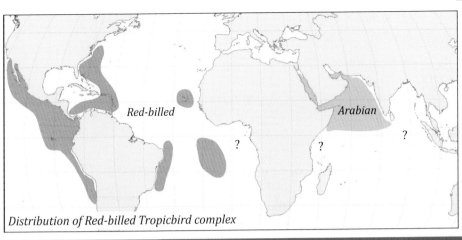

Distribution of Red-billed Tropicbird complex

averages smaller and shorter-tailed than Red-billed, with smaller black mask, blackish cutting edges to bill

adult bill red with black 'lips' and tip

adults

Arabian   Yellow-billed

juv. has yellowish bill, short tail tipped black

barring sparser than Red-billed, but black covert bar bolder; cf. Yellow-billed Tropicbird

Arabian Tropicbird *Phaethon [aethereus] indicus* 40–45cm (+ streamers), WS 90–100cm
Northwest Indian Ocean. Breeds locally on coasts and islands of Arabian Peninsula. At-sea distribution not well known; ranges regularly e. to Sri Lanka (mainly May–Oct); vagrant to NW Australia. Habits much like Red-billed Tropicbird; can be seen in spring–summer from clifftop sites in s. and e. Arabian Peninsula. Voice higher and shriekier than Red-billed, less rasping. Imm. plumages probably parallel Red-billed; note diagnostic black 'lips' even on juv.

FRIGATEBIRDS (5+ species in 1 genus)

Very large, spectacular, light-bodied seabirds of tropical oceans: 3 species widespread, 2 very local, breeding only on single islands. All species have long crooked wings and long, deeply forked tails (often held closed in a point); adult males have inflatable red throat balloons. Plumage predominantly black, with varying degrees of white or rusty depending on species, age, and sex. Adult plumage probably attained in 6–10 years; imm. plumage progressions complex, not well known (for details see Howell 1994, James 2004, Walbridge et al. 2003). Adult female plumages are often the most distinctive, shown opposite.

Frigates soar easily and often high, remaining aloft for days at a time and hanging effortlessly in updrafts over ships. Can range widely, but only exceptionally alight on the sea; typically roost on bushes, trees, cliffs, and human-made structures, including ship rigging. Build stick platform nests mainly in bushes and trees; 1–2 eggs laid. Feed on fish and other marine organisms snatched from near sea surface, and by pirating other seabirds, especially boobies, tropicbirds, and terns. Warbling, chippering, and wheezing calls, plus bill rattling, given mainly on or near breeding grounds.

Great and Lesser exhibit noticeable geographic variation, with species status proposed recently for Lessers breeding on Trindade I., in South Atlantic. Has also been suggested that Galapagos population of Magnificent may represent a cryptic species, averaging larger than mainland populations.

female Great Frigatebird chasing Yellow-billed Tropicbird, Indian Ocean

Magnificent
pp. 288–289

Great
pp. 289–290

Lesser complex
p. 291

Christmas, p. 292

Ascension, p. 293

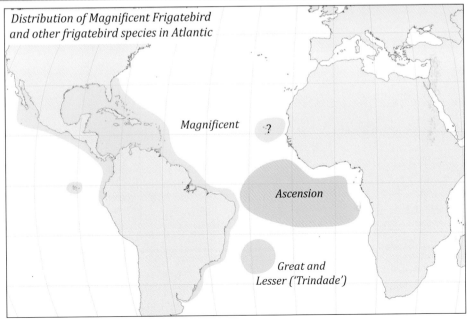

Distribution of Magnificent Frigatebird and other frigatebird species in Atlantic

Magnificent

?

Ascension

Great and
Lesser ('Trindade')

Americas and Atlantic

adult male glossy black overall;
no pale alar bar or armpit scallops

subadult male

adult female has black hood, white chest,
blue-gray bill, blue eyering

subadult female

juv. has white head, chest, and
diamond-shaped belly patch

Magnificent Frigatebird *Fregata magnificens* 90–110cm, WS 200–240cm
Americas and Atlantic. Mainly coastal and inshore, over shelf waters. Locally fairly common
to common along warm-water tropical coasts of the Americas, from nw. Mexico s. to n. Peru,
from se. US s. to Brazil; disjunct populations on Galapagos and (at least formerly) in E Atlantic
on Cape Verdes. Only real ID concern is separation from slightly smaller and stockier Great
Frigatebird, only exceptionally seen along mainland coasts (see adult and imm. comparisons
opposite); juv. Great has gingery head and breast (fading to whitish), rounded white belly patch.

Magnificent Frigatebird versus Great Frigatebird (Eastern Pacific)

frigates often roost on rocky islets; these 3 adult females comprise 2 Magnificent (black hood, blue eyering) and a Great (gray throat, red eyering, pinkish bill)

Magnificent

back plumes coppery, vs. glossy green on Great

paler alar bar **Great**

adult males of all species have inflatable red balloon pouches

pale scalloping

imm. plumages can be very similar; rear of white belly patch broader and often more rounded on Great, which often has rusty smudges on head and chest

early 2nd-cycle

early 3rd-cycle

Magnificent

Great

290

Pacific and Indian Oceans

adult male glossy black overall with pale armpit scallops, pale alar bar

subadult male

adult female has gray throat, white chest; bill blue-gray to pink; eyering red except W and Cen S Pacific, where bluish

2nd-cycle

juv. has rusty head and breast (soon fading to whitish), white belly; some have white armpit tabs

Great Frigatebird *Fregata minor* 82–100cm, WS 190–225cm; also see pp. 287, 289
Widespread, but mainly oceanic; not seen from mainland coasts. Locally fairly common in tropical S Indian Ocean and tropical Pacific; isolated small population in S Atlantic off Brazil. Ranges in tropical oceans, often far out to sea. Occurs widely alongside appreciably smaller and more lightly built Lesser Frigatebird: adults distinctive, but imm. plumages can be very similar: juv. Lesser typically has a more triangular white belly patch, extending out as armpit tabs from the leading edge (Great can have white tabs, but belly patch more rounded); subsequent imm. plumages of Lesser best told by white armpit tabs (lacking in post-juvenile Great), smaller overall size. Cf. Magnificent Frigatebird (inshore, Americas; pp. 288–289).

Cen Pacific to Indian Ocean

adult male glossy black overall with white armpit tabs, pale alar bar

female eyering red

adult female has black head, white hindcollar; bill blue-gray to pink

2nd-cycle

juv. has rusty head and breast, white belly and armpit tabs

Lesser Frigatebird (*Fregata ariel*) **Complex** 70–80cm, WS 175–190cm; also see p. 287 Indo-Pacific. Locally fairly common in equatorial and s. tropical latitudes from Indian Ocean e. to Cen Pacific; ranges into tropical NW Pacific, mainly summer–fall. Ranges in tropical oceans, often far out to sea. Small size apparent when seen with other species; adult male and female distinctive, juv. and subsequent imm. plumages can be confused with Great Frigatebird and very local Christmas Frigatebird; see those species for details.

Relict population of Lesser Frigatebird in S Atlantic recently proposed to be a distinct species, **Trindade Frigatebird** *F. trinitatis* (Olson 2017); ID criteria for this enigmatic and highly endangered taxon await elucidation; most if not all plumages resemble Indo-Pacific Lesser.

very local in E Indian Ocean; relatively large and long-billed

adult male has white belly patch, pale alar bands, shaggy crest; white armpit patches often absent

adult female has black hood, white body, pink bill

white belly, unlike Lesser

juv. has rusty head and breast, white belly and armpit tabs

Christmas Frigatebird *Fregata andrewsi* 95–110cm, WS 200–240cm
East Indian Ocean. Fairly common breeder on Christmas I., with population of about 5000–10,000 birds. At-sea distribution not well known, but ranges over tropical seas n. to Gulf of Thailand and through w. Indonesia, n. to South China Sea. Can be found roosting on offshore islets with appreciably smaller Lesser Frigatebird. Adults distinctive; juv. has larger white belly patch than Lesser with white armpit tabs positioned slightly differently (but beware angle of viewing). 2nd-cycle typically has black patches at sides of chest (lacking on Lesser and Great).

very local in equatorial Atlantic

subadult male, dark morph

adult male glossy black overall, or with big white body patch

dark morphs

light morphs

adult female has wide brownish collar, lacks red throat pouch

subadult female, dark morph

juv. has white head and body, pinkish bill tip; broad dark chest band can be broken

2nd-cycle, dark morph

Ascension Frigatebird *Fregata aquila* 87–97cm, WS 195-215cm; also see p. 287
Equatorial Atlantic. Fairly common breeder at Ascension I., with population of about 25,000–
32,000 birds. Ranges over adjacent tropical seas, rarely e. to Gulf of Guinea. No other frigatebird species normally occurs in its range. Adult of both sexes dimorphic (dark morph common,
light uncommon); light morphs and dark female distinctive if seen well; dark male perhaps
indistinguishable in field from adult male Magnificent. Imm. plumage progression undescribed.
Dark subadult has variable white armpit patches, cf. Lesser Frigatebird complex (p. 291).

GANNETS AND BOOBIES (12 species in 3 genera)

Well-defined family of large, streamlined, plunge-diving seabirds comprising 3 gannets in cooler temperate waters, 9 boobies in warmer tropical waters. Often known as sulids for their scientific family name, Sulidae. Field ID can be challenging, and not always possible for some immatures, although in most cases similar species do not overlap in range.

Ages differ, with adult appearance attained in 3–4 years for most species; sexes similar in most species. Wing molt mainly in non-breeding periods, and proceeds in 2–4 waves within the primaries. Feed by plunge diving for fish and squid, often from a fair height, and some species enter the water with a tall splash that can suggest a whale blow. Some tropical species strongly attracted to ships, which flush prey such as flyingfish. Gannets often scavenge around fishing boats, and several boobies (particularly Red-footed) often rest on ships. Nest on the ground, on ledges, and, for Red-footed and Abbott's Boobies, in trees and bushes. Voices are largely unmusical grunts and brays, but in most boobies the adult male utters high, wheezy whistles, vs. brays and grunts of adult female.

For ID purposes, can be considered in 2 groups: **gannets** (3 species in genus *Morus*), and **boobies** (9 species in genera *Papasula* and *Sula*). Gannets have tapered gapes, lack naked throat areas (useful for cooling) of warm-water boobies.

Red-footed Booby in pursuit of flyingfish

Gannets
pp. 296–299

Boobies
pp. 299–307

Papasula, p. 299

Sula
pp. 300–307

296

GANNETS (3 species in 1 genus)

Large, heavily built sulids of colder-water environments; species readily identified by range. Imm. plumages highly variable, with complex progression to adult plumage in 3–4 years; sexes similar. Nest on ground, usually in dense colonies on flat-topped or gently sloping rocky islands and stacks. Feed mainly over shelf and inshore waters, often in aggregations, at times of 100s or even 1000s around fishing vessels with gulls, albatrosses, and other scavengers. Readily seen from shore, especially in windy weather.

imm. plumages highly variable, see opposite

juv./1st-winter gray-brown overall, with dark underwings, variable white spotting above

adult has white tail and secondaries, 3+ waves of primary molt

Northern Gannet *Morus bassanus* 82–94cm, WS 175–200cm

North Atlantic. Breeds locally Mar–Oct in Atlantic Canada and from Iceland and n. Norway s. to nw. France. Fairly common to locally common at sea in N Atlantic, in summer mainly n. of 45°N, in winter s. to Gulf of Mexico, w. Mediterranean, and NW Africa (mainly imms.), to around 10°N. Distinctive in range, but cf. Masked Booby. Juv. probably not safely separable at sea from Cape Gannet, unless long throat line of Cape can be seen; older imm. and adult Northern attain white secondaries and tail feathers, short throat line visible on white head.

Molt and Age in Northern Gannet

Wing molt in sulids proceeds in waves through the primaries. In Northern Gannet, 1st wave starts with innermost primary in Feb–May, about 6–8 months after fledging, completes in Sep–Feb, 12–18 months after fledging; 2nd wave starts Aug–Sep, 11–12 months after fledging and before 1st wave has finished; 2nd wave typically suspends mid-winter, completes Aug–Feb in 3rd winter; subsequent wing molt typically spans Aug–Feb. Adults replace all primaries via 3–4 concurrent waves of molt, often p1–p3, p4–p7, and p8–10. First head/body/tail molt of Northern Gannet starts mid–late 1st winter, completes Dec–Feb of 2nd winter.

2nd-cycle

throat line

adults

juvs.

Cape Gannet *Morus capensis* 85–93cm, WS 175–195cm
Southern Africa. Locally common, breeding Oct–Mar along coasts of Namibia and South Africa, ranging at sea in cool waters of Benguela and Agulhas Currents; imms. range farther, n. to Gulf of Guinea and around Cape into Indian Ocean, n. to Mozambique; vagrant e. to Amsterdam I. and Australia, w. to South America. Distinctive in range. Juv. has darker underwings than Australasian Gannet; older imms. and adult have diagnostic black throat line (can be hard to see); adult Cape has wholly to mostly black tail, vs. mostly white in Australasian.

juvs.

adults

colony

Australasian Gannet *Morus serrator* 84–92cm, WS 170–190cm
Australian region. Locally common, breeding Aug–Mar from SE Australia to New Zealand, ranging at sea in cooler waters of Tasman Sea and w. to SW Australia; vagrant w. to Marion I. and South Africa. Distinctive in range. Juv. Australasian paler overall, with whiter underwings than Cape and Northern Gannets; adult Australasian has 2–4 black central tail feathers.

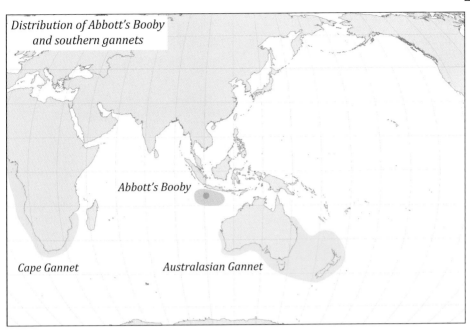

Distribution of Abbott's Booby and southern gannets

Abbott's Booby

Cape Gannet

Australasian Gannet

very local but distinctive sulid of E Indian Ocean; upperwings black overall, center of back white

adult male and juv. bill blue-gray, tipped black

adults

adult female bill pink, tipped black

Abbott's Booby *Papasula abbotti* 79–85cm, WS 160–180cm
Very local in East Indian Ocean. Breeds (mainly Jun–Mar) on Christmas I., with population of about 9000 birds. Nests in canopy of emergent trees on plateau and higher slopes of island. Ranges at sea in surrounding waters and n. to Java. Behavior at sea not well known, perhaps similar to other tropical boobies. Juv. resembles adult, with bill like adult male.

300

BOOBIES (9 species in 2 genera; Abbott's Booby on p. 299)

Smaller and more lightly built sulids of warmer waters, with multiple species occurring together in several areas (but rarely more than 3 species nesting on the same island). ID can be challenging, and not always possible in the field for some imms. Most species attain adult plumage in 2–3 years, but in Abbott's Booby juv. resembles adult male; sexes alike or slightly different. Feed from coastal waters to far offshore, varying with species; often in mixed-species feeding flocks with terns, shearwaters, and frigatebirds in tropical regions, or with cormorants, pelicans, and gulls in subtropical regions. Several species accompany ships at sea. Most species nest on ground, but Abbott's and Red-footed build stick nests in trees and bushes.

widespread, offshore; adult plumages highly variable: body brownish or white, tail dark or white; feet red

adult variation

face and bill colors brightest on breeding birds

Red-footed Booby *Sula sula* 66–76cm, WS 130–150cm

Widespread; rarely seen from shore. Fairly common in tropical Indian and Pacific Oceans; local and less numerous in Atlantic region, mainly in s. Caribbean; also small numbers breed Ascension I. Ranges far out to sea and perches readily on ships. Smallest, most lightly built booby, with crooked wings and very long tail; more agile than other boobies, often catches flyingfish in the air. Both sexes utter guttural brays and chatters. Plumage variation complex, with different morphs predominant in different regions, e.g., black-tailed white morph only in E Pacific.

Red-footed Booby continued (immatures)

1st-cycle of all morphs brown overall, underwings darker than body; often has narrow dark breast band, tail usually tipped white

juv. bill dark gray, becoming pinkish with dark tip

fresh juv.

1st-cycle

2nd-cycle

pale

less crooked wings

Brewster's Brown 1st-cycle

Red-footed 1st-cycle

3rd-cycle attains adult face and bill colors

Comparison of Red-footed and other boobies

note distinctive bill and face colors

Red-footed 1st-cycle

Brewster's Brown female

Nazca 1st-cycle

Blue-footed 1st-cycle

white adult Red-footed (left) shows much less black than adult Masked (right) or Nazca, and most have white tail (black only in E Pacific)

Brown Booby (*Sula leucogaster*) Complex

Treated here as 3 species with distinct geographic ranges. Medium-size, 'generic' boobies with widespread distribution. Ages differ, attaining adult plumage in 2–3 years; adult sexes differ in head and bill patterns, also separable by voice: males whistle, females bray. Feed mainly over shelf waters and along coasts; often seen from shore; dives tend to be shallow angle, not steep from appreciable heights (unlike Blue-footed and Masked Boobies). Mostly return to land for roosting, although also perch and roost readily on fishing boats, harbor markers, jetties. Often nest on steeper and more broken ground than other boobies.

tropical Eastern Pacific

2nd-cycle female

female face pale yellow, bill pinkish

1st-cycle

adults

juv.

variable contrast

juv. body darker than wing linings, feet yellowish to pink, cf. Red-footed

male face dark slaty bluish to blue-green, bill ivory pinkish

female

pale-hooded male

Brewster's Brown Booby *Sula [leucogaster] brewsteri* 68–75cm, WS 135–153cm

Tropical Eastern Pacific. Fairly common to common, locally from Gulf of California s. to Colombia, very rarely s. to Peru; small numbers increasingly n. to California and w. into E Cen Pacific (Hawaii, Palmyra); absent from Galapagos. Averages smaller and more slender-billed than other brown boobies, with slightly paler upperparts; white underwing panel of adult reduced, with dark bar on lesser coverts; adult male crown pale milky (most extensive on s. populations, often including much of neck), usually evident by 2nd cycle.

tropical Atlantic

2nd-cycle male

female face yellow, bill pinkish

subtle contrast

adults

male face yellow with bluish eyering, bill grayish green

1st-cycle throat brighter yellow than other brown boobies

Atlantic Brown Booby *Sula [leucogaster] leucogaster* 68–75cm, WS 135–153cm
Tropical Atlantic. Fairly common locally from e. Gulf of Mexico and Caribbean s. to Brazil; also breeds on Cape Verdes, Ascension, St. Helena, and in Gulf of Guinea. Head and neck slightly darker brown than back, even apparent on some juvs.; white underwing panel of adult has short or no dark bar on lesser coverts.

tropical Indo-Pacific

female face yellow, bill pale greenish

adults

variable contrast, as on other brown boobies

1st-cycle

male face blue, bill yellow

Indo-Pacific Brown Booby *Sula [leucogaster] plotus* 68–75cm, WS 135–153cm
Tropical Indo-Pacific. Fairly common locally from Red Sea and tropical Indian Ocean e. to Cen Pacific; vagrant to islands off w. Mexico. Averages larger and stouter-billed than Brewster's, with larger and cleaner white underwing panel, darker upperparts; adult male has dark brown head and neck.

E Pacific, usually inshore: all ages have dusky neck contrasting with white body; white tail base and center; rather slender gray bill

juv. head and neck brown, soon attaining white streaks

juvs./ 1st-cycle

adults

1st/2nd -cycle

Blue-footed 1st-cycle

Nazca 1st-cycle

note yellowish bill, dark face, whiter underwings of Nazca

adult has white back barring, white nape and rump band

white on adult back variable

1st-cycle with 1st-cycle Brewster's Brown

adult

Blue-footed Booby *Sula nebouxii* 71–79cm, WS 148–166cm; also see p. 301

Eastern Pacific. Fairly common to common in Gulf of California, Gulf of Fonseca, and from Panama s. to n. Peru; also common locally on Galapagos. Ranges in smaller numbers elsewhere along Pacific coast from nw. Mexico s. to n. Chile; associates with Peruvian Booby and Brewster's Brown Booby. Sexes look similar but males whistle, females bray. Mainly inshore (unlikely to be seen far offshore) and often seen from land, regularly in flocks; dives tend to be steep and from high up, unlike Brewster's Brown. Nests on fairly flat ground on rocky islands and stacks.

Humboldt Current, usually inshore; distinctive

adult striking, with clean white head and neck, dark face, scalloped white barring above

juvs.

juv. has dusky head and underparts, dark brown rump and tail, cf. Blue-footed

adults

1st-cycle

attains white head and neck in about 6–9 months

adult has variable white in tail

juvs. with adult

adult has red eyes

Peruvian Booby *Sula variegata* 70–75cm, WS 138–153cm

Humboldt Current. Locally common, breeding from Peru s. to n. Chile. Ranges along coasts and over shelf waters n. to s. Ecuador, s. to Gulf of Ancud, Chile; often seen from shore and readily enters harbors and estuaries. Sexes look alike, but males whistle, females bray. Sometimes in large numbers, with mixed-species feeding flocks of Guanay Shags, Peruvian Pelicans, Inca Terns, and other species. Nests on fairly flat ground on rocky islands.

Masked Booby (*Sula dactylatra*) Complex

Treated here as 2 species, although populations of n. Tasman Sea (with dark-eyed adults) have been considered distinct, as Tasman Booby *S. tasmani*. Largest and most heavily built boobies. Ages differ, attaining adult plumage in 2–3 years; sexes look alike, but males whistle, females bray. Feed mainly offshore and not often seen from mainland; at sea found singly or in small groups, which associate readily with mixed-species feeding flocks of terns, shearwaters, and other boobies. Typically dive from fairly high up; often accompany ships, at times chasing flying-fish. Nest on barren open ground, Masked mainly on flat or gently sloping terrain, Nazca more often on slopes and broken ground.

juv. has brown head and neck, variable white above: soon attains white on head, back, wing coverts

in all ages note yellowish bill, dark face, black tail (rarely some white at base on adults)

adult bill rich yellow to pale yellowish

mostly white

1st-cycle

white hindcollar typical

adults

juvs.

Tasman   west Mexico

black tail cf. Nazca

2nd-cycle

clean white cf. Nazca

'Tasman Booby' adult dark-eyed

Masked Booby *Sula dactylatra* 73–81cm, WS 150–170cm; also see p. 301
Widespread. Fairly common to locally common in tropical Indian and Pacific Oceans, ranging into subtropical latitudes of Pacific; absent from Galapagos, but ranges widely at sea in E Pacific and breeds on islands off Mexico and Chile, n. and s. of range of Nazca Booby. Fairly common locally in e. Gulf of Mexico and Caribbean; also breeds Ascension and St. Helena. '**Tasman Booby**' breeds Lord Howe, Norfolk I., and Kermadecs, ranges in Tasman Sea region; adult has dark eyes (pale yellow on Masked elsewhere); imm. plumages not studied relative to Masked.

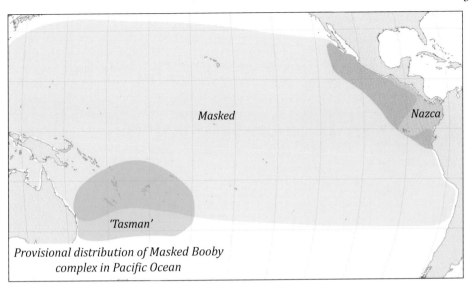

Provisional distribution of Masked Booby
complex in Pacific Ocean

Masked

Nazca

'Tasman'

adult and older imms. from Masked Booby by bill color, but a few
birds intermediate; Nazca usually has much white on central tail

black markings
average heavier
than Masked

adult bill orange
to pinkish orange

shorter neck
'sock' than
Brown Boobies

2nd-cycle

1st-cycle

juvs.

white, cf.
Masked

adult

juv. lacks bold white hindcollar
of most juv. Masked

dark 'shawl'
typical, unlike
Masked

juv. not safely told from darker examples of E Pacific Masked;
distinguishable when develops adult bill colors in 2nd cycle

older
2nd-cycle

Nazca Booby *Sula [dactylatra] granti* 73–81cm, WS 150–170cm; also see p. 301
Tropical Eastern Pacific. Replaces Masked Booby in Galapagos, where common; small numbers
breed n. locally to islands off nw. Mexico and s. to n. Peru. Fairly common in tropical waters n.
to Mexico, where tends to favor shelf waters (vs. more oceanic waters favored by Masked); both
species can be seen from mainland on occasion. Plumage sequences parallel Masked Booby.

SKUAS AND JAEGERS (10 species in 2 genera)

Small family of rather gull-like, predatory seabirds with white wing flashes. Comprise 7 skuas (genus *Catharacta*, breeding mostly at high latitudes in the S Hemisphere, with an outlier in the N Atlantic) and 3 jaegers (*Stercorarius*, breeding on Arctic tundra and wintering at sea); jaegers are also called skuas in much of the Old World. Some authors treat all species in genus *Stercorarius*. South Polar Skua and jaegers are long-distance migrants; other skuas are mostly resident to medium-distance migrants. Field ID often challenging, and many skuas not safely identified to species in the field, a problem compounded by hybridization between some species along with poorly understood immature plumages.

Ages differ slightly (skuas) to strongly (jaegers), and sexes mostly similar, with females averaging larger than males. Adult appearance attained in about 3 years. Wing molt mainly in non-breeding periods (start overlaps with end of breeding in a few species); molt timing can be useful for ID of skua species when combined with age. Flight strong and often fast; feed by pirating other seabirds (mainly shearwaters, storm-petrels, terns, and gulls; also sulids and albatrosses); larger species also scavenge at fishing boats and garbage dumps. Nest in scattered pairs or loose colonies on open ground. Voices are largely unmusical brays, clucks, and mewing whistles, mainly given on nesting grounds and in interactions.

For ID purposes, can be divided into 2 groups: **skuas** (7 larger species in genus *Catharacta*) and **jaegers** (3 smaller species in genus *Stercorarius*).

Skuas
pp. 309–316

Jaegers
pp. 317–321

SKUAS (7 species in 1 genus)

Heavyset, predatory seabirds. Species-level taxonomy vexed. Adult plumages variable, but differ slightly to distinctly between taxa. For species ID check plumage color and pattern, especially on head, neck, back, underwing coverts; awareness of molt timing and age also useful; with experience, structure can be helpful, but hybrids confound ID in some southern species.

Molt and Age. Molts and plumages of Great and South Polar Skuas clarified recently (Newell et al. 2013), but other skuas unstudied. In particular, appearance of birds 1–2 years of age poorly known, as these ages mostly remain at sea. Within a species, 1st-year wing molt differs in timing from older ages: all species appear to have complete molt in 1st year, starting within 6 months of fledging; after this, adult molt cycle begins, with complete prebasic molt after breeding season (start of wing molt can overlap with end of breeding, at least in shorter-distance migrants). Molt of head and neck feathers before breeding may be end of protracted prebasic molt or separate partial molt. Juvs. have uniform fresh plumage, no tail projections, whitish leg blotches (small whitish spots can be retained into 2nd year); subsequent ages have 'messier' plumage, often with different generations of upperwing coverts, and short, blunt, central tail projections.

Hybrids. Subantarctic Skua and South Polar Skua hybridize on the Antarctic Peninsula: 10–16% of pairs in several areas are mixed, and overall about 2% of all breeding skuas on Antarctic Peninsula involve mixed pairs (Parmelee 1988, Ritz et al. 2006). Falkland and Chilean Skuas hybridize along coast of Argentina (Devillers 1978); Chilean Skua and South Polar Skua have hybridized (Reinhardt et al. 1997); but no interbreeding reported among taxa within Brown Skua complex.

Female Subantarctic Skua (left) and male presumed hybrid Subantarctic × South Polar Skua (right). ID of these species is complicated by hybrids, which often resemble Subantarctic Skua in plumage. Most hybrid pairs involve female Subantarctic Skuas mated to male South Polar Skuas. Petermann Is., Antarctic Peninsula, 15 Dec 1994.

310

overall warm-toned; adults have variable buff and rusty spots and streaks on body and wing coverts, often dark-capped; juvs. plainer, usually with darker hood

adults

brighter juv.

plainer than adult

darker juv.

dark hood, cf. adult

juv. has warm, paler edgings above, unlike imm. South Polar

1st-years completing wing molt, Aug

juv., Oct

bleached adult, Oct

Great Skua (Bonxie) *Catharacta skua* 53–61cm, WS 127–146cm

North Atlantic. Breeds May–early Sep on tundra in Iceland, Faeroes, and n. Scotland, with recent spread n. to Norway, Svalbard, Jan Mayen. Winters in N and equatorial Atlantic: adults mainly from seas near s. breeding areas s. to e. US and SW Europe; imms. range farther s., reaching n. Brazil, W Africa, and Mediterranean, and also summer off s. Greenland and Atlantic Canada. Migrants regularly seen from shore in NW Europe, mainly in windy conditions, but only exceptionally from shore in N America. Adult wing molt starts Aug/Oct, ends Jan/Apr; 1st-year wing molt starts Feb/Apr, ends Jul/Sep, followed by 2nd prebasic molt starting Sep/Oct, ending Mar/May. Adult distinctive, but juv. and imm. can be confused with South Polar Skua.

+ 1

light morph adult, Feb

1st-year, Oct

darker 2nd-year, Oct

worn adult, May

overall rather plain and cold-toned; adults vary from dark to blond, often with paler hindneck

fresh subadult, Oct

bleached 1st-year, Aug

bleached adult, Jun

fresh juv., Mar

darker adult, worn plumage, Jun

South Polar Skua *Catharacta maccormicki* 51–58cm, WS 131–148cm
Widespread; transequatorial migrant. Breeds mid-Nov to Mar around Antarctica, mainly in Ross Sea region (light morphs common) and Antarctic Peninsula (light morphs rare). Hybridizes with Subantarctic Skua on Antarctic Peninsula. Migrates n. Mar–Oct (stragglers to Dec or later in tropical waters) to N Pacific, N Atlantic, and Indian Oceans. Most migrate in clockwise loop, n. through w. oceans (reaching Japan and e. US in May) and s. through e. oceans (main numbers off w. US and NW Africa in Aug–Oct). Birds from Antarctic Peninsula (perhaps including some hybrids) migrate to N Pacific, as well as to N Atlantic. Only exceptionally seen from shore n. of breeding grounds. Adult wing molt starts Apr/Jun, ends Aug/Oct; 1st-year wing molt starts Jul/Sep, ends late Nov/Feb; 2nd prebasic molt starts May/Jun, ends Sep/Nov.

Brown Skua (*Catharacta antarctica*) Complex

Provisionally treated here as 4 largely allopatric species, but critical taxonomic study needed. Breeding overlap (and intergrading?) between Chatham Skua and Subantarctic Skua may occur in the under-studied New Zealand subantarctic islands.

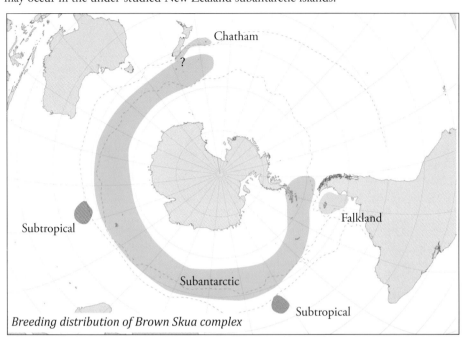

Breeding distribution of Brown Skua complex

Tristan adult

Gough
St. Paul

Gough adults

adults

relatively long-billed and long-legged;
adult variably spotted golden and buff

Subtropical [Brown] Skua *Catharacta [antarctica] hamiltoni* 54–61cm, WS 129–145cm
Breeds (mainly Sep–Jan) on Tristan, Gough, and Amsterdam/St. Paul. Ranges in S Atlantic
mainly 35–45°S; Indian Ocean range not well known. Appears somewhat intermediate between
Falkland and Subantarctic Skuas. Adult wing molt starts Dec/Jan, likely completes Apr/Jun;
imm. wing molt timings need study.

relatively small and small-billed; adult
typically has dark cap, pale neck streaking

imm. (2nd-year?)

adults

adult (juv. behind)

Falkland [Brown] Skua *Catharacta [antarctica] antarctica* 53–60cm, WS 124–138cm
Fairly common breeder late Nov–Mar locally on Falklands; also a few pairs locally on coast of
Argentina (45–47°S), where hybridizes with Chilean Skua. Ranges in S Atlantic, adults mainly
40–55°S, imms. n. to around 20°S off Brazil. Wing molt timings not well known.

plumage tones vary with lighting

many adults rather dark-hooded

adults

broader-winged than South Polar, with shorter tail projections

relatively large and bulky; adult back mottled whitish to buff, forming variable pale saddle

possible subadult

pre-breeding imms. often loaf in 'clubs'

juv. variably warm-toned

adult

Subantarctic [Brown] Skua *Catharacta [antarctica] lonnbergi* 58–66cm, WS 130–155cm
Breeds late Oct–Mar on subantarctic islands from Diego Ramírez Is. e. to New Zealand; also on n. Antarctic Peninsula (where hybridizes with South Polar Skua). Non-breeding range (Mar–Oct; some imms. year-round) mainly 30–60°S, from S Atlantic e. to SW Pacific, n. to S Australia, S Africa, and tropical Indian Ocean; unrecorded Humboldt Current region. Adult wing molt starts Feb/May, completes Jul/Oct; 1st-year wing molt starts Jul/Sep, completes Dec/Apr.

adult relatively plain, with little or no whitish mottling on back; hindneck often contrastingly pale; cf. South Polar Skua

adults

juv.

Chatham [Brown] Skua *Catharacta [antarctica]* undescribed; also see p. 19
New Zealand. Breeds mid-Sep to Feb, locally on Chathams, Snares, and other islands off s. South Island, New Zealand. Most adults remain year-round at breeding islands; imms. may range farther at sea. Breeds cooperatively in trios much more frequently than other skuas. Adult wing molt starts Dec/Jan, likely completes May/Jun; imm. wing molts undescribed.

South Georgia, 1 Apr

at sea n. of Falklands, 5 Mar

Whitish leg patches and relatively fresh primaries on this date indicate a 1st- or perhaps 2nd-year bird, presumably Subantarctic Skua given location; differs from adult in reduced pale mottling on back.

Big whitish leg patches (visible in other images) and fresh plumage point to a 1st-year, but of which taxon? Falkland, Subtropical, and Subantarctic Skuas might all occur in these waters. We suspect Falkland Skua, whose appearance may parallel that of 1st-year Great Skua—but study is needed.

Brown Skua complex immatures
Following their 1st complete molt out of juv. plumage, some 1st-years return to colonies, others remain at sea; retained and faded juv. inner secondaries and obvious whitish leg blotching are good clues to age. 1st-year Subantarctic typically more uniform overall than adult (and thus resembles Chatham Skua), with limited pale mottling on neck, breast, and back; some may have pale buff hindneck streaks. 1st-year Falkland and Subtropical skuas may have dark hoods, similar to 1st-year Great Skuas; 1st-year Chatham Skua undescribed?

316

adult

bright adult

duller adult

juv.

1st-year

relatively long-billed; variable orange plumage tones,
especially on tail coverts and underwing coverts

molting 1st-year can be dull, dark-hooded

pale throat and neck sides contrast
with dark cap and dusky breast band

bright juv.

leucistic head markings not infrequent

adult

Chilean Skua *Catharacta chilensis* 53–61cm, WS 126–141cm

South America. Breeds Nov–Mar from Cape Horn n. along Pacific coast to Chiloé I. (at least
formerly to Gulf of Arauco), along Atlantic coast n. to Chubut, cen. Argentina. Non-breeding
migrant Mar–Nov (imms. year-round), mainly over shelf waters, in Pacific n. to Peru, small
numbers to Juan Fernandez Is.; in Atlantic n. to s. Brazil, very rarely to ne. Brazil and Falklands.
In summer near breeding grounds, often seen along coasts and inland a short distance, loafing
with gulls, feeding at dumps. Adult wing molt starts Mar/Apr, ends Aug/Oct; 1st-year wing
molt starts Aug/early Oct, completes late Nov/Jan.

JAEGERS (3 species in 1 genus)

Adults have bold plumage patterns and long central tail feathers relative to the larger, more heavily built skuas. Imm. plumages highly variable: best species ID features are overall size and structure; bill size and shape; length and shape of any tail projections; pattern of white wing flashes; and to a lesser extent behavior. Feed at sea mainly by pirating other seabirds, especially shearwaters, gulls, terns, and storm-petrels.

Molt and Age (see p. 318). Prebasic molt of head and body feathers mainly fall to early winter, often starting on migration, and wing molt usually on or near wintering grounds: Pomarine starts wing molt Aug/Nov, ends Dec/Apr. Parasitic and Long-tailed start wing molt mainly Oct/Nov and end Jan/Mar. Adult pre-alternate molts mainly Mar–May, involving head and body feathers, plus central tail feathers. Juv. plumage held through fall migration, replaced by complete preformative molt starting Dec/Feb in all species, ending Jun/Sep in Pomarine, Apr/Jul in Parasitic and Long-tailed. Subsequent molt timings similar to adult, although 2nd-cycle molts average a little later.

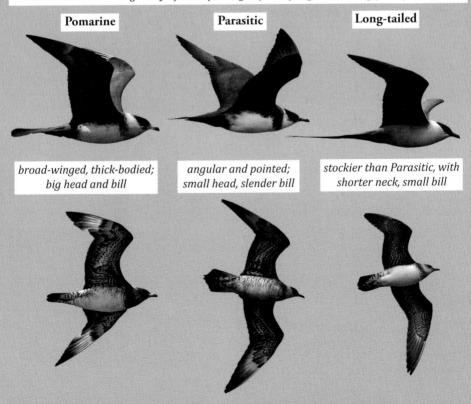

overall structural characters and head/bill proportions of breeding adults (upper row) carry over to the bewildering array of imm. plumages (lower), a good starting point for any ID

Pomarine **Parasitic** **Long-tailed**

broad-winged, thick-bodied; big head and bill

angular and pointed; small head, slender bill

stockier than Parasitic, with shorter neck, small bill

DARK-MORPH JAEGERS

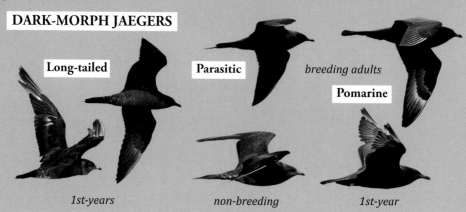

Long-tailed   **Parasitic**   *breeding adults*

Pomarine

1st-years   *non-breeding*   *1st-year*

imm. Long-tailed and all ages of Parasitic and Pomarine have a dark morph, in which paler plumage markings are variably suppressed and even age can be hard to determine; for species ID note structure, especially bill size and shape, and shape of any tail projections

MOLT AND AGE IN JAEGERS (Long-tailed Jaeger shown here)

Aug–Nov   *Mar*

fledge in variable juv. plumage (can be all-dark) with pale tips to upperwing coverts; complete molt from 1st winter into 1st spring/summer

May   *May–Sep*

variable 1st-summer (can be all-dark) resembles juv. but has plain upperwing coverts

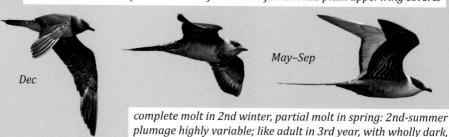

Dec   *May–Sep*

complete molt in 2nd winter, partial molt in spring: 2nd-summer plumage highly variable; like adult in 3rd year, with wholly dark, unbarred underwing coverts (very rarely a few pale bars)

juv. cold-toned; nape mottled

juv.

long, 'spoon-tipped'

breeding adults
male often lacks breast band

2nd-years

1st-years

bleached juv. shafts suggest Long-tailed pattern

non-breeding

largest jaeger, with big bill, broad wings, broad blunt tail projections; all ages can be dark overall, with reduced white wing flashes (see p. 318)

1st-year

with large shearwaters

2nd-year

adult breeding

Pomarine Jaeger (Skua) *Stercorarius pomarinus* 44–51cm (+6.5–11cm tail 'spoons'), WS 110-125cm Widespread. Breeds Jun–Sep on Arctic tundra from Novaya Zemlya and n. Russia locally e. across N America to Baffin I.; often skips breeding in years with poor food. Migrant at mid-latitudes of N Hemisphere mainly Aug–Nov, Apr–early Jun. Non-breeding grounds (mainly Oct–Apr) usually in areas with gulls, large terns, and shearwaters: in Atlantic from Gulf of Mexico s. to Venezuela and off W and SW Africa; in Pacific from cen. California s. to Peru, and from New Guinea to Australia; also N Indian Ocean; smaller numbers widely elsewhere, mainly in tropical latitudes. Often migrates in flocks, especially in spring; unlike smaller jaegers, regularly scavenges at fishing boats and often associates with rafting groups of shearwaters. Chases shorter, but often more aggressive than those of Parasitic Jaeger. Adult dark morph uncommon.

juv. warm-toned; tail projections pointed; nape streaked

juvs.

breeding adults

some lack dark breast band

barring wavier than other jaegers

2nd-summer

non-breeding

1st-years

1st-year chasing Elegant Tern

imms. often more barred below than Long-tailed

medium-size, angular jaeger with sharply pointed tail projections, crescent of 4–8 white shafts on upperwing, slender bill; all ages can be dark overall (see p. 318)

long 'bottle-neck' and small head

Parasitic often shows pale 'headlights'

1st-year

2nd-year

Parasitic Jaeger (Arctic Skua) *Stercorarius parasiticus* 40–44cm (+6–10cm tail points), WS 98–110cm Widespread. Breeds mid-May to early Sep on tundra and moorland from Iceland, n. Scotland, and Svalbard e. across N Eurasia and N America to Greenland. Migrant at mid-latitudes of N Hemisphere mainly late Jul–Oct, Apr–May. Non-breeding grounds (mainly Oct–Apr) usually in areas with concentrations of terns: in Atlantic off s. Brazil and Argentina and off SW Africa, in smaller numbers n. to Gulf of Mexico and SW Europe; in Pacific from Peru to cen. Chile and off Australia and New Zealand, in smaller numbers n. to s. California; also N Indian Ocean; small numbers widely elsewhere, mainly in s. tropical latitudes. Unlike other jaegers, regularly seen from shore s. of breeding grounds, chasing terns off beaches and in harbors; chases often much more persistent and aerobatic than other jaegers. Adult dark morph fairly common.

321

breeding adults

juv.

juv. cold-toned; tail projections bluntly pointed

fall adults often shed tail streamers

often has dusky wedge in white flash, cf. Parasitic

often short, needle-fine

contrasting dark secondaries

molting adult

non-breeding

1st-years

2nd-summer

smallest jaeger, with 2–3 white shafts on upperwing, small bill; adult lacks white underwing flash of other jaegers; imms. can be dark overall (see p. 318)

fall migrants with Sabine's Gulls

1st-year with 1st-year Pomarine (behind left)

adult molting

Long-tailed Jaeger (Skua) *Stercorarius longicaudus* 37–41cm (+14–21cm tail points), WS 94–104cm Widespread. Breeds late May to Aug on dry tundra from Svalbard and Norway e. across N Eurasia and N America to Greenland. Migrant at mid-latitudes of N Hemisphere mainly Aug–early Oct, late Apr–May. Non-breeding grounds (mainly Oct–Apr) mostly in upwelling areas with concentrations of smaller terns and storm-petrels: in Atlantic off Argentina and SW Africa; in Pacific off Peru and n. Chile, and off n. New Zealand and E Australia; small numbers widely elsewhere, mainly in s. temperate latitudes. Often migrates in flocks, frequently in loose association with Sabine's Gulls and Arctic Terns; often feeds while swimming, picking small food items along current fronts. Adult lacks dark morph, but breeding adults in W Eurasia average more extensively dusky underparts than those from e. Russia across N America to Greenland.

GULLS AND TERNS (19+ species in 6 genera)

Widespread group of birds, sometimes treated as 2 families. Of about 50 gull species and 50 tern species worldwide, many are coastal or even inland in distribution and we do not consider them as oceanic birds. Some species are long-distance migrants, others relatively sedentary. Taxonomy of some groups unresolved, especially noddies. ID usually not too difficult with good views, but often inferred by range.

Ages differ distinctly to slightly; sexes appear similar but male gulls average larger. Adult appearance attained in 1–3 years. Most gulls and typical terns exhibit seasonal plumage differences, mostly in head pattern. Wing molt mainly in non-breeding periods (start overlaps with end of breeding in a few species). Feed by picking food from near the sea surface, at times via shallow plunge-dives; kittiwakes also scavenge at fishing boats. Most species nest colonially, gulls and typical terns on the ground or on cliff ledges, noddies also in trees and bushes. Voices are largely unmusical clucks, brays, mews, and chatters, given mainly on nesting grounds and in interactions.

In terms of ID, oceanic gulls and terns can be considered in the following 3 groups (below): **gulls** (4 species in 3 genera); **typical terns** (3+ species in 1 genus); and **noddies** (12+ species in 2 genera).

Typical Terns
pp. 326–328

Gulls
pp. 323–325

Noddies
pp. 329–337

GULLS (4 species in 3 genera)
Well-defined group found worldwide, most diverse in cooler latitudes. Despite the common name 'seagull,' only 4 species are truly pelagic: kittiwakes (genus *Rissa*), Sabine's Gull (*Xema*), and Swallow-tailed Gull (*Creagrus*). Some authors suggest Pacific and Atlantic populations of Black-legged Kittiwake may comprise 2 species, but differences are slight, unlikely to be noticeable in the field; Sabine's Gull shows slight geographic variation in size and gray tone of upperparts, sometimes apparent when extremes are together.

adult has plain yellow bill, clean white head in breeding plumage

translucent

adult non-breeding

fairly small, long-winged gull with short dark legs, solid black wing-tip

juv. has black M on wings, black bill, black hindcollar

colony

adult non-breeding

1st-winter

Black-legged Kittiwake *Rissa tridactyla* 41–46cm
Cold northern oceans. Breeds late Apr/May–Aug/Sep in N Pacific region from Chukchi Sea s. to Kurils and se. Alaska; and in N Atlantic region from Arctic Canada, Greenland, and Franz Josef Land s. to Nova Scotia and W Europe. Ranges at sea in N Pacfic and N Atlantic, n. to limit of sea ice and in winter (mainly Sep/Oct–Mar/Apr) s. to n. China, nw. Mexico, e. US, and NW Africa. Rarely seen from shore s. of breeding range. Nests colonially on cliffs; in N Atlantic also on waterside buildings. Often social at sea, associating readily with other seabirds and resting on ice floes. Laughing and honking calls may suggest small geese and include rhythmic *ketewehk ketewehk*, derivation of English name. 2nd-year like adult but with more black in wing-tip.

adult breeding

darker above than Black-legged Kittiwake, with stubby bill, red legs

non-breeding adult has dark ear-crescent

dusky

breeding adults

juvs.

no black in tail

1st-summer

contrasting white

broad white trailing edge

Red-legged Kittiwake *Rissa brevirostris* 39–43cm

Bering Sea region of North Pacific. Breeds mid-Jun to Sep, locally on Commanders, Pribilofs, Aleutians; in summer ranges over shelf break and offshore waters of Bering Sea and N Pacific. Winter range presumed offshore in N Pacific; vagrant s. to Japan and w. US. Habits much like Black-legged Kittiwake, but wingbeats often a little quicker and jerkier; the 2 species can be found nesting and feeding together. 2nd-year like adult but with more black in wing-tip.

non-breeding/imm.

distinctive small gull with bright white triangle on upperwing, forked tail

adult breeding

juv. has brown cowl and upperparts

complete molt over 1st-winter into plumage like non-br. adult

Sabine's Gull *Xema sabini* 32–35.5cm

Widespread. Breeds late May/Jun–Aug, locally on low-lying Arctic tundra of E Asia, N America, Greenland, Svalbard. Migrant at mid-latitudes of N Hemisphere mainly Aug–Oct, Apr–May, mostly E Pacific and E Atlantic. Non-breeding grounds mainly off W South America (Peru and n. Chile) and SW Africa; smaller numbers n. in Pacific to cen. Mexico; rare in W Pacific and W Atlantic. Flight buoyant and tern-like. Mostly in small groups or singly, but fall and winter flocks can number 100s, rarely 1000s. Breeds in small colonies, often near Arctic Terns.

adult breeding

juv.

molting

1st-cycle

non-breeding

black 'goggles' accentuate large eyes

large, unmistakable gull with bold wing pattern, forked tail

Swallow-tailed Gull *Creagrus furcatus* 56–61cm

Eastern Pacific. Breeds year-round on Galapagos (cycle less than annual); also small numbers on Malpelo I., Colombia. Ranges off W South America from s. Colombia s. to Peru, rarely s. (mainly Dec–Apr) to cen. Chile and n. (mainly Mar–Jun) to s. Cen America. Flight unhurried and buoyant, on broad cupped wings; often appears very white at long range and can suggest a large egret. Feeds at night (attracted to ship lights); rests during day on the water, typically in groups, rarely flocks of 100s. Breeds on ledges and in crevices on rocky islands.

Swallow-tailed Gull

adult breeding

326

TYPICAL TERNS (3 species in 1 genus)

Most terns were formerly treated in the genus *Sterna*, but these dark-backed, ocean-going tropical terns are now placed in the genus *Onychoprion*. Despite its wide range, Sooty Tern shows only slight geographic variation, but the more sedentary Bridled Tern comprises 2 distinct groups, provisionally considered here as separate species. Gray-backed Tern has no described geographic variation.

adult with adult Sooty Tern, which is slightly larger and broader-winged

extensively white underwing

extensive dark tip on Sooty

Gray-backed Tern

distinctive tropical tern with silver-gray upperparts, long white brow

juv.

adult breeding

non-breeding/imm.

Gray-backed (Spectacled) Tern *Onychoprion lunatus* 32–35cm + 5–6.5cm tail streamers
Tropical Western and Central Pacific. Local breeder from n. Marianas and Hawaii (where present mainly Feb–Oct) s. and e. to Fiji and Tuamotus. Ranges over shelf and pelagic waters, often with feeding flocks of other terns, boobies, shearwaters. Unlike Sooty Tern, often rests on coconuts and floating debris, less often on the sea. Nests colonially on ground, at times in association with Sooty Terns. Non-breeding and juv. resemble bridled terns but with grayer back, narrower dark trailing edge to underwing. Clucking calls similar to Sooty Tern, distinct from bridled terns.

Western — adult breeding — Eastern

distinctive tropical terns with dark brown to gray-brown upperparts, long white brow

Eastern darker and browner above than Western, with less white in tail, reduced or absent pale hindcollar

Western juv.

Eastern imm.

Western non-breeding

Western adult breeding

Bridled Tern (*Onychoprion anaethetus*) **Complex** 30–35cm + 4–6.5cm tail streamers
Local in tropical oceans, comprising 2 allopatric cryptic species: **Western Bridled Tern** *O. [a.] melanoptera* (Atlantic and E Pacific; 32–35cm) fairly common but local breeder in W Africa from s. Morocco s. to Gulf of Guinea; in Caribbean (s. to Venezuela, w. into Gulf of Mexico); and along Pacific coast of Americas from cen. Mexico s. to Ecuador. **Eastern Bridled Tern** *O. [a.] anaethetus* (Indian Ocean and W Pacific; 30–33cm) fairly common but local from Red Sea and Madagascar to w. India, and from Indonesia and Australia n. to s. Ryukyus, e. to Melanesia.

Ranges mainly over shelf waters (e.g., n. in Gulf Stream to ne. US in late summer–fall), not far out to sea. Often along weedlines and current breaks, where perches on coconuts, boards, floating debris. Colonies can number 100s; at sea mainly singles or small loose groups, at times with mixed-species feeding flocks of other terns, boobies, shearwaters. Small numbers sometimes nest with colonies of Sooty Tern; nest typically hidden among coral rubble, under bushes, or in crevices. Braying and clucking calls lower and more grating than Sooty Tern calls.

328

distinctive tropical tern with blackish upperparts, white forehead patch; juv. has whitish underwings, cf. noddies

adult breeding (non-breeding similar or with some pale tipping above, messier face pattern)

dark primaries, cf. bridled terns

Indo-Pacific adult belly clouded smoky-gray

Atlantic adult belly clean white

juvs.

complete molt over 1st-year produces imm. plumage resembling messy adult

juv.

extent of white and buff spotting variable

Pacific adult breeding

upperparts can look brown in strong light, cf. bridled terns

Sooty Tern *Onychoprion fuscatus* 36–39cm + 6–7.5cm tail streamers
Widespread in tropical oceans. Fairly common to locally common throughout tropical Atlantic, Indian, and Pacific Oceans. Ranges n. to waters off se. US in summer–fall. Breeds on open ground, often in dense colonies numbering 1000s of pairs; breeding cycle 9–12 months, depending on location. Usually in flocks at sea, at times of 100s, feeding over schooling tuna or dolphins, often with shearwaters, petrels, noddies, etc. Flocks often spook easily, circling high when disturbed or when searching for food. Rests on sea, rarely on flotsam. Adult has varied clucking calls, including *wed-a-wek* or 'wide-awake'; juv. gives high lisping whistles.

NODDIES (12+ species in 2 genera)

Tropical terns, traditionally considered 4–5 species in 3 genera, but genus *Procelsterna* here subsumed into *Anous* (Cibois et al. 2016), and a more realistic treatment is 12+ species in 2 genera: *Anous* (Brown, Black, and Blue-gray Noddy complexes) and *Gygis* (White Noddy complex).

Brown Noddy (*Anous stolidus*) Complex

Treated here as 2 species of overall brown, white-capped tropical terns: the widespread Common Brown Noddy and localized Galapagos Brown Noddy of E Pacific. Other cryptic species may be involved, although not readily distinguished in the field. Brown noddies differ from black noddies (pp. 331–333) in their larger size, deeper bills, and browner adult plumage, appreciated readily when the 2 are seen together. Fresh plumage grayer and darker than worn (and imm.) plumage.

Feeding flight low to the water, swooping to pick prey from near the sea surface; out at sea, rarely soars high like Sooty Tern. Direct flight strong and typically fairly low, more direct and less fluttery than flight of black noddies, and can suggest a small jaeger. Unlike black noddies, not usually in dense flocks; often rest on logs, coconuts, sea turtles, less often on the sea. Mainly range over seas near breeding islands, but sometimes far out at sea, especially in non-breeding season. Low gutteral growls, grunts, and chatters rarely heard away from breeding grounds. Nests built in bushes or on rock ledges and cliffs.

worn adult, molting

Galapagos region

juv.

adult

paler-capped adult

Galapagos Brown Noddy *Anous [stolidus] galapagensis* 37–41cm

Common endemic in Galapagos Is., Ecuador. Ranges at sea in equatorial E Pacific, but pelagic distribution not well known. Darker and slatier overall than Common Brown Noddy, with muted, paler ashy cap (which can look whitish in strong light) that often includes a narrow whitish 'bridle' over base of bill. Juv. dark brown overall, often with pale gray patches on forehead or narrow pale gray eyebrow. 1st-year resembles adult but browner, with duller crown.

with adult Atlantic Black Noddy (right)

note smaller size, finer bill, and darker plumage of Atlantic Black

medium-size, brown tropical tern with long tapered tail, whitish cap

adult Caribbean, worn plumage

adult E Pacific

adults

wing-tips blacker than back, cf. black noddies

adult Cen Pacific, fresh plumage

juv.

faded imm.

Common Brown Noddy *Anous [stolidus] stolidus* 36–42cm
Widespread in tropical oceans. Fairly common to common but local from Caribbean and Gulf of Guinea s. to Gough I., S Atlantic; and throughout tropical Indian and Pacific Oceans, except Galapagos. For habits, see introduction to brown noddy complex (p. 329). Atlantic populations average slightly paler and browner than Indo-Pacific birds. Adult darker and slatier in fresh plumage; juv. brown overall, typically with narrow whitish eyebrow and variable white streaks on forehead; 1st-year like adult but browner, with duller whitish cap. Cf. black noddies, small jaegers, juv. Sooty Tern, Bulwer's Petrel.

Black Noddy (*Anous minutus*) Complex

Treated here as 4 largely allopatric species found throughout tropical oceans. Black noddies differ from brown noddies in smaller size, finer bills, and darker plumage (worn adult plumage and 1st-year browner than fresh adult), readily appreciated when the 2 are seen together (opposite).

Feeding flight low to the water, swooping and swirling to pick prey from near the sea surface. Direct flight typically low over the sea, more fluttery and less strong than flight of brown noddies; can suggest a large dark storm-petrel. Unlike brown noddies, often feed in dense flocks and commonly rest on the sea. Mainly range over seas near breeding islands, but sometimes far out at sea, especially in non-breeding season. Harsh brays and growls higher-pitched than brown noddy calls, rarely heard away from breeding grounds. Nests built in bushes or on rock ledges and cliffs.

small, blackish tropical tern with long slender bill, contrasting white cap

adults

adult

cap smoothly demarcated at back, vs. messy on 1st-year

juv.

Atlantic Black Noddy *Anous [minutus] americanus* 31–33cm

Tropical Atlantic. Fairly common to locally common. Breeds locally from n. Venezuela to equatorial Atlantic, e. to Gulf of Guinea, s. to St. Helena; ranges in adjacent seas, rarely nw. into Caribbean region, including Florida Keys (mainly Apr–Aug). Similar to Pacific Black Noddy (no range overlap) but adult blacker overall, with more contrasting white cap, especially at nape. Juv./1st-year browner overall, but still with bright white cap (unlike juv. brown noddies).

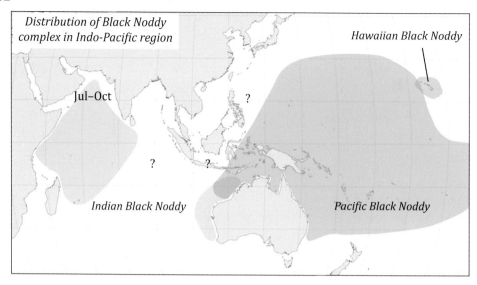

Distribution of Black Noddy complex in Indo-Pacific region

Hawaiian Black Noddy

Jul–Oct

?

?

?

Indian Black Noddy

Pacific Black Noddy

small, blackish tropical tern with long slender bill, white cap, dark lores

often rafts on water

plumage tones of all black noddies vary with lighting and wear

tail can be slightly paler gray than back

worn adult browner

Pacific Black Noddy *Anous [minutus] minutus* 31–34cm

Tropical Pacific. Fairly common to locally common. Breeds locally from NW Australia and Micronesia e. to nw. Hawaii (where nests in bushes, unlike Hawaiian Black Noddy) and Tuamotus, disjunctly in E Pacific on Clipperton, Cocos, and perhaps Malpelo. Indian Black Noddy (range overlap off NW Australia) slightly smaller and paler, more grayish overall, with slightly longer bill, pale lores on typical adult. Cf. Hawaiian Black Noddy, Bulwer's Petrel, dark storm-petrels. Juv./1st-year browner overall, but still with bright white cap (unlike juv. brown noddies).

endemic to main Hawaiian Is.; adult has diagnostic pale gray tail, orangey legs and feet

1st-year

adults

Hawaiian Black Noddy *Anous [minutus] melanogenys* 32–35cm
Endemic to Hawaii; fairly common. Breeds on cliffs in se. Hawaiian Is., nw. to Niihau, where can occur alongside Pacific Black Noddy (unclear if the 2 breed or interbreed at the same colonies); at sea range poorly known. Averages larger and paler than Pacific with contrastingly pale ashy-gray tail, paler head and neck, orangey legs and feet. Imm. has dark legs and feet, darker tail; criteria for separation from imm. Pacific Black Noddy await elucidation.

Indian Ocean: small, dark tropical tern with very long slender bill, white cap, pale lores

black eye stands out in pale face

adult with Pacific Black Noddies

Indian Black (Lesser) Noddy *Anous [minutus] tenuirostris* 30–33cm
Tropical and subtropical Indian Ocean. Breeds from Mascarenes n. to Seychelles and Maldives; also off W Australia (including small numbers among Pacific Black Noddies at Ashmore Reef). Ranges to waters off Madagascar and E Africa, very rarely n. to Oman. Cf. slightly larger and darker Pacific Black Noddy, Bulwer's Petrel, dark storm-petrels. Juv./1st-year browner overall with more strongly defined white cap offset by gray lores. Rare examples of Indian Black Noddy have dark gray lores, but not as contrastingly black/white as lores of Pacific Black Noddy.

Blue-gray Noddy (*Anous (Procelsterna) ceruleus*) Complex

Treated here provisionally as 3 species; Silver Noddy has been considered a race of Blue Noddy, despite plumage and latitudinal habitat differences. Plumage tones vary slightly within groups, but appearance can also vary greatly with lighting; juvs. variably washed brownish above. Birds often stay near breeding grounds year-round, and thus very localized. Often in flocks, swooping and swirling low over the water to snatch prey from near the surface; associate readily with feeding flocks of other noddies, terns, shearwaters. Breed on rocky stacks and cliffs, usually in colonies, nesting on ledges and in crevices.

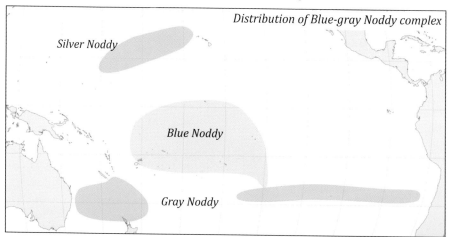

Distribution of Blue-gray Noddy complex

Silver Noddy

Blue Noddy

Gray Noddy

subtropical S Pacific

plumage tones vary with lighting

typical adults

darker adult

imm.

Gray Noddy (Ternlet) *Anous [ceruleus] albivittus* 25–28cm

Subtropical South Pacific; very local. Breeds Sep–Feb from Lord Howe e. to Kermadecs and from Rapa e. to Desventuradas, Chile. Smoky-gray overall (can look whitish in bright light, cf. White Noddy), paler on head and underparts; underwing coverts whitish. Cf. Blue Noddy.

equatorial Cen Pacific

plumage tones vary with lighting

Blue Noddy (Ternlet) *Anous [ceruleus] ceruleus* 23–25cm
Equatorial and tropical South-Central Pacific; very local. Breeds (possibly year-round, depending on location) from Ellice and Fiji e. to Marquesas and Gambiers. Blue-gray overall (little contrast on underwing), slightly paler on head and underparts, with contrasting white postocular crescent and often a diffusely paler crown; population in Gambiers has head, upper chest, and underwing coverts paler gray (vs. overall blue-gray in other populations).

tropical N Pacific   *plumage tones vary with lighting*

Silver Noddy (Ternlet) *Anous [ceruleus] saxatilis* 22–24cm
Tropical North Pacific; very local. Breeds (mainly Dec–Mar in Hawaii) from Marcus and Marshalls e. to nw. Hawaii. Pale blue-gray to whitish head and underparts paler than grayish upperparts, but white postocular crescent contrasts (especially in shade); whitish underwing coverts often contrast more strongly with dark underside to remiges than on Gray Noddy.

336

White Noddy (*Gygis alba*) Complex

Treated here as 3 species, usually identified easily by range; presumed competition for nest sites on smaller islands in the Marquesas may result in hybridization there between Indo-Pacific and Little. Range widely in tropical oceans, often far from land. At sea found singly or in loose groups, often with feeding flocks of other noddies, boobies, shearwaters, etc. Feed by dipping to the surface, but also fly high above the sea, when can be mistaken for distant tropicbirds; occasionally rest on sea. Single egg laid on tree branch, rocky ledge, or other surface. Juv. has variable gingery-brown edgings and wash to upperparts, which fades quickly and is rarely noticeable at sea. Also known as Fairy Tern or White Tern.

tropical Indian and Pacific Oceans

with Common Brown Noddies

juvs. variable

tail fork varies with how tail is spread

adults

Indo-Pacific White Noddy *Gygis [alba] candida* 32–34cm

Tropical Indian and Pacific Oceans. Fairly common to common from Indian Ocean e. to Cen Pacific (Hawaii, and throughout Polynesia); disjunctly on Clipperton, Cocos, and probably Malpelo in E Pacific. Adult has relatively deep bill with bluish base; juv. bill blacker, smaller, and finer than adult bill, soon develops bluish at base. Pitcairn adults average reduced black eyering, paler legs and toes. In Marquesas, overlaps and may hybridize with Little White Noddy.

tropical S Atlantic

juv.

adults

Atlantic White Noddy *Gygis [alba] alba* 32–35cm
Tropical South Atlantic. Fairly common but local, breeding from islands off ne. Brazil to Ascension and St. Helena. No similar species in range. Relative to Indo-Pacific White Noddy, Atlantic averages larger, with shallower bill (little or no gray-blue at base), shallower tail fork.

very local in tropical S-Cen Pacific

juv.

adult

Little White Noddy *Gygis [alba] microrhyncha* 26–28cm
Very local in tropical South-Central Pacific. Fairly common in Marquesas; may also occur on other islands w. to Phoenix; vagrant n. to Hawaii. Occurs alongside Indo-Pacific White Noddy; Little is slightly smaller and has more fluttery flight, lacks dark shafts to primaries, tail has shallower fork, and bill is smaller, finer, and all-black (beware juv. Indo-Pacific).

PHALAROPES (2 species in 1 genus)

Phalaropes are small sandpipers that swim. Most sandpipers spend their lives on land, although many migrate over the open ocean, but 2 species of phalaropes are pelagic in their non-breeding periods. They nest at high latitudes in the Northern Hemisphere and spend most of their year at sea, sometimes far from land. Flocks form silvery strings and swaths on the water and in flight.

Ages differ; distinct seasonal plumages, with breeding-plumage females brighter than males (seen mainly on spring migrants and on breeding grounds). Attain adult appearance in 1 year. Wing molt protracted at sea in non-breeding periods, but molt of head and body feathers rapid in late summer–fall, again in spring. Nest in scattered pairs beside ponds and lakes. Chip calls given year-round; also wheezy and squeaky chatters, mainly on breeding grounds.

molting Red Phalarope (back left) with molting Red-necked Phalaropes; late July, California

If seen up close, together, Red-necked and Red Phalaropes can look quite different (below), but from a bouncing boat it can challenging to distinguish the two species in non-breeding and molting plumages, even when together (above). The larger size of Red, different call notes, and needle-fine bill of Red-necked are often the most useful features.

Red Phalarope (left) is appreciably larger than Red-necked (right), rides higher in the water, has a thicker bill (usually pale at base), and is paler, more silvery overall in non-breeding plumage

non-breeding Red and faded juv. Red-necked

plain silvery back, unlike Red-necked

with 2 Red-necked Phalaropes

non-breeding

breeding plumage

non-breeding

female

male

Red (Grey) Phalarope *Phalaropus fulicarius* 20–22cm
Widespread. Breeds Jun–Aug, locally on Arctic tundra across E Eurasia, N America, Greenland, Iceland, Spitsbergen. Pelagic migrant at mid-latitudes of N Hemisphere mainly Jul–Nov and Apr–early Jun. Widespread in winter, mainly in E Pacific from Mexico s. to cen. Chile, and in E Atlantic off NW Africa and SW Africa. Often in flocks, locally of 1000s, mixing readily with Red-necked Phalarope. Flight mainly low over water, but towers in swirling clouds when hunted by jaegers. Off w. US, non-breeding plumage sometimes mistaken for Fork-tailed Storm-Petrel. Call a high, slightly tinny *tink*, distinct from lower chip of Red-necked Phalarope.

juv. dark above

juvs.

non-breeding; note needle-fine bill

breeding plumage

Red-necked Phalarope *Phalaropus lobatus* 17–19cm
Widespread. Breeds mid-May to Aug on arctic tundra across Eurasia, N America, Greenland, s. locally in NW Europe to n. Scotland. Migrant at mid-latitudes of N Hemisphere mainly Jul–Oct, Apr–May; N Atlantic breeders appear to cross Cen America to winter in E Pacific. Non-breeding grounds mainly in E Pacific from Mexico s. to Peru, in NW Indian Ocean from Arabian Sea s. to NE Africa, and in W Pacific from Philippines s. to New Guinea region. Habits much like Red Phalarope, but tends to favor warmer, nearshore waters, and a regular migrant inland. Call a clipped *plik*, lower than Red Phalarope.

APPENDIX A: GEOGRAPHIC LOCATIONS

The following maps show islands and other regions mentioned in the species accounts. Some island groups that mostly or wholly comprise widely scattered small islets and atolls (such as the Maldives and Tuamotus) are located roughly by the

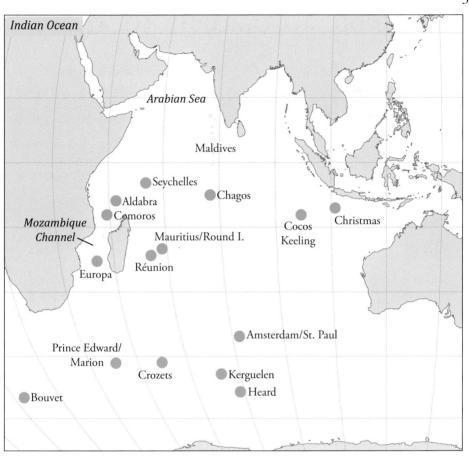

Indian Ocean

Arabian Sea

Maldives

Seychelles

Chagos

Aldabra
Comoros

Mozambique
Channel

Mauritius/Round I.

Cocos
Keeling

Christmas

Europa

Réunion

Amsterdam/St. Paul

Prince Edward/
Marion

Crozets

Kerguelen

Heard

Bouvet

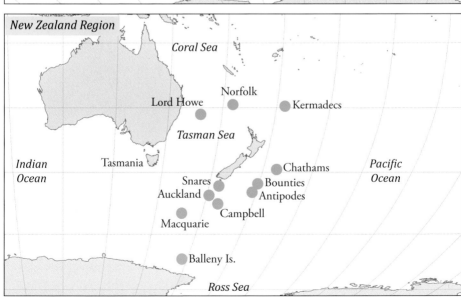

New Zealand Region

Coral Sea

Norfolk

Lord Howe

Kermadecs

Tasman Sea

Indian
Ocean

Tasmania

Chathams

Pacific
Ocean

Snares

Bounties

Auckland

Antipodes

Campbell

Macquarie

Balleny Is.

Ross Sea

name and are not indicated with blue dots that could misleadingly restrict their location.

More so in the Pacific than in other oceans, numerous island names have been changed in relatively recent times, usually as independent nations are established and decide to rename islands; conversely, presumably to promote tourism, Isla Masatierra in Chile has been officially renamed Isla Robinson Crusoe! Given that

343

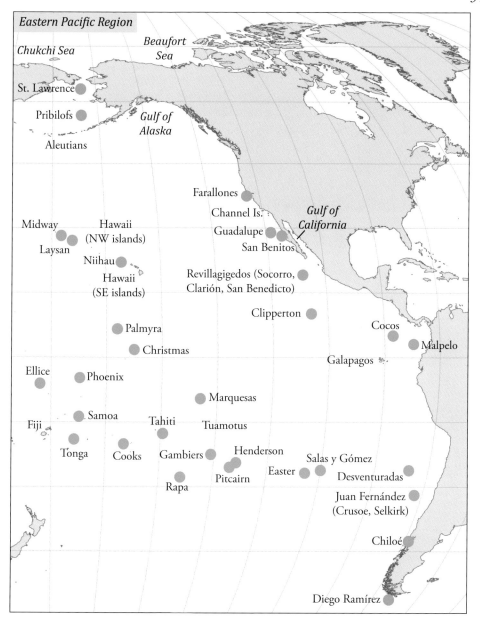

Eastern Pacific Region

Chukchi Sea

Beaufort Sea

St. Lawrence

Pribilofs

Gulf of Alaska

Aleutians

Farallones

Channel Is.

Gulf of California

Midway

Hawaii (NW islands)

Guadalupe

Laysan

San Benitos

Niihau

Hawaii (SE islands)

Revillagigedos (Socorro, Clarión, San Benedicto)

Clipperton

Cocos

Malpelo

Palmyra

Christmas

Galapagos

Ellice

Phoenix

Marquesas

Samoa

Tahiti

Tuamotus

Fiji

Tonga

Cooks

Gambiers

Henderson

Salas y Gómez

Pitcairn

Easter

Desventuradas

Rapa

Juan Fernández (Crusoe, Selkirk)

Chiloé

Diego Ramírez

this is an English-language guide, we have not attempted to keep apace with such bureaucracy and have mostly used what we consider the most familiar English names found in the majority of recent bird-related literature, whether or not they find favor with the oxymoronic politically correct.

APPENDIX B:
TAXONOMY AND ENGLISH NAMES

Keeping apace with discoveries in the bird world is proving a challenge in terms of formally naming new entities. And as E. O. Wilson (2014:125) has noted, the glacial rate at which biodiversity is being classified is a disgrace of the biological sciences, one that hinders both study and conservation.

However, as birders free from the bureaucratic molasses that taxonomists have created for themselves, we believe it helpful to recognize biodiversity regardless of 'official' taxonomic status. Therefore we have treated many populations (several of them formally unnamed) as separate entities, provisionally often as species. While today these views may seem radical, we suspect in years to come our approach may be viewed as quaint and conservative. Only time will tell. Regardless, observers can if they wish (and if practically possible) distinguish and appreciate distinctive forms of oceanic birds in the field. The bureaucrats can catch up later.

TAXONOMY

Seabird taxonomy lags behind landbird taxonomy (pp. 14–20 summarize recent taxonomy for oceanic birds). For example, only in the past 15 or so years have we come to accept the 'revelations' of species-level differences among taxa that occur in relatively well-studied areas, as with northern 'Soft-plumaged Petrels' (now Zino's, Desertas, and Cape Verde Petrels), or with 'Dark-rumped Petrels' (now Hawaiian and Galapagos Petrels, with the latter surely comprising further cryptic species). And witness the recent genus- and species-level revisions among birds as easily studied as albatrosses. But with smaller and less familiar groups such as prions, diving-petrels, small shearwaters, and storm-petrels we are only starting to scratch the surface. For example, witness the recent discovery by biologists of an abundant new prion taxon at a 'well-studied' seabird breeding island in the South Atlantic (Ryan et al. 2014).

Genetic studies have fueled much recent taxonomic work and helped resolve some patterns of diversification. They have been less successful, however, for establishing species limits. Added problems for seabirds are that specimens may be scattered through the world's museums and difficult to amass for proper study; that specimens can be misidentified (e.g., Wallace et al. 2017 used a specimen of Black Storm-Petrel mislabeled as Markham's, which thus produced spurious results; N. Rice, pers. comm.); and that voucher specimens may not exist, simply enigmatic tissue samples whose identity cannot be verified (e.g., Cibois et al. 2015). Genetic studies often take on faith previous studies and recycle the same sequences, which can lead to a house of cards where errors become harder to trace. And while lab ornithologists who wouldn't know their study species if they found it in the toilet bowl are assigning species and genus limits left and right, it is unclear whether the genes studied, and differences found within them, have any bearing on factors that determine speciation and reproductive isolation. Field ornithologists and birders, who appreciate the behavior, vocalizations, and habitats of birds in life, can be equally placed to make informed decisions about species limits and other relationships. Ideally these two camps should combine forces to make sense of the burgeoning literature being produced.

The most dramatic changes in recognition of 'new' species have come with storm-petrels. For example, until the 2000s most authors considered the widespread 'Band-rumped Storm-Petrel' as a monotypic species. However, recent genetic and vocal studies have revealed complex diversity among various Band-rump populations, with numerous cryptic species being involved (e.g., Robb et al. 2008, Smith et al. 2007). And in the 2010s, the Leach's Storm-Petrel complex was finally acknowledged to comprise 3 species. As for less familiar and less accessible taxa, such as white-bellied storm-petrels, diving-petrels, and small tropical shearwaters, we can only imagine what the future holds when careful studies are undertaken. Our work for this book highlighted that even in some larger and relatively conspicuous species, such as boobies, tropicbirds, and noddies, not-so-cryptic species are staring us in the face yet are not widely accepted as such.

Even when taxa are formally described, the attribution of scientific names can be messy or ambiguous. For example, the recognition of cryptic taxa (such as two seasonal populations [species?] of band-rumped storm-petrels breeding in the Galapagos Islands) can make it unclear which population the type specimen refers to, and which population requires a name—in theory, a quick genetic analysis could address this question. For type specimens in South Atlantic members of the white-bellied storm-petrel complex, measurements indicate the presently used names may be reversed: *leucogaster* likely refers to Gough birds, and *melanoleuca* to Inaccessible birds, not the other way round (Howell 2010a). There is little glamor in bureaucracy, however, so these and other such questions remain to be formally answered or addressed.

ENGLISH NAMES

For birders, scientists, and conservationists to work with entities they need names, and our treatment of numerous populations as species or potential species required us to coin some English names. We gave considerable thought to new names and consulted colleagues around the world, recognizing that names are simply handles for communication, and rarely perfect. For example, Kermadec Petrel nests on many islands, not just the Kermadecs; Fork-tailed Storm-Petrel is not the only storm-petrel with a forked tail; and so on.

Descriptive names based on plumage are of little use for birds that are often very similar in appearance, such as storm-petrels. As a rule, we opted for geographic names (often islands where taxa breed) or for names that honor persons who discovered, named, or studied the species or related groups, or whose contribution to ornithology (especially seabirds) is worthy of recognition. We prefer not to lose a sense of history or poetry by invoking cumbersome, quotidian names such as 'Lesser Southern White-faced Storm-Petrel,' or 'Hot-season Azores Band-rumped Storm-Petrel' and instead favor more evocative names. Who wouldn't want to see a Titan Storm-Petrel, or an Inaccessible Storm-Petrel, or a Silver Noddy?

RECENTLY DESCRIBED AND PROVISIONALLY SPLIT SPECIES

The following list explains new or potentially unfamiliar names we have used in this book; see pp. 14–20 for more information on recent seabird taxonomy.

Rockhopper Penguin *Eudyptes chrysocome* complex (pp. 40–41). Treated as 3 species, named for geographic regions where they occur: **Northern Rockhopper Penguin** *E. moseleyi*, **Southern Rockhopper Penguin** *E. chrysocome*, and **Eastern Rockhopper Penguin** *E. filholi*.

Little Penguin *Eudyptula minor* complex (p. 46). Species status as *E. novaehollandiae* proposed recently for Australian population (Grosser et al. 2015). Split may be valid, but publication was weak, critical study still needed.

Kuril Guillemot *Cepphus [columba] snowi* (p. 59). Provisional split from Pigeon Guillemot; named for the island chain where it breeds.

South Georgia Diving-Petrel *Pelecanoides georgicus* (p. 68). Species status as *P. whenuahouensis* proposed recently for relict population breeding on Codfish I., New Zealand (Fischer et al. 2018). Split may well be valid, but critical study still needed. The 'English' name of Whenua Hou Diving-Petrel was suggested, but this is a Maori name, not English; **Codfish Diving-Petrel** is instead an appropriate English name and parallels the name South Georgia Diving-Petrel.

MacGillivray's Prion *Pachyptila macgillivrayi* (p. 90). Cryptic taxon of prion sometimes treated as a race of Broad-billed Prion or of Salvin's Prion, but more realistically considered a species.

Black-capped Petrel *Pterodroma hasitata* complex (pp. 110–112). Treated provisionally as 2 species: **White-faced Petrel** *P. [hasitata] hasitata* and **Black-faced Petrel** *P. [hasitata]* undescribed.

Vanuatu Petrel *Pterodroma occulta* (p. 121). Cryptic taxon of White-necked Petrel described as a species in 2001; named for the islands where it breeds.

Great-winged Petrel *Pterodroma macroptera* complex (pp. 140–141). In recent years, New Zealand taxon is usually treated as a separate species, **Gray-faced Petrel** *P. [macroptera] gouldi*, distinct from **Great-winged Petrel** *P. [macroptera] macroptera* of Atlantic and Indian Oceans.

Herald Petrel *Pterodroma heraldica* complex (pp. 146–147). In recent years, distinctive Atlantic population known as **Trindade Petrel** *P. arminjoniana* (named for the main island where it breeds) usually split from **Herald Petrel** *P. heraldica* of the Pacific. Dark-morph Herald Petrels nesting on Henderson Island suggested in

Bryan's Shearwater (left) is a distinctive species of small shearwater described in 2011, and found breeding in Japan in 2015. Pincoya Storm-Petrel (right) was described as new to science from Chile in 2013, but its taxonomic status remains vexed, its breeding grounds unknown. How many other undescribed oceanic birds remain?

1996 to represent a cryptic species, **Henderson Petrel** *P. [heraldica] atrata*.

    Audubon's Shearwater *Puffinus lherminieri* complex (pp. 180–181). Formerly included many warm-water taxa worldwide, an unrealistic grouping that was partially redressed by Austin et al. (2004). Within the Audubon's complex of the N Atlantic, we recognize 3 species, following Robb et al. (2008) and Howell (2012), who used and explained the English names we use here: **Audubon's Shearwater** *P. lherminieri*; **Barolo Shearwater** *P. baroli*; and **Boyd's Shearwater** *P. boydi*.

    Tropical Shearwater *Puffinus bailloni* complex (pp. 182–185). Here treated as 5 groups, provisionally species: **Seychelles Shearwater** *Puffinus nicolae*, named for the main islands where it breeds; **Baillon's Shearwater** *Puffinus bailloni*, named for French naturalist Jean Baillon (1744–1802); and 3 Pacific Ocean taxa named for the regions they inhabit: **Melanesian Shearwater** *Puffinus gunax*, **Micronesian Shearwater** *Puffinus [dichrous] dichrous*; and **Polynesian Shearwater** *Puffinus [dichrous] polynesiae*. Traditionally all of these taxa were subsumed into the Audubon's Shearwater complex.

    Galapagos Shearwater *Puffinus subalaris* (p. 186). Distinctive taxon, named for the islands where it breeds; may comprise further cryptic species. Traditionally subsumed into Audubon's Shearwater complex.

    Bryan's Shearwater *Puffinus bryani* (p. 189). Poorly known taxon, described in 2011; named for US natural scientist E. H. Bryan (1898–1985).

Rapa Shearwater *Puffinus myrtae* (p. 190). Distinctive but poorly known taxon, best treated as a full species; named for the island where it breeds. Described originally as a large race of Little Shearwater; genetic studies suggest it may be more closely related to Newell's Shearwater.

Little Shearwater *Puffinus assimilis* complex (pp. 192–193). In recent years, distinctive **Subantarctic Shearwater** *P. elegans* is usually split from **Little Shearwater** *P. assimilis*, which may comprise further cryptic species.

Wandering Albatross *Diomedea exulans* complex (pp. 202–212). Treated as 5 species, retaining the name 'Wandering' as a helpful association for the group, as done by Tickell (2000). We prefer **Gough Wandering Albatross** for *D. dabbenena*, named for the island where it still breeds (Tickell 2000); some authors use Tristan Albatross, named for an island whence humans have extirpated the species.

Campbell Albatross *Thalassarche [melanophris] impavida* (p. 219). A recent split from Black-browed Albatross; named for the island where it breeds.

Buller's Albatross *Thalassarche bulleri* complex (pp. 222–223). Treated as 2 species, named for their geographic distribution: **Northern Buller's Albatross** *T. [bulleri] platei* and **Southern Buller's Albatross** *T. [bulleri] bulleri*.

European Storm-Petrel *Hydrobates pelagicus* complex (pp. 235–236). Split suggested by Robb et al. (2008), who used the English names we adopt here: **British Storm-Petrel** *H. [pelagicus] pelagicus*, named for main breeding islands; and **Mediterranean Storm-Petrel** *H. [pelagicus] melitensis*, named for breeding range.

Leach's Storm-Petrel *Hydrobates leucorhous* complex (pp. 237–241). Split proposed by Howell (2012), who used and explained the English names we use here: **Leach's Storm-Petrel** *H. [leucorhous] leucorhous;* **Townsend's Storm-Petrel** *H. [leucorhous] socorroensis*; and **Ainley's Storm-Petrel** *H. [leucorhous] cheimomnestes*.

Band-rumped Storm-Petrel *Thalobata castro* complex (pp. 243–247). North Atlantic taxa were covered by Robb et al. (2008) and Howell (2012), who used and explained the English names we use here: **Madeiran Storm-Petrel** *T. [castro] castro*; **Monteiro's Storm-Petrel** *T. [castro] monteiroi*; **Grant's Storm-Petrel** *T. [castro]* undescribed; and **Cape Verde Storm-Petrel** *T. [castro] jabejabe*.

For S Atlantic taxa of Band-rumps we have adopted the following names: **St. Helena Storm-Petrel** *T. [castro] helena*, named for the main island where it breeds; and **São Tomé Storm-Petrel** *T. [castro]* undescribed, named for the island where it is presumed to breed.

For Galapagos populations of Band-rumps we suggest **Darwin's Storm-Petrel** (cool season) and **Spear's Storm-Petrel** (hot season), commemorating British naturalist Charles Darwin (1809–1892) and American marine ornithologist Larry Spear (1945–2006), who dedicated his life to the study of oceanic birds. The type specimen of 'Galapagos Band-rumped Storm-Petrel' was collected at sea in February, and has not been assigned to a population. When its affinities are known, a new scientific epithet will be needed for the remaining population.

For the 2 other Pacific taxa of Band-rumps, we suggest **Hawaiian Storm-Petrel** *T. [castro] cryptoleucura*, named for the islands where it breeds; and **Japanese Storm-Petrel** *T. [castro] kumagai*, named for the islands where it breeds.

Wedge-rumped Storm-Petrel *Halocyptena tethys* complex (pp. 248–249). Names used here for the 2 taxa are long-standing, used by Murphy (1936): **Galapagos Storm-Petrel** *H. [tethys] tethys*, named for the islands where it breeds; and **Peruvian Storm-Petrel** *H. [tethys] kelsalli*, named for the region where it breeds.

Wilson's Storm-Petrel *Oceanites oceanicus* complex (pp. 250–253). Names used here for 3 taxa are long-standing (see Murphy 1936): **Lowe's Storm-Petrel** *O. [gracilis] galapagoensis*, named for British ornithologist Percy Lowe (1870–1948); **Elliot's Storm-Petrel** *O. [gracilis] gracilis*, named for American ornithologist Daniel Elliot (1835–1915); and **Fuegian Storm-Petrel** *O. [oceanicus] chilensis*, named for the Fuegian zone, i.e., the area of fjords and islands in s. Chile, as in Tierra del Fuego. **Pincoya Storm-Petrel** *O. [oceanicus] pincoyae* was described formally in 2013; named for a local sea goddess in Chile.

'New Caledonia Storm-Petrel' *Fregetta* undescribed? (p. 257). A streaked storm-petrel found at New Caledonia in 2008 may prove to be the same taxon as *Thalassidroma lineata*, described in 1848 by US naturalist T. R. Peale (1800–1885) and later moved into the genus *Pealea*. Should this be the case, we suggest using the English name Peale's Storm-Petrel.

White-bellied Storm-Petrel *Fregetta grallaria* complex (pp. 258–262). Species limits remain vexed, but provisionally we recognize 6 species: **Black-bellied Storm-Petrel** *F. tropica*; **Gough Storm-Petrel** *F. [tropica] 'melanoleuca'* (probably *leucogaster*, cf. Howell 2010a), named for the main island where it breeds; **Inaccessible Storm-Petrel** *F. [grallaria] 'leucogaster'* (probably *melanoleuca*, cf. Howell 2010a), named for the main island where it breeds (also breeds at St. Paul, in Indian Ocean, an island ostensibly inaccessible to most people); **Titan Storm-Petrel** *F. [grallaria] titan*, named for its large size, the name proposed by Howell (2014); **Juan Fernandez Storm-Petrel** *F. [grallaria] segethi*, named for the main islands where it breeds; and **Tasman Storm-Petrel** *F. [grallaria] grallaria*, named for the Tasman Sea region, where it breeds.

White-faced Storm-Petrel *Pelagodroma marina* complex (pp. 264–266). Comprises 6 taxa that we provisionally treat as 4 species: **Cramp's Storm-Petrel** *P. [marina] hypoleuca*, named for British ornithologist Stanley Cramp (1913–1989) and including Bourne's Storm-Petrel *P. [marina] eadesi*, named for British ornithologist W. R. P. Bourne, who described the taxon; **Latham's Storm-Petrel** *P. [marina] marina*, named for British ornithologist John Latham (1740–1837), who described the taxon (includes Maori Storm-Petrel *P. [marina] maoriana*, named for New Zealand breeding range); **Australian Storm-Petrel** *P. [marina] dulciae*; named for its breeding range, which lies wholly in Australia; and **Kermadec Storm-Petrel** *P. [marina] albiclunis*, named for the islands where it breeds.

White-tailed Tropicbird *Phaethon lepturus* complex (pp. 282–283). Comprises at least 2 species-level taxa: **Catesby's Tropicbird** *P. [lepturus] catesbyi*, named for British naturalist Mark Catesby (1683–1749); and **Yellow-billed Tropicbird** *P. [lepturus] lepturus*, an old name for the species, which helpfully distinguishes it from the orange-billed Catesby's.

Arabian Tropicbird *Phaethon [aethereus] indicus* (p. 285). Split from Red-billed Tropicbird, and largely endemic to the Arabian Sea.

Lesser Frigatebird *Fregata ariel* (p. 291). Species status as *F. trinitatis* recently proposed for relict and highly endangered population breeding at Trindade in S Atlantic; **Trindade Frigatebird** seems an obvious English name.

Brown Booby *Sula leucogaster* complex (pp. 302–303). Comprises 3 distinct groups best considered as species: **Atlantic Brown Booby** *S. [leucogaster] leucogaster*, named for the region it inhabits; **Indo-Pacific Brown Booby** *S. [leucogaster] plotus*, named for the region it inhabits; and **Brewster's Brown Booby** *S. [leucogaster] brewsteri*, named for American ornithologist William Brewster (1851–1919).

Brown Skua *Catharacta antarctica* complex (pp. 312–315). Treated provisionally as 4 species, with names reflecting geographic distribution: **Falkland Skua** *C. [antarctica] antarctica*, **Subtropical Skua** *C. [antarctica] hamiltoni*, **Subantarctic Skua** *C. [antarctica] lonnbergi*, and **Chatham Skua** *C. [antarctica]* undescribed.

Bridled Tern *Onychoprion anaethetus* complex (p. 327). Treated provisionally as 2 species with names reflecting geographic distribution: **Western Bridled Tern** *O. [a.] melanoptera* and **Eastern Bridled Tern** *O. [a.] anaethetus*.

Brown Noddy *Anous stolidus* complex (pp. 329–330). Treated as 2 species, with names reflecting distribution: widespread **Common Brown Noddy** *A. [stolidus] stolidus;* localized **Galapagos Brown Noddy** *A. [stolidus] galapagensis*.

Black Noddy *Anous minutus* complex (pp. 331–333). Treated as 4 species, with names reflecting geographic distribution: **Atlantic Black Noddy** *A. [minutus] americanus*, **Indian Black Noddy** (also known by the inappropriate name of Lesser Noddy) *A. [minutus] tenuirostris*, **Pacific Black Noddy** *A. [minutus] minutus*, and **Hawaiian Black Noddy** *A. [minutus] melanogenys* .

Blue-gray Noddy *Anous ceruleus* complex (pp. 334–335). Treated as 3 species, with names alluding to plumage coloration: the equatorial **Blue Noddy** *A. [ceruleus] ceruleus*, southern **Gray Noddy** *A. [ceruleus] albivittus*, and northern **Silver Noddy** *A. [ceruleus] saxatilis* (latter often subsumed into Blue Noddy, but differs in plumage and biogeographic affinities).

White Noddy *Gygis alba* complex (pp. 336–337). Usually known as White Terns, but genus *Gygis* is part of the noddy clade, distinct from typical terns. Treated here as 3 species, named for geographic distribution and relative size: **Atlantic White Noddy** *G. [alba] alba*, **Indo-Pacific White Noddy** *G. [alba] candida*, and **Little White Noddy** *G. [alba] microrhyncha*.

ACKNOWLEDGMENTS

Steve. This book could never have been considered without the invaluable knowledge gained over months of research cruises in the Pacific and Indian Oceans with my seabird mentors Larry Spear and David G. Ainley, and from many birding tours I have led world-wide for WINGS, supported by Will Russell, Matt Brooks, and all at the WINGS office.

Among fellow tubenose enthusiasts, Elaine Cook is a good friend and well-organized traveling companion who has shared sundry seabirding trips from Madeira and Oman to New Zealand and Polynesia; in Hatteras, North Carolina, pelagic comrades in arms Brian Patteson and Kate Sutherland are remarkable seabird observers who have taught me much.

The wide-ranging seabird work of Hadoram Shirihai and colleagues, and the careful work of Robert L. Flood and colleagues in the North Atlantic and elsewhere have been invaluable and inspirational; both Hadoram and Bob have answered many questions, offered advice, and helped in tracking down literature.

All at the Palomarin Field Station of Point Reyes Bird Observatory (now Point Blue) were supportive throughout, especially Renée Cormier, Mark Dettling, Ryan DiGaudio, Megan Elrod, Tom Gardali, and Diana Humple.

Last but not least, little did my parents know that the trips they took me on as a kid to the seabird breeding islands of Pembrokeshire, in South Wales, would lead to a lifelong love affair with the ocean. Without their support for so many years, this book could never have come to pass.

Kirk. Many photos for this guide came from expeditions made to remote locations with other seabird aficionados. Special acknowledgment goes to Robert L. Flood for his mentorship, friendship, and inspirational knowledge of seabirds; and to Mike Danzenbaker, the most affable of traveling companions, as well as a highly skilled seabirder and photographer. No expedition is complete without Bob and Mike. Thanks also to Hadoram Shirihai for his logistical support with many of those trips, which would not have been as successful without his generous guidance. And without Didier and Sophie Watterlot and their yacht *Sauvage*, many of my very best days at sea would not have been possible; I thank them for their dedication to making our ventures the successes they have been.

Angus Wilson and John Shemilt are great friends and seabirding companions. Angus is an especially skilled observer, and as a scientist he provides a thoughtful element to every marine encounter. John provides a stylish and distinguished touch to our adventures and is a legend for his introduction of the 'asspad' to long-range pelagic expeditions. Geoff Jones is a remarkably skilled photographer and I am proud to have him as a 'mate.' His lust for life and ability to entertain have saved me from lunacy on more than one steaming-hot day on a becalmed tropical ocean—thank you, Geoff, for just being you. John and Jemi Holmes, your kindness, patience, and enthusiasm make you great companions, and it is an honor to be your friend. Colin Rogers, your friendship, humor, and skill as a seabirder are all appreciated, and I look forward to future travels together.

Finally, I would like to acknowledge my father, Bill Zufelt. His tales of birding adventures as a youth with Rich Stallcup and others to exotic locations such as Attu and the Dry Tortugas were the spark that ignited my lifelong quest to seek out adventure, culminating in my great love of the remote seas and the creatures that call those places home. For that gift I am forever grateful.

Both. Many others have helped in this project, and we apologize to anyone we have inadvertently omitted. For company in the field, thoughtful discussions, responses to questions, and help while visiting far-flung sites we thank: Albatross Encounter New Zealand, Tom Blackman, Ned Brinkley, John Brodie-Good, Ian Bullock, Licia Calabrese, Chris Collins, Chris Corben, Jeff Davis, David J. Fisher, Michael Force, Pete Fraser, Doug Hanna, the Russ family at Heritage Expeditions, Terry Hunefeld, Alvaro Jaramillo, Matt Jolly and the entire Jolly family at Stoney Creek Shipping, Meghan Kelly, Yann Kolbeinsson, Fabrice Lebouard, Bruce Mactavish, Todd McGrath, Gary Melville, Pete Morris, Killian Mullarney, Michael O'Brien, Dave Pereksta, Kenneth Petersen, H. Douglas Pratt, Peter Pyle, Magnus Robb/The Sound Approach, Danny Rogers, John Ryan, Peter Ryan, Sav Saville and Brent Stephenson at Wrybill Birding Tours, Fabrice Schmitt, Debra Shearwater, Dave Shoch, Adrian Skerrett, Brian L. Sullivan, Adam Walleyn, and Sophie Webb.

For their careful review of the manuscript, along with helpful comments, corrections, and suggestions for improvement, we thank Ned Brinkley, Elaine Cook, Jeff Davis, and Robert L. Flood. On the Princeton team, our commissioning editor, Robert Kirk, was encouraging and patient throughout the process, while copy-editor Laurel Anderton and production editor Karen Carter massaged the text into better shape and style, and shepherded the book through the final production stages. Any remaining errors are ours.

Most of the 2200 or so images used are our own, but we thank the following for help filling gaps: Pronoy Baidya, Robin W. Baird/Cascadia Research Collective, Kevin Bartram, Paul Brooks, Peter Chadwick, Rohan Clarke, Chris Collins, Mike Danzenbaker, Michael Force/NOAA/SWFSC, Marc Guyt/AGAMI, Rob Hamilton, Doug Hanna, Phil Hansbro, Beatrice Henricot, Peter W. Hills/worldbirdphotos.com, Fred Jacq, Andy Johnson, Tom Johnson, Geoff Jones, Matt Jones, Kazuto Kawakami, Meghan Kelly, Douglas B. Koch, Daniel López-Velasco, Richard Lowe, Bruce Mactavish, Todd McGrath, Pete Morris, Killian Mullarney, Victor Paris, Joe Pender, Dave Pereksta, Mark J. Rauzon, Juan Sagardía, Chris Sanderson/Wildsearch Photography, Fabrice Schmitt, Hadoram Shirihai, Brian L. Sullivan, Hiroyuki Tanoi, Gary Thoburn/garytsphotos.zenfolio.com, Will Wagstaff, and Sophie Webb. Thanks also to Jeff Davis, Bob Flood, Jessica Law/Birdlife International, Brian Sullivan, Dani López-Velasco, and Tadao (Ted) Shimba for their help in tracking down images.

Despite being a photo field guide, this book could not have been written without reference to museum specimens, and for their generous assistance we thank personnel at the California Academy of Sciences; the Museum of Vertebrate Zoology, University of California, Berkeley; the British Museum, Tring; the North Carolina State Museum of Natural Sciences; the San Diego Natural History Museum; the National Museum of Natural History (Smithsonian Institution), Washington, DC; the American Museum of Natural History, New York; and the Natural History Museum of Los Angeles County.

And last but far from least, we thank all those who will use this book to improve our pitifully meager knowledge of oceanic birds. In the same way that our copies of the pioneering books by Peter Harrison (his 1983 classic *Seabirds of the World*, and the follow-up photo guide in 1987) are falling apart, covered in scrawled comments and corrections, we hope that before long copies of this work will be marked by similar scrawl, such is the ongoing development of knowledge concerning oceanic birds.

REFERENCES

Abbreviations: AMNH: American Museum of Natural History; BOC: British Ornithologists' Club. Publications with 7 or more coauthors are cumbersome to cite and are simply noted as, for example, 'Yew, F., & 6 coauthors.'
* indicates works useful for drafting range maps.

Alexander, W. B. 1928. Birds of the Ocean. Putnam, New York.

Austin, J. J. 1996. Molecular phylogenetics of *Puffinus* shearwaters: preliminary evidence from mitochondrial cytochrome *b* gene sequences. Molecular Phylogenetics and Evolution 6:77–88.

Austin, J. J., V. Bretagnolle, & E. Pasquet. 2004. A global molecular phylogeny of the small *Puffinus* shearwaters and implications for systematics of the Little–Audubon's Shearwater complex. Auk 121:847–864.

Banks, J., A. Van Buren, Y. Cherel, & J. B. Whitfield. 2006. Genetic evidence for three species of rockhopper penguins, *Eudyptes chrysocome*. Polar Biology 30:61–67.

Barros, R., F. Medrano, R. Silva, & F. de Groote. 2018. First breeding site record of Hornby's Storm Petrel *Oceanodroma hornbyi* in the Atacama Desert, Chile. Ardea 106(2):203–207.

*Bartle, J. A., D. Hu, J-C. Stahl, P. Pyle, T. R. Simons, & D. Woodby. 1993. Status and ecology of gadfly petrels in the temperate North Pacific. Pp. 101–111 in K. Vermeer, K. T. Briggs, & D. Siegel-Causey (eds.). The status, ecology, and conservation of marine birds of the North Pacific. Canadian Wildlife Service Special Publication, Ottawa.

*BirdLife International. 2017. IUCN Red List for birds. Downloaded from http://www.birdlife.org on 17/07/2017.

Bolton, M., & 7 coauthors. 2008. Monteiro's Storm-Petrel *Oceanodroma monteiroi*: a new species from the Azores. Ibis 150:717–727.

Bretagnolle, V., & H. Shirihai, 2010. A new taxon of Collared Petrel *Pterodroma brevipes* from the Banks Islands, Vanuatu. Bull. BOC 130:286–301.

Brooke, M. 2004. Albatrosses and Petrels across the World. Oxford Univ. Press.

Brooke, M. de L., & G. Rowe. 1996. Behavioural and molecular evidence for specific status of light and dark morphs of the Herald Petrel *Pterodroma heraldica*. Ibis 138:420–432.

Brown, R. M., & 7 coauthors. 2011. Phylogenetic relationships in *Pterodroma* petrels are obscured by recent secondary contact and hybridization. PLoS ONE 6(5): e20350.

Chambers, G. K., C. Moeke, R. Steel, & J. W. H. Trueman. 2009. Phylogenetic analysis of the 24 named albatross taxa based on full mitochondrial cytochrome *b* DNA sequences. Notornis 56:82–94.

Cibois, A., J-C. Thibault, M. LeCroy, & V. Bretagnolle. 2015. Molecular analysis of a storm petrel specimen from the Marquesas Islands, with comments on specimens of *Fregetta lineata* and *F. guttata*. Bull. BOC 135:240–246.

Cibois, A., J-C. Thibault, G. Rocamera, & E. Pasquet. 2016. Molecular phylogeny and systematics of Blue and Grey Noddies (*Procelsterna*). Ibis 158:433–438.

*Cramp, S., and K. E. L. Simmons (eds.). 1977. Handbook of the Birds of Europe, the Middle East, and North Africa. Oxford Univ. Press.

Cristidis, L., & W. E. Boles. 1994. The taxonomy and species of birds of Australia and its territories. Royal Australian Ornithologists Union Monograph 2, Melbourne.

Devillers, P. 1978. Distribution and relationships of South American skuas. Gerfaut 68:374–417.

Dinechin, M. de, R. Ottvall, P. Quillfeldt, & P. Jouventin. 2009. Speciation chronology of rockhopper penguins inferred from molecular, geological and palaeoceanographic data. J. Biogeography 36:693–702.

Fischer, J. H., & 10 coauthors. 2018. Analyses of phenotypic differentiations among South Georgian Diving-Petrel (*Pelecanoides georgicus*) populations reveal an undescribed and highly endangered species from New Zealand. PLoS ONE 13(6): e0197766.

*Flood, B., & A. Fisher. 2011. Multimedia identification guide to North Atlantic Seabirds: Storm-petrels & Bulwer's Petrel. Pelagic Birds & Birding Multimedia Identification Guides, Penryn, UK.

*_____. 2013. Multimedia identification guide to North Atlantic Seabirds: *Pterodroma* Petrels. Pelagic Birds & Birding Multimedia Identification Guides, Hockley, UK.

_____. 2016. Multimedia identification guide to North Atlantic Seabirds: Albatrosses & Fulmarine Petrels. Pelagic Birds & Birding Multimedia Identification Guides, Hockley, UK.

*Flood, R. L., & A. C. Wilson. 2017. A New Zealand Storm Petrel *Fregetta maoriana* off Gau Island, Fiji, in May 2017. Bull. BOC 137(4):278–286.

Flood, R. L., A. C. Wilson, & K. Zufelt. 2017. Observations of five little-known tubenoses from Melanesia in January 2017. Bull. BOC 137(3):226–236.

Force, M. P., S. W. Webb, & S. N. G. Howell. 2007. Identification at sea of Hawaiian and Galapagos petrels. Western Birds 38:242–248.

Gil-Velaseo, M., G. Rodríguez, S. Menzie, & J. M. Arcos. 2015. Plumage variability and field identification of Manx, Yelkouan, and Balearic Shearwaters. British Birds 108:514–539.

Grosser, S., C. P. Burridge, A. J. Peucker, & J. M. Waters. 2015. Coalescent modelling suggests recent secondary contact of cryptic penguin species. PLoS ONE 10(12): e0144966.

Hailer, F., & 6 coauthors. 2010. Long-term isolation of a highly mobile seabird on the Galapagos. Proc. Royal Soc. B doi: 10.1098/rspb.2010.1342.

Harris, M. P. 1969. The biology of storm petrels in the Galapagos Islands. Proc. California Academy of Sciences 37:95–166.

Harrison, P. 1983. Seabirds: An Identification Guide. Houghton Mifflin, Boston.

_____. 1987. Seabirds of the World: A Photographic Guide. Helm, London.

Harrison, P., & 12 coauthors. 2013. A new storm-petrel species from Chile. Auk 130:180–191.

Hinchon, G. 2017. Presumed Pigeon Guillemots of subspecies *snowi* off Hokkaido, Japan, in February 2016. Dutch Birding 39:87–89.

Howell, S. N. G. 1994. Identification of Magnificent and Great frigatebirds in the eastern Pacific. Birding 26:400–415.

_____. 2010a. Identification and taxonomy of White-bellied Storm Petrels, with comments on WP report in August 1986. Dutch Birding 32:36–42.

_____. 2010b. Molt in North American Birds. Houghton Mifflin, Boston.

*_____. 2012. Petrels, Albatrosses, and Storm-Petrels of North America. Princeton Univ. Press.

_____. 2014. Titan Storm Petrel. Dutch Birding 36:162–165.

Howell, S. N. G., & J. B. Patteson. 2008. Variation in the Black-capped Petrel—one species or more? Alula 14:70–83.

Howell, S. N. G., & F. Schmitt 2016. Pincoya Storm Petrel: comments on identification and plumage variation. Dutch Birding 38:384–388.

Howell, S. N. G., T. McGrath, W. T. Hunefeld, & J. S. Feenstra. 2010. Occurrence and identification of the Leach's Storm-Petrel (*Oceanodroma leucorhoa*) complex off southern California. North American Birds 63:540–549.

James, D. 2004. Identification of Christmas Island, Great, and Lesser Frigatebirds. Birding Asia 1:22–38.

*King, W. B. (ed.). 1974. Pelagic studies of seabirds in the central and eastern Pacific Ocean. Smithsonian Contributions to Zoology 158.

López-Suárez, P., C. J. Hazevoet, & L. Palma. 2012. Has the Magnificent Frigatebird *Fregata magnificens* in the Cape Verde Islands reached the end of the road? Zoologia Caboverdiana 3(2):82–86.

Manly, B., B. S. Arbogast, D. S. Lee, & M. Van Tuinen. 2013. Mitochondrial DNA analysis reveals substantial population structure within the endangered Black-capped Petrel (*Pterodroma hasitata*). Waterbirds 36(2):228–233.

*Marchant, S., & P. J. Higgins (eds.). 1990. Handbook of Australian, New Zealand, and Antarctic Birds, vol. 1. Oxford Univ. Press.

*Mays, G., Durand, J-M., & Gomez, G. 2006. Première nidification du Puffin cendré [*Calonectris diomedea*] sur la façade atlantique française. Ornithos 13(5):316–319.

*Menkhorst, P., D. Rogers, R. Clarke, J. Davies, P. Marsack, & K. Franklin. 2017. The Australian Bird Guide. Princeton Univ. Press.

Monteiro, L. R., & 7 co-authors. 1997. Seabirds of São Tomé e Príncipe. Progress Report to BP/BirdLife International/Fauna & Flora International Conservation Programme.

Murphy, R. C. 1927. On certain forms of *Puffinus assimilis* and its allies. AMNH Novitates 276.

*_____. 1936. Oceanic Birds of South America. 2 vols. AMNH, New York.

Murphy, R. C., & F. Harper. 1921. A review of the diving petrels. Bull. AMNH 44, art. 17:495–554.

Murphy, R. C., & S. Irving. 1951. A review of the frigate-petrels (*Pelagodroma*). AMNH Novitates 1506.

Murphy, R. C., & J. M. Pennoyer. 1952. Larger petrels of the genus *Pterodroma*. AMNH Novitates 1580.

Newell, D., S. N. G. Howell, & D. López-Velasco. 2013. South Polar and Great Skuas: the timing of primary moult as an aid to identification. British Birds 106:325–346.

Nunn, G. B., & S. E. Stanley. 1998. Body size effects and rates of cytochrome *b* evolution in tube-nosed seabirds. Molecular Biology and Evolution 15:1360–1371.

Nunn, G. B., J. Cooper, P. Jouventin, C. J. R. Robertson, & G. G. Robertson. 1996. Evolutionary relationships among extant albatrosses (Procellariiformes: Diomedeidae) established from complete cytochrome-*b* sequences. Auk 113:784–801.

Olson, S. L. 2017. Species rank for the critically endangered Atlantic Lesser Frigatebird (*Fregata trinitatis*). Wilson Journal of Ornithology 129:661–675.

Onley, D., & P. Scofield. 2007. Albatrosses, Petrels, and Shearwaters of the World. Princeton Univ. Press.

*Paiva, V. H., A. I. Fagundes, V. Romão, C. Gouveia, & J. A. Ramos. 2016. Population-scale foraging segregation in an apex predator of the North Atlantic. PLoS ONE 11(3): e0151340.

Parmelee, D. F. 1988. The hybrid skua: a Southern Ocean enigma. Wilson Bulletin 100:345–356.

Penhallurick, J., & M. Wink. 2004. Analysis of the taxonomy and nomenclature of the Procellariiformes based on complete nucleotide sequences of the mitochondrial cytochrome *b* gene. Emu 104:125–147.

*Pitman, R. L. 1986. Atlas of seabird distribution and relative abundance in the Eastern Tropical Pacific. Nat. Marine Fisheries Service Admin. Report LJ–86-02C.

*Pratt, H. D., P. L. Bruner, & D. G. Berrett. 1987. A Field Guide to the Birds of Hawaii and the Tropical Pacific. Princeton Univ. Press.

*Pyle, R. L., & P. Pyle. 2017. The Birds of the Hawaiian Islands: Occurrence, History, Distribution, and Status. B. P. Bishop Museum, Honolulu, Hawaii, USA, Version 2 (1 January 2017). http:/hbs.bishopmuseum.org/birds/rlp-monograph/

Reinhardt, K., K. Blechschmidt, H.-U. Peter, & D. Montalti. 1997. A hitherto unknown hybridization between Chilean and South Polar skua. Polar Biology 17:114–118.

Ritz, M. S., S. Hahn, T. Janicke, & H-U. Peter. 2006. Hybridization between South Polar Skua (*Catharacta maccormicki*) and Brown Skua (*Catharacta antarctica lonnbergi*) in the Antarctic Peninsula region. Polar Biology 29:153–159.

Robb, M., K. Mullarney, & The Sound Approach. 2008. Petrels Night and Day. The Sound Approach, Poole, Dorset.

Robertson, B. C., & 7 coauthors. 2016. Phylogenetic affinities of the *Fregetta* storm-petrels are not black and white. Molecular Phylogenetics and Evolution 97:170–176.

Robertson, C. J. R., & G. B. Nunn. 1998. Towards a new taxonomy for albatrosses. Pp. 13–19 in G. Robertson & R. Gales (eds.). Albatross Biology and Conservation. Surrey Beatty & Sons, Chipping Norton.

Ryan, P. 2017. Guide to Seabirds of Southern Africa. Struik Nature, Cape Town.

Ryan, P. G., K. Bourgeois, S. Dromzée, & B. J. Dilley. 2014. The occurrence of two bill morphs of prions *Pachyptila vittata* on Gough Island. Polar Biology, doi 10.1007/s00300-014-1473-2.

Schaugnessy, P. D. 1975. Variation in facial color of the Royal Penguin. Emu 75:147–152.

*Shirihai, H. 2007. A Complete Guide to Antarctic Wildlife, 2nd ed. A&C Black, London.

_____. 2008. Rediscovery of Beck's Petrel *Pseudobulweria becki*, and other observations of tubenoses from the Bismarck archipelago, Papua New Guinea. Bull. BOC 128:3–16.

Shirihai, H., & V. Bretagnolle. 2010. First observations at sea of Vanuatu Petrel *Pterodroma (cervicalis) occulta*. Bull. BOC 130:132–140.

_____. 2015a. The poorly known Mohéli Shearwater *Puffinus (persicus) temptator* at the Comoro Islands, western Indian Ocean. Bull. BOC 135:216–223.

_____. 2015b. *Bulweria* petrels off the Comoros, south-west Indian Ocean. Bull. BOC 135:348–351.

Shirihai, H., V. Bretagnolle, & F. Zino. 2010. Identification of Fea's, Desertas, and Zino's Petrels at sea. Birding World 23:239–275.

Shirihai, H., T. Pym, J. Kretzschmar, K. Moce, A. Taukei, & D. Watling. 2009. First observations of Fiji Petrel *Pseudobulweria macgillivrayi* at sea: off Gau Island, Fiji, in May 2009. Bull. BOC 129: 129–148.

Shirihai, H., T. Pym, M. San Román, & V. Bretagnolle. 2014. The Critically Endangered Mascarene Petrel *Pseudobulweria aterrima*: identification and behaviour at sea, historical discovery of breeding sites, and breeding ecology on Réunion, Indian Ocean. Bull. BOC 134:194–223.

Shirihai, H., M. Schweizer, G. M. Kirwan, & V. Bretagnolle. 2017. The type of Rapa Shearwater *Puffinus (newelli?) myrtae* from the Austral Islands, Polynesia, with remarks on the morphological variation of the taxon. Bull. BOC 137:127–134.

Smith, A. L., & V. L. Friesen. 2007. Differentiation of sympatric populations of the Band-rumped Storm-Petrel in the Galapagos Islands: an examination of genetics, morphology, and vocalizations. Molecular Ecology 16:1593–1603.

Smith, A. L., L. Monteiro, O. Hasegawa, & V. L. Friesen. 2007. Global phylogeny of the Band-rumped Storm-Petrel (*Oceanodroma castro*; Procellariiformes: Hydrobatidae). Molecular Phylogenetics and Evolution 43:755–773.

*Spear, L. B., & D. G. Ainley. 2007. Storm-petrels of the eastern Pacific Ocean: species assembly and diversity along marine habitat gradients. Ornithological Monographs no. 62.

*Spear, L. B., S. N. G. Howell, & D. G. Ainley. 1992. Notes on the at-sea identification of some Pacific gadfly petrels (genus: *Pterodroma*). Colonial Waterbirds 15:202–218.

*Spear, L. B., D. G. Ainley, N. Nur, & S. N. G. Howell. 1995. Population size and factors affecting at-sea distributions of four endangered procellariids in the tropical Pacific. Condor 97:613–638.

Steeves, T. E., D. J. Anderson, H. McNally, M. H. Kim, & V. L. Friesen. 2003. Phylogeography of *Sula*: the role of physical barriers to gene flow in the diversification of tropical seabirds. Journal of Avian Biology 34:217–223.

Tennyson, A. J. D., C. M. Miskelly, & S. L. Totterman. 2012. Observations of Collared Petrels (*Pterodroma brevipes*) on Vanua Lava, Vanuatu, and a review of the species' breeding distribution. Notornis 59:39–48.

*Tickell, W. L. N. 2000. Albatrosses. Yale Univ. Press, New Haven.

Tomkins, R. J., & B. J. Milne. 1991. Differences among Dark-rumped Petrel (*Pterodroma phaeopygia*) populations within the Galapagos archipelago. Notornis 38:1–35.

Viot, C. R., P. Jouventin, & J. Bried. 1993. Population genetics of some southern seabirds. Marine Ornithology 2:1–25.

Walbridge, G., B. Small, & R. Y. McGowan. 2003. Ascension Frigatebird on Tiree—new to the Western Palearctic. British Birds 96:58–73.

Wallace, S. J., J. A. Morris-Pocock, J. González-Solís, P. Quillfeldt, & V. L. Friesen. 2017. A phylogenetic test of sympatric speciation in the Hydrobatinae (Aves: Procellariiformes). Molecular Phylogenetics and Evolution 107:39–47.

Wilson, E. O. 2014. The Meaning of Human Existence. Liveright Publishing, New York.

*Zajková, Z., T. Militão, & J. González-Solís. 2017. Year-round movements of a small seabird and oceanic isotope gradient in the tropical Atlantic. Marine Ecol. Progress Series 579:169–183.

INDEX

NOTES

NOTES

SOME ANATOMY AND PLUMAGE TERMS

rump patch (technically, uppertail coverts)

upperwing band

M-pattern (across both wings)

hindcollar

cap

secondaries

primaries

half-collar

scapulars

bonnet

elbow

bend of wing

cowl

underwing margins